"*Let the Legends Preach* is a gift to tl
My friend, Dr. Jared Alcántara, has l
gospel giants, along with their sermc
reuniting with old friends, and to others they will be sorely needed introductions. And to all, we will find deep refreshment as each preacher takes us deeper into the well of God's word. My hope is that this book will gain a wide reading, particularly in those spaces where African American preaching and preachers have been ignored."

—**Bryan Loritts**, author of *The Dad Difference*

"In his book, *Let the Legends Preach*, Dr. Jared Alcántara allows us to eavesdrop on the preaching prowess of twenty-four homiletical giants who were selected as 'living legends' at the E. K. Bailey International Conference on Biblical Preaching. With the wit and wisdom of a sage and seer, each of these great proclaimers etched rich insights onto the fabric of the preaching community. Read the sermons of these 'Pulpit Statesmen,' and let God light a fresh fire in you to preach!"

—**Maurice Watson**, Senior Servant, Metropolitan Baptist Church, Largo, Maryland

"Jared Alcántara has brought in harmony a legendary ensemble of voices. Some have only read summaries of these voices. Others have only heard them from a distance. I have the distinct privilege of saying that I knew most of these legends personally. Their voices taught me how to sing. For in me, you will hear the lyricism of A. L. Patterson's alliteration, the tenor of Gardner Taylor's poetic form, the bass of Harry Wright's imagination, the baritone of Robert Smith's explication, and the pause of James Massey's sermonic delivery. These and many other E. K. Bailey legends have helped me articulate the gospel's song. For this reason, it is my tremendous pleasure to offer my affirmation and highest endorsement of this volume of sermons. In these times, we need to listen to the melody of this legendary chorus."

—**Ralph Douglas West**, Senior Pastor, The Church without Walls, Houston, Texas

"With so many competing visions for black preaching, history needs a documented witness of the prowess and potential of authentic black preaching. *Let the Legends Preach* is a diamond extracted from the vaults of the brightest of black preaching. Classrooms and congregations are the richer for this resource."

—**Charlie Dates**, Senior Pastor, Progressive Baptist Church, Chicago; Affiliate Professor, Trinity Evangelical Divinity School

"It is with heartfelt gratitude that I applaud and appreciate Dr. Bryan Carter, the visionary, Dr. Jared Alcántara, and the compilation team on this commemorative project. Preaching was the life and breath of my beloved husband, E. K. Bailey. From the time that we met in 1965 at Bishop College, until God transitioned him to his heavenly reward in 2003, he loved God's word and preaching for the salvation and edification of all people throughout the world. His passion for Christ to be made known to all people exuded from everything he did to impact the kingdom. This quest would cause him to spend countless hours in prayer, research, sermon structuring, compiling illustrations, considering personal applications, and refining sermons that he would be privileged to preach in America and abroad. He established the E. K. Bailey Preaching Conference with pastors, ministers, and communicators of the gospel in mind and the motif was established, 'Imparting the Word to impact the world.' His desire was for the preacher to not only hear premier preachers in the E. K. Bailey Preaching Conference, but to be prepared by the best theological and practical minds. His desire was also that preachers would not only 'preach good,' but would desire to be good people, possessing moral integrity while maintaining a loving relationship with his/her spouse and children. Some of the legends in this book were his mentors who helped shape his ministry. They all represent people who are called by God, who demonstrated discipline, and excelled in applying the mandate, 'Preach the Word! Be ready in season and out of season. Correct, rebuke and encourage with great patience and careful instruction' (2 Tim 4:2)."

—**Sheila Bailey**, President of Sheila B. Ministries

"As someone who has been attending the E. K. Bailey Preaching Conference for many years, one of the highlights I've most enjoyed is the annual recognition of a 'living legend'—a pulpit veteran whose preaching ministry has influenced the church well beyond his own congregation. The list of recipients is a 'who's who' of masterful pulpiteers, and it is a delight to see this new collection of the sermons these pulpit giants preached at the conference. The gathering of these powerful sermons in one volume makes this resource a treasure that will benefit anyone who loves great preaching."

—**Michael Duduit**, editor of *Preaching*; Dean, Clamp Divinity School
at Anderson University, Anderson, South Carolina

Let the Legends Preach

Let the Legends Preach

Sermons by Living Legends at the E. K. Bailey
Preaching Conference

EDITED BY
Jared E. Alcántara

FOREWORD BY
Joel C. Gregory

WIPF & STOCK · Eugene, Oregon

LET THE LEGENDS PREACH
Sermons by Living Legends at the E. K. Bailey Preaching Conference

Wipf & Stock
An Imprint of Wipf and Stock Publishers
199 W. 8th Ave., Suite 3
Eugene, OR 97401

www.wipfandstock.com

PAPERBACK ISBN: 978-1-7252-6689-6
HARDCOVER ISBN: 978-1-7252-6690-2
EBOOK ISBN: 978-1-7252-6691-9

03/22/21

To the Bailey Family:

Dr. Bailey's vision for equipping preachers in expository preaching
continues to live and flourish today

Contents

             Living Legend 2018

Chapter 24   Lloyd C. Blue | 241
             Living Legend 2019

             Recommended Reading | 251

             Bibliography | 253

Foreword

"Let the Legends Preach"

ON THE SUNDAY AFTER July 4th, the storied downtown Dallas Fairmont Hotel relinquishes its commercial guests and undergoes a transfiguration. Nearly one thousand preachers, largely but not exclusively African American, appropriate its two towers for the E. K. Bailey International Conference on Biblical Preaching. Founded by the lauded and legendary African American proclaimer Rev. Dr. E. K. Bailey, it is now under the stewardship of his able successor, Pastor Bryan Carter. For many of us, the event is more like a family reunion or university homecoming. For twenty-four years, I have given and received joyful greetings in the spacious lobby, had intense conversations about preaching in the hallways, and enjoyed the high point of the year—the Living Legend Luncheon.

Dr. Bailey's vision, when weighed in the assessment of history, may well be the most decisive impact on African American preaching in the late twentieth and early twenty-first centurues. Comparisons fail. There are several regional and national conferences, but the E. K. Bailey has endured for a quarter-century, withstood the lamented loss of its visionary founder, and now serves a new generation of young Black preachers. At the same time, it has steadily attracted an enlarging group of preachers other than African Americans. From the historic churches of New York City to the vital churches of Chicago, from the crossroads of rural southern states and little wooden worship houses to urban megachurches, pastors keep coming to listen to and learn the craft of expository preaching.

What was the Bailey vision? He never wished to bleach out the native vitality, a holy American artform, of African American preaching. There is nothing in the world like it. The call and response, the hypnotizing runs of rhetoric, the native narrative drama, and the closing intonation all stand alone in the history of Christian preaching. Dr. Bailey never wished to replace any of those distinctive marks. What he did want to do was to shine a bright light on the natural biblical content of Black preaching and polish to a gleaming reality what is already there. In a sense, the conference brings vividly to the front of the preacher's mind what may move to back of mind amid ministry. His goal was to make a good thing better, a great thing greater. By the example of preaching in the plenary sessions and the didactic content of the breakout sessions, Dr. Bailey called us all back annually to the centrality of the text. At the same time, the vision was not to make that an end, but rather that which points to Christ.

He would be the first to note that his was not a solitary vision and others made the rough places smooth. A generation before him in the academy and the pastorate, persons such as Rev. Drs. Henry Mitchell, J. Alfred Smith Sr., A. Louis Patterson Jr., James Earl Massey, and others were harbingers of Dr. Bailey's vision. The conference took these scattered rays, filtered them through the magnifying glass of his soaring personality, and set the vision ablaze in downtown Dallas. He put before the conference inimitable personalities such as the Rev. Drs. Gardner C. Taylor and William J. Shaw, carved on the Mount Rushmore of preaching forever. He set forth preachers of stunning individuality such as the Rev. Drs. Manuel L. Scott Sr. and Caesar Arthur Walker Clark Sr. It may be said with confidence that no conference has set before its listeners such a collection of personalities in the name of biblical exposition.

To be personal, I was at a time of untold transition in the middle of a now fifty-five-year-long preaching ministry. Ironically, having resigned the church across the street from the Fairmont Hotel, I did not know what was next. Dr. Bailey was almost alone in calling me and insisting that I continue preaching. He invited me to preach for the first time at the conference. I went to the conference expecting a seminar room comfortably filled with preachers. When I walked into the gallant ballroom, I saw nine hundred expectant Black preachers. I decided I had better preach. I preached on 2 Corinthians 4:6, the passage on a treasure in earthen vessels. God visited the moment. No other moment changed the rest of my life so much. To this day, I cannot explain what happened. The brothers and then the sisters of color across the nation invited me to preach at churches, conventions, conferences, and schools. Any fool can count how many seeds are in an apple; only God knows how many apples are in a seed. The E. K. Bailey Conference changed my life and ministry in that crowded hour those many years ago.

The biographies of the preachers in this volume are pithy, well-stated, and insightful. A few remarks may help get our arms around the twenty-four persons so honored. One thread through the years is the influence of Bishop College. Eight honorees were Bishop men and at least one other had a connection with the school. When the history of American preaching is written later in this century, the influence of that Dallas HBU, now closed since 1988, will be a fascinating study. Its graduates have told me of the parade of prominent proclaimers that came through the high hour of its chapel. Something about Wright and Mangrum and Rollins and Williams and others the reader could name stamped itself onto honorees of the past and those who will inevitably be honored in the future. The award has also been national in its honorees. Manhattan and Brooklyn, Los Angeles and San Francisco, Chicago hugging Lake Michigan and Atlanta sprawling across the woods of Georgia have commended their sons of ministry for the honor. Rural roots and beleaguered poverty, demonic prejudice and orphaned loneliness all mark the lives of some. The conference has presented three Whites with the honor, a noble gesture that humbled the recipients into silent gratitude. Academicians such as Drs. Mitchell, Massey, Robinson, J. Alfred Smith Sr., and Robert Smith Jr., along with many other honorees who have served as adjunctive professors highlight the halls of the academy.

An appealing aspect of the conference has been its certification track. This has afforded the opportunity to men and women to be certified in homiletics over a series of conferences. The creativity and accountability of this program has given weight and value to the accomplishment of those who come year after year. They belong to a fraternity and sorority of ministers who have had the tutelage of some of the best preachers in the world. The more recent dedication of the conference to a single book of the Bible each year has only strengthened the certification and focused the teaching. Tens of thousands of persons sitting in the pews of hundreds of churches have heard better preaching and more of it because of the breakout sessions. Deacons have said so, as well as preachers' spouses.

When Dr. Bailey, so early and so lamented, so earnestly prayed for in his illness and grieved for in his so-soon departure, left us, many feared for the future of the conference. Under the watchful stewardship of the elegant and eloquent Dr. Sheila M. Bailey, the conference continued in several years of transition. Yet, the preachers came, the proclaimers preached with power, the spirit of the conference survived the loss of its founder, and a great sigh of relief and gratitude ascended from the chandeliered ballroom of the Fairmont.

Then, the mantle fell on Dr. Bailey's chosen and able successor at Concord, Pastor Bryan Carter. With his legendary humility, gifted sagacity beyond his years, and powerful, pastoral preaching, he has shepherded the conference into the new century with the best of the past but a definite turn to the future. Pastor Carter took the torch from one generation and passed it to the next with flawless grace and easy pace. George W. Truett used to say, "Hats off to the past and coats off for the future." Pastor Carter has demonstrated a genius in balancing the conference on the fulcrum of the past in order to leverage the best of the future.

May I hazard a guess? The storied Yale Lyman Beecher Lectures were founded in 1871. Although they no longer need to have police to control the crowds as they once did, they continue unabated these 129 years. If Christ delays his promised, personal, and bodily return, and the nation abides, the E. K. Bailey Conference will, in all probability, be meeting with ministers not yet born, pastoring churches not yet founded, in places not yet named, with Living Legends not yet conceived, all for the glory of God and the sacred art of biblical exposition. May it be so.

Joel C. Gregory, PhD

Holder of the George W. Truett Endowed Chair of Preaching and Evangelism
Director of the Kyle Lake Center for Effective Preaching
Baylor's George W. Truett Theological Seminary
Waco, Texas

Editor's Preface

I CONSIDER IT A tremendous honor, a profound delight, and a humble privilege to serve as the editor for the volume that you are about to read, *Let the Legends Preach: Sermons by Living Legends at the E. K. Bailey Preaching Conference.* I still remember the first conversation that I had about this book over the breakfast table with a dear friend about two and a half years ago in November 2018. I had only been living in Texas for a short while. I had just moved my family from Chicago a few months prior in order to join the faculty at Baylor University's George W. Truett Theological Seminary in Waco. I do not remember all of the reasons why I was scheduled to be in the Dallas-Fort Worth area that day, perhaps to pick someone up at the airport, but I *do* remember how excited I was to reconnect over breakfast with a good friend and dear brother in Christ, Rev. Dr. Bryan Carter. He is the distinguished senior pastor of the Concord Baptist Church, Dallas, and the inimitable host of the Annual E. K. Bailey Expository Preaching Conference (EKBPC). Unfortunately, despite my best attempts to make it to the conference in past years, I had never been able to attend. I was also new to that part of the country. Not only did Pastor Carter welcome me to Texas with open arms, but he invited me to join him at the conference the next year as a workshop leader and a plenary session preacher.

Pastor Carter is a gifted pastor, preacher, leader, and a generous friend; no doubt, he is also a forward-thinking organizer and visionary. That morning over breakfast, he told me about his dream for a book that would simultaneously preserve the sermons of the distinguished recipients of the Living Legend award for excellence in preaching, celebrate the milestone of the twenty-five-year anniversary of the conference, and honor the legacy of his predecessor, the visionary behind the conference itself, its namesake, the late Rev. Dr. E. K. Bailey (1945–2003). When Pastor Carter asked if I would consider coming alongside him to bring the book to completion, I remember how thankful I was to be considered for it and how humbled I felt at the opportunity to take part in such a hallowed project, one that honored the Living Legends represented in this volume.

This book would not have been possible, and it most certainly would not have been completed, were it not for the hard work and dedication of so many. Let me rush to thank my family, especially my wife, Jennifer, for your prayers, your support, your love, and your sacrifice. You are my first and best team! I also want to thank my colleagues at Baylor's Truett Theological Seminary: my Dean and Associate Dean, Dr. Todd Still and Dr. Dennis Tucker, for throwing your support behind this project and for allocating student worker hours to the long and arduous task of transcription; my distinguished colleagues in homiletics, Dr. Scott Gibson, for the feedback you provided, and Dr. Joel C. Gregory, for the excellent foreword that you wrote to this volume, and how honest and open you were about how much this conference has meant to you. Thank you to the many student "worker bees" at Truett who spent long hours behind the scenes transcribing twenty-four audio sermons: Daniel Gregory, Claire Kent, Tyler Phillips, Mackenzie Rock, Maddie Rarick, Joshua Sharp, Adam Thompson, and Ruby Wayman. I want to give a special shout-out to my graduate assistant, Charlie Campbell, who came to understand in an all-too-personal way what it means to "eat, sleep, and breathe" a book project. #thisishowwetruett

I also want to offer my appreciation and gratitude to the team at Wipf and Stock and the team at the Concord Baptist Church in Dallas. Thank you to Michael Thomson, my acquisitions editor, and to the many fine leaders at Wipf and Stock who supported the project, in particular, James D. Stock and Jim Tedrick. To my colleagues at Concord, I am most grateful to you as well. Thank you to Ms. Camille Roberts, Ms. Aquilla Allen, Ms. Tracie Cavitt, Ms. Summer Galvez, Pastor Aaron Moore, and Pastor Michael Greene. Without these two teams of wonderful, talented people working collaboratively and creatively in concert, this book would most certainly not have been published.

Just before sending the final manuscript to press, I spoke again with Pastor Carter about how much the conference has meant to him. He gave me permission to share with you what he shared with me. He said,

> This book is for every preacher who has ever attended the E.K. Bailey Expository Preaching Conference. Thank you for your support throughout the years and your commitment to biblical exposition. We have been honored to partner with you in your preaching ministry, one that has strengthened the church and exalted Christ. We dedicate this book to the family of Dr. E.K.

Bailey; his vision for equipping preachers in expository preaching continues to live and flourish today. Dr. Bailey's vision was built on instilling in preachers the authority of Scripture, the centrality of Christ, and dependence on the Holy Spirit. He gave his life to teaching preaching, encouraging preachers, and modeling preaching, for which we are eternally grateful.

It has been a single honor to be a part of the E.K. Bailey Expository Preaching Conference since 1998. I first came as an attendee at the invitation of my older brother; he purchased my registration as a college graduation gift and allowed me to sleep on his couch and drive to the conference each day. I had no idea that one day, I would have the joy and privilege of serving as the conference director, serving since 2009. It has been a great honor to host such an esteemed gathering of biblical expositors. This conference has changed the trajectory of my life in many ways. I am forever indebted to the members of the conference faculty who have invested in my life and the life of every attendee. Every preacher is a student first, and this conference has provided me and others with the tremendous opportunity to be a student who could grow and develop as a proclaimer of the gospel. My prayer is that God will continue to raise up generations of preachers that exalt Christ in their preaching on every occasion.

Thank you, Pastor Carter, for exalting Christ in *your* preaching, honoring your predecessor's legacy, and for introducing a new generation of preachers to the rich and timeless sermons preserved in this volume. Also, thanks for picking up the check for breakfast. Next time, I will pay. In the meantime —let the legends preach!

Jared E. Alcántara, PhD

Holder of the Paul W. Powell Endowed Chair in Preaching
Baylor's George W. Truett Theological Seminary
Waco, Texas

Chapter 1

Ervin Kinsley (E. K.) Bailey (1945–2003)

The Preacher

REV. DR. ERVIN KINSLEY (E. K.) Bailey (1945–2003) impacted several generations of pastors and Christian leaders through his preaching, teaching, mentoring, equipping, and training. Born on December 19, 1945, in Marshall, Texas, he died on October 22, 2003, after a prolonged battle with nasal cancer. He began his pastoral ministry in 1969 at Mt. Carmel Missionary Baptist Church in Dallas, Texas. Then, in June 1975, he became the founder and senior pastor of Concord Missionary Baptist Church in Dallas, where he served until his death in 2003. In the 1980s, Dr. Bailey rose to national prominence when he launched E. K. Bailey Ministries, Inc. as a vehicle for mentoring Christian leaders in the areas of preaching, personal change, discipleship, and social change. Out of E. K. Bailey

1

Ministries, Inc., arose The Institute on Church Growth, Discipling the African American Male and Female Conferences, and the International Conference on Expository Preaching. His impact on expository preaching continues to be felt through the E. K. Bailey Preaching Conference, now celebrating its twenty-fifth year.

Dr. Bailey received his BS degree in Religion from Bishop College, his doctor of ministry degree from United Theological Seminary, and two honorary doctorate degrees from Dallas Baptist University and Criswell College. Some of his best-known sermons are available in print such as *Confessions of an Ex Cross-Maker*, *The Preacher and the Prostitute*, and *Testimony of a Tax Collector*. He also coauthored *Preaching in Black and White* with Warren W. Wiersbe.

He and his wife, Dr. Sheila M. Smith Bailey, were married for thirty-four years and reared two daughters, Cokiesha B. Robinson and Shenikwa M. Cager, and one son, Emon Kendrick Bailey. In 2005, his wife and one of his daughters, Cokiesha, co-published a book designed to capture his homiletical wisdom and autobiographical journey entitled *Farther In and Deeper Down*. The inspiration for the title to the book originates in the sermon that appears in this chapter. Delivered in 2001, it was the first sermon that Dr. Bailey preached at Concord just weeks after being diagnosed with nasal cancer.

The Sermon

Recently, we had our International Expository Preaching Conference. During that conference, Robert Smith gave a lecture. He talked about the kind of preaching that is needed today, and he used for his subject on preaching, "Farther In and Deeper Down." I want to borrow Robert Smith's subject from his preaching lecture and attach it to this twelfth chapter of 2 Corinthians because I think it has a word for this pastor and people as we go through this time of crisis. So, I want to talk today about farther in and deeper down.

The date was October 4, 1987. The place was Midland, Texas. The girl's name was Jessica McClure. She was two and a half years old as she sat in her backyard, dangling her feet over what seemed to have been a harmless ground depression. Her aunt left her only for a few moments, but that's all it took, for when Jessica attempted to stand up, she fell thirty feet into an abandoned oil well shaft. A rescue team was dispatched with heavy equipment, and for the next fifty-eight hours, they worked feverishly to dislodge Jessica's body from the abandoned shaft.

A man by the name of O'Donnell was assigned as the primary rescuer. He was small in frame but strong in upper body and, after digging a parallel shaft alongside of the original oil shaft, they let Mr. O'Donnell down thirty feet and then five feet across as they drilled through sheer rock. O'Donnell got down there—he was able to touch Jessica's body; he was able to even get her vital signs, but just as everything was appearing to go so well, suddenly, disaster struck. For the record is, as O'Donnell reached for Jessica, she slipped and went further in and deeper down.

They pulled O'Donnell up out of the shaft where they restructured and recast their strategy. And the doctors were saying, "Time is of essence. We only have a few more hours." The pediatricians told them, "Whatever you're going to do, you must do quickly for she will not live and last much longer." So, they put O'Donnell back down in the shaft and, this time, when he reached little Jessica a voice was heard up top that cried out, "O'Donnell, pull hard! You may have to break her in order to save her!"

O'Donnell was caught because he knew how fragile the two-year-old girl was, but he knew that if he did not pull hard, he would not save her. So, complying with the request of the voice from above, he pulled her and as he pulled little Jessica began to cry. Can you imagine what his heart was feeling like? He pulled hard—so hard it messed up one of her toes, but he kept on pulling. He pulled hard until it scratched up her face, but he kept on pulling. And, finally, as he made one last tug, her body was dislodged from the shaft. They put her in the apparatus and they pulled her back to safety on top of the ground.

Now, no one accused O'Donnell of child abuse. They had to amputate one toe, but nobody said he was too rough. She had to have plastic surgery along her face and around her head, but nobody said he was too rough. Because everybody knew that if he did not scar her, he would not save her.

Pull hard. I want you to know that every now and then, God has to pull hard. He may call us to amputate some things, he may even scar us up a little bit where we may need some plastic surgery, but God knows if he doesn't pull hard, if he doesn't scar us, he may not save us.

The apostle Paul, in our text today, tells us of an experience he had when God carried him further in and deeper down. Paul said, "I had that experience because God told me how much I was going to have to suffer . . . ," he said, ". . . because the greater God plans to use you, he's got to carry you further in and deeper down."

There are several things I want to look at today. At the "A" part of verse 7, it says, "*And because of the surpassing greatness of the revelation and for this reason.*" Stop right there. He says "because" and "for this reason."

God is calling us further in and deeper down into the mystery of suffering. Now if this is not relevant to you, you just listen in as I talk to myself. God uses suffering to take us further in and deeper down into his mystery. Have I got a witness?

As we look out across the landscape of our human existence, we see suffering everywhere. We see suffering in our families when a mother can drown her children, when a father can take a gun and kill his wife, shoot his children, and then take his own life.

We see suffering everywhere. We see it in our homes etched in the face of ailing loved ones. We see it in our streets as we see it being perpetrated against victims of crime. We see it on the news while every day we see war-torn countries experiencing unusual suffering. But, then, we see it in our hospitals and we even see it in ourselves as our bodies break down under the weight of time, and we ask the question, "Why? Why me? Why not somebody else, God? Why me?" What we discover is that suffering is couched—suffering is shrouded—in the veil of mystery. I said it's shrouded in mystery. Let me see if I can unravel a little bit of that.

Paul here says that he knew a man. It's amazing that he uses the third person here to describe an experience that happened to him, but it's an attempt not to brag. He puts it in the third person. He says, "I knew a man about fourteen years ago, and he was rhapsodized up into the heavenlies and as he was in the heavenlies, he saw visions of paradise, and he saw things that were unlawful to talk about back on planet Earth." He said it was a mysterious kind of experience.

Suffering does carry with it great mystery. But, I want you to see a couple of things here as we unravel the mystery of suffering. One is suffering disciplines our morality. Somebody ought to get that. I said that suffering disciplines our morality. Listen, when God created the world—after he created—the Bible tells us that God created angels and then God later created man. But, he gave man something that he did not give to angels. He gave us—he made us free moral agents. Now, what that means is that we are free to enthrone, and we are free to dethrone God.

Satan decided to dethrone God. Adam decided to follow Satan's pattern, and they both dethroned God. Sin came into the world and, after sin came into the world, suffering followed sin. We have experienced suffering in our human existence ever since Adam sinned. I don't care who you are or where you're from, the day will come when you will experience some suffering.

The old Black preacher used to say when man sinned, he fell from essence into existence. When man sinned, the lion jumped on the lamb. When man sinned, the dog barked at the cat. When man sinned, the grass turned brown. When man sinned, the leaves turned brown and fell from the trees.

When man sinned, oceans started throwing hurricanes at the land. For sin affected all of nature; it affected all of our relationships. When man sinned, it opened a door to suicide, homicide, and fratricide. When man sinned, it disturbed the relationship of everything in this world.

So, God in his infinite wisdom uses suffering to discipline our morality. You show me a person who has never gone through anything, and I'll show you a shallow person. If you've never been through anything, if you've never experienced any hard times, if you don't know anything about suffering, I want you to know God cannot use you very much. All those that God really uses he carries further in and deeper down. Somebody ought to help me here. You don't have to take my word for it. You know I quote the poem all the time:

> I walked a mile with pleasure,
> she chatted all the way,
> but left me none the wiser
> for all she had to say.
> I walked a mile with sorrow,
> but never a word said she;
> but, oh the things I learned from her
> when sorrow walked with me.

God uses the spade of sorrow to dig the well of joy. Oswalt Chambers says to us, "You can't drink grapes; they must be crushed." God has a way of taking his Jehovistic hand and laying it on our heads. For God knows there is something in us that he needs to crush in order to release the sweet nectar of the Holy-Spirited vine.

Not only that, but God says to us a second thing here under this mystery. Not only does God use suffering to discipline our morality, God uses suffering to define our mortality. Look what Paul says. Paul says, "I went to the third heaven. I was exalted above anything any other man in history had ever experienced. No human being had ever gone to heaven and lived to tell about it."

Paul said, "I had reason to brag, but even before that I had other reasons to brag. I was circumcised on the eighth day. I'm a Hebrew of Hebrews, I'm of the tribe of Benjamin, the elite tribe. I've got reason to boast. You want to brag? I've got bragging rights. I know how to toot my own horn. I know how to brag. I'm a Pharisee. I lived so correctly that I was able to touch the law. I was found blameless. I could toot my own horn. Then, I had this unusual experience of going to heaven."

You want to brag? You ever been to heaven and came back to tell about it? Paul says, "I've got something to brag about." He said, "But I refuse to do it because of this thorn in my flesh, because every time I thought about getting conceited, God used the ministry of the thorn to remind me of my mortality."

You see, sometimes, we can get into the situation of surpassing greatness. We can get a false impression of who we are and how great we are. We use this word "great" rather easily, and we use this word "great" rather quickly.

God says, "Listen. I'm going to give you a little suffering to remind you of how much you need me. I'm going to put this thorn in your flesh to keep you leaning and depending on me."

What kind of great experiences have you had in life? What kind of exaltation have you experienced? Degrees and accomplishments and all of those things are good, but if you want to know how really great you are, someone said, stick your finger in a pail of water. When you pull it out, if it leaves a hole in the water, then you are really great, but if you pull your finger out of that water, and that water goes back together, then you're just like everyone else. Someone ought to help me here. Have I got a witness?

Understand that we are mortal. Life is like a vapor. It's here today, and it's gone tomorrow. But, then, Concord, I believe God is going to see me through this cancer and this crisis. But, I also believe that he did this for me and for you because God has allowed me to experience some heavenly things since I've been on this Earth. I won't call the roll of the great things God has allowed me to experience, have my name on this place and that place, and the kind of places I've preached in, and the people I've shaken hands with.

But now, he's put something in my body to make me realize it's not about me. It's not about the people I know because all of the big folk I know, they can't help me now. Not even the doctors I know can help me now if God doesn't show up.

But I want you to know something. He didn't do this just for me. He did it also for you. As a member of this church so often we as people, we depend on the pastor a little too much. We let the pastor do our praying for us. We let the pastor do our Bible study for us. We let the pastor do our church service for us.

God says, "I will put a thorn in your flesh just to let the folk know you won't be here forever." I asked the Lord, "Give me another twenty even thirty years, and I don't know how long he's going to do it, but this thorn in the flesh is just a sign that someday this church will have another pastor. It's just a sign that someday times will change. People come and people go but the Bible says that Jesus is the same yesterday, today, and forever more. Don't put your hope in no man, not even a preacher or a pastor. Put your hope in Jesus. Suffering tells you every man is mortal and will soon pass away.

But he says something else here. He says, "I'm going to take you further in and deeper down into the agony of suffering." Notice in the seventh verse. He said, "Because of this surpassing revelation, to keep me from exalting myself, there was given me a thorn in the flesh, a messenger of Satan to buffet me."

He takes us further in and deeper down into the agony. I know it's agony because when you do an etymological study of the word "thorn," it wasn't just something you picked up out on the field, that little small, the old folks used to say, "Tee-nin-chi."[1] But, it was more like a stake—the agony of a stake being permanently put in his side. He says, "That was given to me, and it was given to me a messenger of Satan."

I'm God's child! Satan can't touch me without God's permission. But here this great man of God, Paul, perhaps the greatest Christian who lived since Jesus, and he says, "There was given me a thorn in the flesh." Are you walking with me? Don't miss that little passive phrase, "There was given to me," because that's saying this was according to God's will. He's saying that this thorn was a gift. When was the last time you thought your affliction was a gift?

Now, understand the Bible because, in Job 2, God and Satan work on the same thorn with different motives. Satan was going to and fro and came to God and said, "How about Job? You've got that hedge around him, what's up with that?"

God said, "Well, he's a servant of mine."

[Satan] said, "I dare you to take the hedge down."

"Why is that?"

"Because I'll make him curse you to your face."

"Oh no, not Job."

Satan said, "Let's put him to the test. I will make him curse you to your face."

And God said, "Alright, let's try it." Now God permitted it, but Satan implored it.

That's the same thing God does with us. Nothing can come into your life unless it is God-sent or God-allowed. I don't care what the problem is. I don't care what the affliction is or what the sickness is. God has to allow it!

Both God and Satan will have their hand on the thorn, but they will have different motives. You see, Satan wants the thorn to hurt you, but God wants the thorn to help you. Satan wants the thorn to buffet you while God wants it

---

1. A made-up word that Dr. Bailey heard older people use and that he also used often. It is a way of saying that something is small.

to bless you. They both have their hand on the thorn but they have different motives. Somebody ought to help me here. Are you walking with me?

Look at the extent of the suffering. He said, "There was given to me a thorn in the flesh." The extent means the size of the suffering you have to endure. The extent means the longevity, the degree of suffering you have to go through. Now, some people have to go through more than some other folk, and the reason some of you aren't going through anything is because God can't use you. You haven't made yourself available to God. Kahlil Gibran says, "Until you have been carved in two, you'll never have the capacity to hold joy." In other words, there has to be some cutting going on.

You don't have to take it from Khalil Gibran. Jesus said just about the same thing over there in John 15:1–8. Jesus says, "Every now and then, I've got to prune you. I've got to cut away some dead stuff. Even when you are blooming and producing, I've got to prune you because I want more than what you're giving out." But listen, don't think God is mad with you when he starts cutting. One writer said, "The Father is never so close as when he is pruning the vine." You see, in order to prune, he has to get close to you. He has to touch you. He has to feel you to know where to cut.

Now listen. You ever seen a pruned tree? It never looks good. You aren't going to look good when God is cutting. Folk may look at you or point at you or they might even talk about you because you don't look good when God is pruning you. You may lose all your hair when chemotherapy gets through with you. You aren't going to look too good when God's cutting up on you. You look cut up! You look bruised! Look like you've been assaulted! But if you wait awhile: "*They that wait upon the Lord shall renew their strength, mount up on wings like eagles, run and not be weary, walk and not faint.*"

Look again at the verse. It says, "This thing was given to me." He says, "Paul, this thing is from me." Now, you go to your thorn. We don't know what Paul's thorn was. Martin Luther thought that it was the opposition and persecution that Paul faced. John Calvin thought that it was spiritual temptation. Others argue that Paul's thorn was eye trouble stemming from the bright light Christ put in his face on the Damascus Road. Some think Paul's thorn was malaria, epilepsy, insomnia, and depression. But, we don't know what his thorn was so there's no point in speculating. I'm glad God didn't tell us what his thorn was so that we can put our own experience in the place of his thorn that was given to me.

There was given to me nasal cancer. What's your thorn? Are you having financial difficulty today? I mean money wars. Are you having financial problems? Listen, God says, "This thing is from me because I am your purse bearer, and I want to teach you how to lean and depend on me."

Anyone going through a difficult circumstance? God says, "This thing is from me because I am the God of circumstances and you didn't come to where you are accidentally. There is divine intentionality behind your life."

Anybody going through the long night of suffering? Sorrow? God says, "This thing is from me. I have not allowed other people to comfort you because I want you to learn how to turn to me."

Have you been given a difficult assignment? God says, "This thing is from me because I want to teach you like nobody else can teach you."

Have your friends betrayed you? God says, "This thing is from me because you've been looking to your friends for counseling. I want to teach you how to say, 'Father, I stretch my hand to thee. No other help I know.'"

Interruptions are divine instructions. Now don't you waste your time trying to figure out why God is taking me through this. "Well, pastor, is there sin in your life?"

"Yeah there's sin in yours, too."

"Is that why God is taking you through this?"

"I'm not sure but I'm looking. I'm examining it so I can deal with it."

But understand Paul was not given a thorn because he had sinned, he was given a thorn to keep him from sinning. Not only do I want you to see the extent of suffering, I want you to see the effect of suffering. Let me slow down because I want you to get this, before I head on to the close. The word "effect" means "result." What's the result of one's suffering? The answer is, "It all depends."

There are those who will go through suffering triumphantly, and there are those who will be defeated by suffering. And some of you I am looking at right now. You have been defeated by your affliction.

Watch me now. Listen. When pain becomes resentment, the consequence is depression. When pain becomes resistance, the consequence is despair. But, when pain leads to prayerfulness, the consequence is maturity, and when pain leads to patience, the consequence is victory.

Notice how Paul handled his. "Three times," he says, "I entreated the Lord." That doesn't mean that he did that three times; it is a phrase—a Hebrew idiom—that means that he prayed about it over a long period of time. He says, "I talked to the Lord about it." It does not say he complained to the Lord. It says three times he prayed.

Now, when you pray in the midst of your pain it leads to maturity. That's what he wants you to do and how he wants you to handle your thorn so that it leads to maturity.

What is the result? It all depends on how you respond to your pain. It's amazing that folk can sit up in the church twenty years, and when mama dies, they try to crawl in the grave with her. Don't misunderstand me. I'm not belittling the pain of death. I've sat in that front row more times than I have fingers, so I've been through it, and I know how painful death is. But, we don't weep as men who have no hope. We've got a hope beyond the grave. Although I cry, and I have pain, my hope is in Christ Jesus, and I know that he has the power to carry me even beyond this local pain. The effects of suffering all depend on how much you crawl into the Master's lap and let him minster to you as only he can.

Paul said, "God said to me." In other words, God said, "Paul, I've told you I'm not going to remove the thorn." In other words, "Quit asking because I've already answered. I'm not going to remove the weakness, but I'll tell you what I will do. My grace is sufficient."

Grace means getting what you need when you don't deserve it. Grace means overshadowing mercy. Grace means extraordinary goodness. "I'm going to give you my grace and my grace is sufficient." Sufficient means aplenty. Sufficient means enough. Sufficient more than you can use. Sufficient means continually available to you. God did not give Paul what he asked for, but he gave him something better. Paul asked for relief, but God gave him grace. Have you ever had grace to deal with a situation?

When I was at Mount Carmel, I remember vividly. I went to an elderly member's house. She was dying, and I went over to encourage her. And Pastor Haynes, when I got there, she was sitting up smiling. They told me the woman was near death and a few days later she did die. I expected that woman to be moaning and groaning, but when I got there—"Hi, Pastor, how are you doing?"

I said "I'm doing fine, how are you?"

She said, "It's so good to see you. You know I've been on this road a long time, and it won't be long until I'm going to see Jesus." That's what she told me. She said, "I can't wait to see my Master's face."

I went to encourage her, but she ended up encouraging me. For God had given her something that he hadn't given me. God gave her dying grace. She had grace to do what I didn't have grace to do because it wasn't my time.

A lot of people have said to me, "Pastor, thank you for being so strong" but my strength is not within me! You don't believe me. Let me show you in the book. Paul says, "Most gladly, therefore, I would rather boast about my weaknesses that the power of Christ may dwell in me." My power doesn't come from me. In fact, whenever you see human strength, God's power is nowhere around. So, stop trying to be so strong in your flesh keeping a stiff upper lip. God's power is not in that. God's power shows up when you're weak. God's strength is made complete in your weakness. That's how you get the power of God. Have I got a witness? Somebody ought to help me as I prepare to close this little message.

Look what he says. *"Therefore, I'm well content with weakness, with insults, distresses, persecutions, difficulties for Christ's sake,"* because he's going to take us further in and deeper down into the victory of suffering.

Now, there is a mystery in suffering. There is an agony in suffering. But, praise be to God! There is victory over suffering. First of all, God is going to test you. You can't have a testimony without a test. Some folks get tested a lot. Some folk "testi-lie" because they've never been through anything.[2] God has to test you. And look what Paul says through the test. "I am well-content in my weakness. I can handle insults, distresses, persecution, difficulty, because I know it's all about him and not about me." I'm so thankful today that we have Paul's example so I can come to this pulpit to say, "Lord, whatever you decide is alright with me."

I'm not that strong. In fact, I'm weak. I cried when I heard that I had cancer. My wife and I got together. We cried together. But, God looked down and saw how weak we were, and I caught her hand, and I said, "Let's pray." As we called on the Lord, I got up at 4:00 in the morning, made my way in to the living room, got into the word. I heard David say, "It was good that I was afflicted." Have I got a witness here? Because when God carries you further in and deeper down, he's about to do something special with you. Have I got a witness? "Lord, I don't like it, and it hurts, but if you can get glory out of it, here's my body. Do what you have to do." Have I got a witness? I've got to hurry up and close here now.

But, let me tell you one last thing that he says about this victory. He says, "When I am weak, then I am strong." Have I got a witness? I'll tell you what you do. When your thorn is causing you pain, find you a praying ground. Tell the Lord, "I've got pain in my side," and watch the Lord work it out. Have I got a witness? I've got to hurry up and close here now. I've already been here too long.

But, there was a new farmer, and he hired a well digger to dig a new well on his farm. They decided they would charge the landowner by the foot. He said, "Build me a well, and I'll pay you by the foot." Fortunately, about nine feet down, they hit water.

The well digger told him, "This well will last through some good years."

But the farmer asked, "When the dry season comes, will this well be deep enough to make it through?"

The well digger said, "No, this well is for the normal season. This well is for the normal rain. This well is for the normal environment. But when the dry season comes, this well will not be deep enough to bring you water."

---

2. Dr. Bailey would often say that some people testify to what God has done and other people lie about what has happened to them, as in they "testi-lie."

The farmer said, "Then, keep on digging. I want you to dig a little deeper."

The well digger said, "If I dig deeper, it's going to cost you some more."

He said, "I know. Every time you go deep, it's gonna cost you something. But keep on digging! I don't care how much it costs. I want to get way down." So, he kept on digging thirty feet down and he hit a wellspring. Have I got a witness?

The farmer said, "It's alright. I'll pay the price. But I need a well that can handle the dry season." Have I got a witness?

You need a well that can handle your dry season. If you stay on the surface, you will be shallow in your life. If you stay on the surface, you will blow away with the wind. But if you keep on digging, dig in the word of God, dig in your prayer, dig in your churchgoing, dig in blessing other folks, then when the dry season comes, you'll be deep enough to have water coming out from a very deep well.

Jesus was on Calvary, but he kept on digging. Have I got a witness? Because he knew that no other mountain would carry him deep enough. But, he kept on digging. He dug until he hit redemption. He dug until he hit salvation. He dug until he hit justification. He kept on digging. He dug until he hit a second chance. He dug until he hit mercy. He dug until he hit grace. Already. Early Sunday morning, he got up. He said, "That's deep enough!" Because he wants to carry you further in and deeper down in his will.

Will everyone stand, please? All eyes right here. I don't know what tomorrow holds, but I know who holds tomorrow. I want my life to count for him. Any time you walk out on God's word, he's going to test you, but understand there's rest in him. He'll first give you the test, but then his power will rest upon you.

Listen. Electric power comes from pressure. Steam power comes from fire causing water to expand and pressure. Every kind of power you know about is a result of pressure. Spiritual power is the result of God causing some pressure in your life. Whether or not that power will be operative depends on how you respond to it.

So, don't come telling me about who you know that died with what I have. I don't want to hear it. I'm not going through this looking forward to dying. I'm going through it looking forward to living.

I believe the God I serve is just not through with me yet. One day I will die, but I don't believe it's now. I trust God. So, when you see me don't look at me with a long face. I have the joy of the Lord, and the joy of the Lord is my strength. What you see that God has given me, he's no respecter of persons, he'll give to you if you respond by trusting him.

Chapter 2

Caesar Arthur Walter (C. A. W.) Clark Sr. (1914–2008)

Living Legend 1996

The Preacher

Rev. Dr. Caesar Arthur Walter (C. A. W.) Clark Sr. (1914–2008) was the beloved pastor and leader of the Good Street Baptist Church in Dallas, Texas, where he served from 1950 until his death in 2008. An only child born on December 13, 1914, to tenant farmer parents in Shreveport, Louisiana, Clark had to drop out of school in the seventh grade in order to work on the farm. Converted at the age of thirteen, he was ordained as an itinerant preacher shortly thereafter at the age of fourteen. Then, as a young adult, he pastored city and rural churches in and around Shreveport. One of the first churches that he served, the Israelite Baptist Church in Longstreet, Louisiana, called him in 1933. When he took the bus to Longstreet, he would walk four miles from the station to the church and, when he had to take the train, he would walk six miles. They paid him $2.50 per month. Another church that he served, the Little Union Baptist Church of Shreveport, counted among its membership the family the late Johnnie Cochran Jr., the renowned defense attorney and civil rights activist.[1]

Self-taught and highly motivated, he applied and gained entrance to Bishop College in Texas where he graduated in 1946. Also in the 1940s, he met the woman who would become his wife, Mrs. Carolyn Clark. Together, they had one son, Caesar A. W. Clark Jr., and he was also stepfather to Carolyn's children, Tonya and Maurice.

In 1948, Dr. Clark accepted a call from the Good Street Baptist Church in Dallas. Under his leadership, the church became a voice for fair and equal housing for African Americans in Dallas, it purchased and renovated a housing complex for local residents, it established a primary school, and it also launched a learning center, a community center, a legal advocacy clinic, a credit union, and a nonprofit charitable foundation. In 1958, at a major turning point in the Civil Rights struggle, Dr. Clark also welcomed Rev. Dr. Martin Luther King Jr. to preach at Good Street. During his years at the church, he gained so much respect and esteem among ecclesiastical and civic leaders that, in 2003, the United States Congress voted to name a local post office after him, an honor that is almost always granted posthumously.

Clark also established himself as a gifted preacher, evangelist, and revivalist. He averaged approximately thirty week-long revivals per year. On one occasion, he preached to more than fifty thousand people in the Houston Astrodome. Not only has his style been emulated by many preachers who have followed him but, according to some experts, he is "by far one of the best whoopers the African American community has produced."[2]

1. In Cochran's autobiography *Journey to Justice*, he describes his earliest memories as a little boy walking to the church one block from his three-bedroom rented house in Shreveport's Lakeside section. He also recounts his vivid memories of Dr. Clark: "Our father sat apart with the other deacons, but I hardly noticed since my eyes, like those of the rest of the congregation were riveted on the diminutive man who bestrode Little Union's pulpit like a colossus . . . .No matter how warm the day, when C.A.W. Clark preached, no head nodded, no eyes wandered in search of distraction. He never used a note, because he had committed the Bible to memory and the Scriptures were alive on his tongue." This is a brief expert from a longer account of Dr. Clark's preaching and Sunday morning worship. See Cochran, *Journey to Justice*, 10.

2. Simmons and Thomas, *Preaching with Sacred Fire*, 627. For more on Clark's life and preaching, see also Alcántara, "Past Masters: Caesar A.W. Clark."

The Sermon

In the book of Proverbs, the thirtieth chapter, there is this word: *"The ants are people not strong, yet they prepare their meals in summer. The conies are but feeble folk, yet they make their houses in the rocks. The locusts have no king, yet go they forth all of them by bands."* And this is the text. *"The spider taketh hold of the hands and is in kings' palaces."*

I want to talk about a conversation I had with a spider. Now, in order to grasp what I shall attempt to say, you will need to put your imagination to work. Use your imagination, and I believe you will be able to grasp the meaning of my conversation with the spider. Oh, brothers and sisters, the spider teaches us that wisdom is not the peculiar possession of the bee. The spider teaches us that wisdom is not the exclusive possession of the great. The spider teaches us that wisdom is not the sole treasure of the strong. The spider is small. The spider is weak. But the spider is wise. And somehow, the wisdom of the spider turns her little nest into greatness. Somehow, wisdom turns her weakness into strength.

Now, when I saw this spider, I observed on the basis of the text that it was a female spider. The spider taketh with *her* hands. Female spider. Her—she—a symbol of femininity. She—a symbol of motherliness. She—a symbol of tenderness. She—a symbol of comfort. She—a symbol of understanding. The text says, "She taketh hold." Now, look at that. She taketh hold. Oh, brothers and sisters, if we could just get some people to take hold. She taketh hold.

And in a minute, we will move on to what she takes hold with. Give consideration to the fact that she taketh hold. Think of all of the wonderful opportunities we have to be and to do. But we refuse to take hold. Think of how much further along we could be as a people, but we refuse to take hold. Think of how much further along we could be economically, but we refuse to take hold. Think of how much further along we could be politically, but we refuse to take hold. Think of how much further along we could be educationally, but we refuse to take hold. The opportunities present themselves to us but, for some reason, we refuse to take hold.

Could it be that we lack the wisdom of the spider? The spider was where she was because she had taken hold.

Oh, brothers and sisters, think of how many churches refuse to take hold. They have pastors spend the long hours in prayer and meditation and in planning programs designed to advance the church. But in so many instances, churches refuse to take hold.

Oh, brothers and sisters, we know that in many instances, when we want to give ourselves a biblical basis for criticizing the pastor, the church is not doing as well as she ought to be doing. We lay this on the pastor: "Where there is no vision, the people perish." And we take that as the pastor lacking vision. But I was thinking about that two weeks ago, and it just occurred to me that not only must the pastor have vision, the people must have enough vision in order to see the pastor's vision and take hold. It does not matter how much vision the pastor has. If the people refuse to take hold, then advancement will not take place, no matter how much vision the pastor has. If the people refuse to take hold, then the promise will not be forthcoming. The object of this effort is to reclaim the backsliders and then to win them all.

In a little while, Pastor Bailey will come with a special appeal. And then, our hope is, our prayer is, that somebody will take hold. You all gonna take hold tonight? Tonight, hope is coming this way. The lifeline has already been thrown. Somebody ought to take hold. Now, I wouldn't bother you about it if I hadn't taken hold myself.

Back in my native state of Louisiana, one Tuesday afternoon, at the Greenville Baptist Church, I took hold. And then, I told you this before. I think I want to tell you again. Since I have taken hold, I don't feel no wastin' time. I've been preaching fifty-three years. I've been a pastor forty-nine years. I don't feel no wastin' time. I've come too far from where I was. Nobody told me how hard the road would be. It's not been easy. But he's brought me this far, to here. If there is a backslider here this evening, will they please take hold? If there is any saved man, woman, or child present this evening when the appeal is made, take hold. Tomorrow has not come. And yesterday is gone. The only time you have is right now.

Now, my brothers and sisters, notice when you read this, that the spider is small. Yes, you know bigness is a mark of American culture. We go for big things, not necessarily for useful things, just so they're big. Yes, we go after big things. Not necessarily what we need, but something big. We have the notion that, if we possess something big, then that makes us big. If we are lacking for something essential on the inside, then we get something big on the outside to compensate, to make up for our lack.

A great many of us are in debt now that we really shouldn't be in, but we just had to have something big. And not really what we need, but something big. Some of us feel, yes, that to get something big is to have a ride. My brothers and sisters, the biggest thing is not necessarily the best thing. The newest thing is not necessarily the most enduring. The spider is small, but she does not allow her size to determine her station in life.

Oh, brothers and sisters, yes, I saw a spider in my travels. I saw this spider in a place, yes, where, in my opinion, at the time when spiders were not supposed to be. And I saw this spider in a palace! I had seen spiders before, but the spiders I had seen before were in the poor man's cottage. I had seen spiders in barns. I had seen spiders in fence corners. I had seen spiders in weeds. I had seen spiders under the side of the house. But never before had I seen a spider in a king's palace.

Now, let's take a quick look around at the palace. Behold, the ornate decorations. Behold, the oriental rugs. Yes, behold the stained-glass windows. Behold, the courtiers attending the kings. Behold, the lavish appearance of the furnishings. Behold, the chandeliers. When the wind blew through the palace, the chandeliers made music like the old harps, and, by gentle breeze. I enjoyed touring the palace. And I was almost ready to leave and, lo and behold, I saw a spider.

I had seen spiders before, but I never saw spiders that had the nerve to spin a web in the king's palace. Well, my brothers and sisters, when I saw this spider, I didn't strike up a conversation at once. I just looked at the spider and tried to figure out why she would be there. Something told me that aspiration is not the exclusive possession of the great, and something told me that hope is not confined to the great.

Well, after having looked at this spider for a while, I went over—and use your imagination—and you can tune in on our conversation. I said, "Spider, now what are you doing here? Spider, you have a lotta nerve to be in this place." Well, then, the spider said to me, "I know I am a spider." Well, yes. You see, when you know who you are, believe so much.

I heard that great Brooklyn preacher Gardner Taylor say, "When we forget whose we are, we forget who we are." Well, when you forget who you are, you behave in a strange fashion.

You see, the demoniac in the land of the Gadarenes didn't know who he was. You see, brothers and sisters, the stars tell us that many are suffering an identity crisis. You see the beasts of the farmers don't have to know who they are, and the fowl of the air don't have to know who they are. But a man has to know who he is.

Now, I already told you I'm old and slow. Well, yes, the spider said to me, "I know I am a spider." Well, you ought to know who you are. If you don't know who you are, you ought to find out before you leave from here. I would like to tell you. I know I'm a child of the king. I know, yes, I know I've been born from above. And my name is written in the Lamb's Book on high. I know I am his and he is mine. And every now and then, yes, I am reminded from within that I am a child of the king. Because I'm a child of the king, I don't worry. I'm not uneasy for being his child. If it be his will for me, he can cool the fiery furnace because I am his child. If it is in keeping with his will, he can stop the mouth of the lions for me.

Well, the spider said, "I know I'm a spider. But then, in spite of my spiderhood, I have hopes and I have aspirations. And I been a long time getting here."

"Well," I asked the spider, "How long have you been on your way in to the king's palace?"

And the spider said to me, "I don't know exactly how long it's been, but to give you some idea of how long I've been on my way to this place, you seen some of my ancestors out in the country. Some of my ancestors never got any farther than the barn. Some of my ancestors never got any farther than the fence corner. Now, they had a desire to make it here, but they never quite made it. But they transferred to me their hopes and their aspirations."

Well, when the spider spoke about hopes and aspirations, I could understand that. For I, too, have come a long way with hopes and aspirations. You see, I was born without a name. Yes, I hope you'll be patient with me. I was born without a name for the man that fathered me was not married to my mother. Society looked at me and assigned me the category of the illegitimate. Well, I don't quite understand what makes a baby illegitimate. For, you see, nobody consulted the baby. Nobody asked the baby for his choice. When the baby knew anything, he was already here.

Well, my brothers and sisters, I was born without a name. I had to borrow a name. And in Louisiana, we didn't have but three months' schooling. The cotton folk didn't have but three months. Well, I've never seen a high school diploma with my name on it. But that is not to encourage anyone not to go to school. It is to show you what the Lord can do.

Well, my brothers and sisters, I dropped out after second grade. That's as far as I ever learned in the public school. In 1942, when I went on to the campus at Bishop College in Marshall, Texas, at that time I didn't have a high school diploma. But the late dean, Melvin J. Banks, took me in hand and gave me an examination, and then admitted me on a probationary basis. Well, I would understand the spider's hopes and aspirations.

Well, you know, you don't have to have as much as you think you have to have. When I went to Bishop College, my money was short. I lived many a week on one dollar. Now, don't tell me it can't be done. I've already done it. Well, yes, a great many people are worried over budget cuts, but that doesn't bother me. For I picked up the Bible the other day and turned to where it says, "Trust in the Lord. He'll keep you. The soul shall thou dwell in the man, and therein thou shalt be fed." Well, not only did I have aspiration, but I had hope. I still do. For I stand here on Jesus' name. "On Christ the solid rock I stand. All other ground is sinking sand."

Well, the spider said to me, "I've been a long time getting here. I didn't start out in the king's palace. I used to be in fence corners. I used to be in the weeds. I used to be in barns. But, even while I was in the fence corner, I dreamed of the palace. Even while I was in the weeds—yeah—I didn't think weed thoughts. I thought palace thoughts. Even while I was down in the ditch, I didn't think ditch thoughts. I thought palace thoughts."

Well, I noticed—and I've been coming here a long time—I believe I noticed this year more children, more teenagers, and more young adults attended this meeting than ever before. And that's a healthy sign. That's a good sign, and it's also a challenge.

I say to the children, the teenagers, and the young adults: you may be living in the ghetto, but you don't have to think ghetto thoughts. Well, you may be living in a shabby place, but you don't have to think shabby thoughts. You may be living in a run-down building, but you don't have to think run-down thoughts. Well. Yeah.

You recall in your reading. They put John or whoever wrote the Revelation on a barren isle. Yeah. They bound his body, but they couldn't bind his mind. They bound his body, but they could not bind his spirit. Yeah.

Well, keep on thinking palace thoughts. You'll make it after a while. Keep on thinking high thoughts. You'll make it after a while. Yes.

The spider told me that even while she was in an out-of-the-way place, she dreamed of a better place. Well, brothers and sisters, I gotta leave that spider now, and say something else.

You see, you and I are mixtures of dust and divinity. We're not all divine on the one hand, not all dust on the other hand. We are mixtures of dust and divinity. And, the dust, yes, tries to block our way. But the divinity helps us to keep on climbing. Every now and then, yeah, we give in to the dust and yield to temptation. David gave in to the dust. Divinity told David, "Don't do it, king. She belongs to another man. Don't do it, king." That's divinity talking. But, the dust kept on pulling, and the dust won out. Yeah. But, you know, the dust never wins ultimately. The dust never wins finally. For, I hear David saying, "Create in me a clean heart, and renew within me a right spirit." Yeah.

Then, Paul has trouble with that dust. And, I hear him saying, "Oh, wretched man that I am. Who shall deliver me from the body of this death?" But, then divinity won out. And I hear him saying, "There is, therefore, now no condemnation to them that are in Christ Jesus who are not after the flesh but after the spirit."

Well, thank God. The spider kept on climbing until she reached the king's palace. And, the text says, she took hold with her hand. You see, much of what happens to you in this life will be determined by what you do with your hands. Much of what happens to you in this life will be determined by how you use your hands. You see, hands can do evil. But, I want my hands to be clean. I want my hands to do good.

Every now and then, I ask the Lord, "Precious Lord, take my hand. Precious Lord, it's an uphill journey. Precious Lord, take my hand. The day is dreary. Take my hand. The night is dark. Take my hand. The burden is heavy. Take my hand. My heart's full of sorrow. Take my hand. My eyes are full of tears. Take my hand. Trouble's all around. Precious Lord, take my hand. Precious Lord, take my hand. Lead me on. Let me stand."

Every now and then, "Father, I stretch my hand to thee. No other help I know. If thou withdraw thyself from me, oh, whither shall I go?"

Well, thank God, the spider made it to the king's palace. Oh, brothers and sisters, I started out a long time ago, to make it to the king's palace. I've been sometimes up and sometimes down, sometimes weak and sometimes strong, sometimes right and sometimes wrong. I don't know how you feel about it.

But, I———I'm on my way to the king's palace, sometimes weak and sometimes strong, sometimes up on the mountain and sometimes down in the valley.

But, I———I am determined to make my way to the king's palace. Sometimes I just steal away, and I ask myself, Why should I feel discouraged? Why should the shadows come? Why should my heart be lonely and long for heaven and home when Jesus—I———I—Jesus is my portion, my constant friend is he. His eye———e—his eye————e is on the sparrow, and I———I know he watches me. I———I sing because I'm happy. I———I. I———I sing because I'm free. His eye———e. His his eye———e is on the sparrow.

Chapter 3

Manuel L. Scott Sr. (1926–2001)

Living Legend 1997

The Preacher

Rev. Dr. Manuel L. Scott Sr.'s preaching ministry extended far beyond the walls of the churches that he pastored. Born in Waco, Texas, on November 11, 1926, he grew up poor in the South during the Great Depression and Jim Crow era segregation. At the age of nine, he became a Christian through the influence of a neighbor named Mrs. Tommye Jackson, a woman who invited him to a church service at the historic Toliver Chapel Baptist Church. As a result of her invitation, and through the mentoring he received from more than one pastor at Toliver Chapel, Scott answered the call to preach in 1944, becoming licensed and ordained as a minister of the gospel at the age of eigh-teen. Soon after his ordination, he enrolled as a student at Bishop College in Marshall, Texas. He also married his childhood sweetheart, Mrs. Thelma Scott, to whom he remained married for over forty years before she passed away from cancer. They reared six children together.

In 1949, he took his first church, Calvary Baptist Church of Los An-geles, California, where he remained for thirty-three years (1949–1982). He also pastored a second church, St. John Baptist Church in Dallas, Texas, where he served for thirteen years (1982–1995) and remained until his retirement.

Over his decades-long ministry, Dr. Scott built a national and inter-national reputation as a dynamic preacher and evangelist. *Ebony* listed him twice as one of the top fifteen Black preachers in America (1984, 1993).[1] In the words of Cleophus J. LaRue, Scott was a "a 'royal peculiar' who brought dignity and grace to the office of pastor and held high the standards of the black preaching enterprise."[2] Scott also possessed a special gift for reaching people in many different types of contexts. He preached frequently for city-wide revivals in Los Angeles and Dallas, and he also preached at conferences, conventions, or evangelistic crusades for the National Baptist Convention, Inc., the Billy Graham Evangelistic Association, the Southern Baptist Con-vention, and the International Congress on World Evangelization. In ad-dition, he served as the executive secretary of evangelism for the National Baptist Convention, USA, Inc., and was at one time the director of the Con-gress of National Black Churches, Inc. in Washington, DC.

Besides preaching, he ministered to countless people through his pub-lications, writing numerous book chapters and articles, and two books: *From a Black Brother* and *The Gospel for the Ghetto*. Two of Scott's sons went into full-time pastoral ministry. In 2010, one of his sons, the Rev. Dr. Manuel L. Scott Jr., published a wonderful collection of his father's sayings and sermons, *The Quotable Manuel Scott Sr.: Words from a Gospel Genius*.

The Sermon

In the brief period that we have, I want to speak to the urgency of the gospel and its decisiveness for human destiny. You may recall that Walter Cronkite used to end all of his reporting on CBS with the expression, "And that's the

1. See "America's 15 Greatest" and "15 Greatest Black Preachers."

2. From the dedication page in LaRue, *Power in the Pulpit*, iv. For more on Scott's preaching, pastoral ministry, and biography, see Alcántara, "Past Masters: A Poet in the Pulpit"; Scott, *The Quotable Manuel Scott Sr.*

way it is." I want to pull that as an umbrella over the message this morning: *And that's the way it is.*

If we would vote for what could be called "everybody's text," if we had to vote for a verse in the Bible that would be called the "Credo of Christianity," if we had to vote for a verse that could be described as "the gospel in the Gospels," if we were called upon to select a sentence from Scripture on which it could be said that all of the Bible hangs, if we were called upon to pick a verse that expresses the essence of the church's message, if we had to choose a rhetoric that would round out the reigning truths of our religion and the requirements for salvation through Jesus Christ, if we had to vote for a verse that would nestle the good news of the gospel and that would embrace the dominant sentiment of the Bible and the church, if we had to pick everybody's text, I would surmise that most of us would vote for John 3:16.

You know how it reads, don't you? *"For God so loved the world that he gave his only begotten Son, that whosoever believeth in him should not perish, but have everlasting life."* Here is the truth of Scripture in a teaspoon of terms. Here are both positives and negatives. "Shall not perish." Negative. "But have everlasting life." Positive. Here it is in John 3:16. Here is God's initiative. God's coming for us. "God so loved the world." But here also is man's response: "Whosoever *believeth* in him shall not perish." That's the response.

Here is the gold of the gospel: *"For God so loved the world that he gave his only begotten Son, that whosoever believeth in him should not perish, but have everlasting life."* And this verse is as instructive by what it does *not* say as much as it is by what it *does* say. It does not say that "God so loved the world that he gave his only begotten Son, that whosoever believeth in him should not perish, but have health." It does not say that! I wish we could say that if you believed in Jesus, you'd never get sick. That isn't what the verse says! And it does not say that we shall have happiness. No, it doesn't say that! Not happiness in any sense of what we're talking about. And it does not say that we shall have houses! It does not say that! It is a key verse, the key verse of Scripture! It is a crown of the gospel, but it does not say that! Believe in Jesus, and yet you might live in a shack! And it does not say that we shall have human help. Live in Jesus and believe in Jesus and folk will hate you without a cause! It does not say that! No! All this capitalistic cultural continental talk, all of this Western civilization wording. The weight of your gift for believing in Jesus shall have everlasting life. That's what we'll have.

Oh, now, I'm not about to be so irrational or impractical or unpragmatic so as not to say that if one believes in Christ, it enhances his equipment for the acquisition for life's acknowledged goods. It does that, but that's not what the spotlight is on. Jesus said: "God so loved the world that whosoever believeth in him should not perish but have everlasting life." And what is that? What is everlasting life?

Now, you know that I'm not smart enough to tell you because the Scripture says that eyes have not seen, and ears have not heard, nor has it entered into the heart of man what good things God has prepared for people who love him! Now, you know that I can't tell you. I don't know enough. But I can hint at it. Oh yeah, everlasting life is energy for coping victoriously with this life.

Now, I tell you if you come to church and you feel kinda played out, or if you look played out, I tell you, for the exhaustive business of dealing with existential dates, Jesus offers energy for this life. And just a little talk with him sometimes gives you resources just when you need them most, just when the lights are flickering, just when the days are too much for you to deal with, just when inadequacy and insufficiency dog your footsteps by day and by night. Jesus gives you energy!

That's everlasting life. Everlasting life expresses itself in the earthly context. You don't have to wait 'til you get to heaven. You can shout down here! Don't have to wait. And then everlasting life, I must hold it close. But everlasting life is endless life, endless duration. I tell you what we Christians have found. We've found a way to live always. Shall *never* die! And maybe I can't get a house or no healthiness or no money down here, but I can believe in Jesus and have life endlessly!

What a text this is! It's got so many components. You can walk through any door and lay your hand on some treasure. Look at that first door: "For God so loved . . ." That's quite a door, isn't it? What a component!

Now, I know about Auschwitz, and I know about Buchenwald where six million Jews were slain, and I know about Nagasaki and Hiroshima, where we dropped the atomic bomb. I know about black slavery and its bitterness and second-class citizenship and its hardships. I do know about that. And I know about starvation in Ethiopia and poverty, pressing poverty in India. I know about injustices! I do know, just like you, I belong. I identify with you! But I tell you. It is still true. God loves! God loves this world! Go home with that here.

But it simply doesn't talk about God's unqualified, unconditioned essence. This text has another compartment: "Loves the world . . ." God's universality. What a compartment that is! That God is no parochial, particular racist. God is tall enough to see over the fences that divide mankind, and He's everywhere present!

Now, look at another compartment. There is our unmerited response. He didn't say, "Whosoever acts like him"! No! No! Some of you came to church this morning perhaps trying to make up your mind to go with Jesus and you're not acting like him. But, that isn't what it says! It says, "Whosoever *believes* in him"! Believes that God is what he said God is. And believes that what he says doeth, we ought to do. And believes that what he claims is what is true for himself, shall not perish but have everlasting life. What a grand and splendid possession! Everlasting life! And this morning, *you* can have it! You can leave here with more energy for living, and with a passport to perpetuity to never end you! You can leave here with that.

Maybe you came here and your sins are too heavy for you. I saw—you know I like Westerns, and if I don't answer my phone on Saturday, it may be because that's the Westerns day. I saw a Western yesterday that had a criminal who had worshiped his gold for twenty years and had waited for twenty years to get out and get his hands on his gold. Then, when he got it, he recognized that it was his enslavement. And so, he laid it down where the Sheriff could get it. He said: "It's too heavy for me!"

I just want to tell you, if your sins are too heavy for you, lay 'em down! Take them, Jesus! He died for those sins. And then if your situation, you're not being able to get along with your wife, with your children, with your community, your situation is too heavy for you, lay it down at the feet of Jesus.

"God so loved the world." Ain't that good news? I wish somebody here this morning would say, "I believe that, and I'm gonna try." And I tell you, your load will get lighter! And your way will get brighter! For Jesus is the light of the world! He's the hope of all ages.

I went to Washington, first of the week, and Jewel Mackenzie is up there with her sister, Iris Carr. They met me at the airport on my arrival and, of course, she's got a mighty fine car. She made the car and Jewel and herself available to me in Washington the whole time I was there. Wasn't that nice? On my arrival, they were there. And all during my stay, they were available. And then when I got ready to make my departure, they were at my hotel taking me to the airport.

I said, "That's what Jesus does." Hallelujah! He was with me at conviction wall, at conversion center when I arrived. And you know he's been available to me the whole time I've been around! Oh, I'm sure he's been available to you. Oh, yeah. Available to me. Any time I need him, I just ring him up. Tell him, "Come see about me." He's available.

And one of these days, I'm going to have to make my departure. Like everybody else, I've got to lay down and die. But the same Jesus who's been available will be there to see me off on my departure! When the earthly journey's over, all of my labors, all over, Jesus will be right there to make up my dying bed! Right there, I tell ya! I love his name! I know him, and he knows me!

God Almighty, I wish somebody here this morning would just believe in him. The choir's going to sing, and I wish you'd just get up out of your seat, and say, "You know what? I want you, Jesus, to be at my arrival, and I want you to be available for me because I might have some blinded eyes that I need somebody to open. I might have some withered hands that I need somebody to heal. I might have some deceased friend that I have to have released from the dead. Or I might have some stormy waters that I need somebody to make hush! And won't you, Jesus, won't you, Jesus, abide with me? And I might end up in some lonely spot, and I need somebody to go with me always. Won't you, Jesus?"

Won't you try him today? Won't you believe in him today? Oh, yeah! Won't you get up out of your seat and let him take your sins and take your situations and take yourself? He's able! Won't you get up and come on? Sing that tune! That's the gospel! Sing that! That whosoever. Come on, that's right! Sure enough! They shall have. That's right, you come on! That's right, you come on this way! What a splendid sentence! What reigning rightness, God tell ya! What incomparable speech! Listen to it! You get up and shout today! You come! You come, today!

Chapter 4

Gardner C. Taylor (1918–2015)

Living Legend 1998

The Preacher

BORN ON JUNE 18, 1918, as the only child of an educated mother and a Baptist preacher father in Baton Rouge, Louisiana, Gardner Calvin Taylor (1918–2015) embarked on a journey in which he became one of the most significant preachers of the twentieth century.[1] His peers named him the

---

1. For more on Dr. Taylor's life, ministry, and preaching, see Thomas, *African American Preaching*; Carter, "The Audible Sacrament"; Alcántara, *Crossover Preaching*; and Alcántara, *Learning from a Legend*. See also the series of books edited by Edward L. Taylor that features Dr. Taylor's lectures, essays, sermons, and addresses, in Taylor, *The Words of Gardner Taylor*.

greatest African American preacher in *Ebony* magazine in 1984 and again in 1993.[2] In 1996, Baylor University listed him as one of the 12 most effective preachers in the English-speaking world.[3] In 2000, President Bill Clinton granted him the Presidential Medal of Freedom, the highest honor that a civilian can receive.

Dr. Taylor spent his teenage years as an agnostic until his involvement in a 1937 car accident in which a man died. The incident functioned as a transforming moment in his life, disrupting his initial plans to attend law school at the University of Michigan, and calling him forward into pastoral ministry. As a result, he enrolled in the Oberlin Graduate School of Theology in 1937, where he also met and married his wife, Mrs. Laura Bell Scott Taylor. They had one daughter, Martha Taylor LaCroix. While at Oberlin, he pastored part-time at Bethany Baptist Church in Elyria, Ohio, from 1938 to 1941. Then, he pastored full-time in Louisiana, first at Beulah Baptist Church in New Orleans (1941–1943), and then at Mt. Zion Baptist Church in Baton Rouge (1943–1948), the same church that his father had pastored years earlier. Then, in 1948, when he was only thirty years old, he and Mrs. Taylor left Louisiana so that he could answer the call to become the next senior pastor at Concord Baptist Church of Christ in Brooklyn. He remained there until his retirement in 1990, presiding over that congregation for forty-two years. During his years there, he also taught at as an adjunct professor at prominent divinity schools including Harvard, Yale, and Princeton, and he taught and preached internationally in countries such as South Africa, Australia, Japan, Brazil, Israel, and the United Kingdom.

Taylor actively advocated for civil rights, social change, and self-reliance as pastor of four different churches. He allied himself with Dr. Martin Luther King Jr. and the progressive civil rights wing of the National Baptist Convention, USA, Inc. Taylor sought the presidency of the National Baptist Convention in 1961. After a defeat that involved much controversy surrounding the results, he helped cofound the Progressive National Baptist Convention, Inc. (PNBC).

In addition to his preaching, teaching, lecturing, and advocacy work, Dr. Taylor also published widely, writing numerous articles, essays, book chapters, and books. Some of his published books include *How Shall they Preach?*, *The Scarlet Thread*, and a book that he co-wrote with Dr. Samuel D. Proctor titled *We Have This Ministry*.

He and his first wife, Mrs. Laura Scott Taylor, were married for over fifty years until she passed away in 1995. On July 30, 1996, he married his

---

2. See "America's 15 Greatest" and "15 Greatest Black Preachers."

3. See "Baylor Names."

second wife, Mrs. Phillis Strong, to whom he remained married for nearly nineteen years until his death on Easter Sunday, April 5, 2015, at the age of ninety-six.

The Sermon

Expository preaching represents the true gem of the preaching undertaking. But, like all gems, it must be treated with care and purpose. You must be careful that you do not leave dark corners which many expository preachers have left on the corner of the passage. They shine the light where they want it to be seen, but they leave much of the passage in shadows.

I had a conversation with a man who was dean of the Duke University Chapel whose name escapes me now. He has gone on to the Father's house. We talked one night in Gettysburg, I remember about the parables of our Lord which were dealt with here just a few minutes ago. He was talking about the emphasis on the one. That emphasis is there. Any gospel that does not begin with one does not begin. But, any gospel that ends with one ends. He was talking about the emphasis on one sheep, one boy, one coin. It came to me and I pointed it out to him.

In each instance, the one was restored to the group. The lost coin was returned to the family budget. The lost sheep, after much searching across thin and glen, and through briers, until the shepherd's hands were torn and his feet were torn and, in this case, his brow was torn and, in this case, his side was torn, he got that sheep to bring it back to the fold. In the case of the lost boy, he was returned to the family table.

To be honest to itself, expository preaching must keep both sides of the great terms of the gospel, to the individual and to the group. The failure of many expository preachers has been to focus on one, to throw the light on one part and not let the whole passage be seen for what it's worth.

Of course, those of us who come out of the African American community, as Henry Mitchell tellingly told us last night, ought never forget that we have to give a certain complexion to exposition. It is a combination of Athens and Jerusalem. The remembered Black preachers—J. H. Jackson, William Holmes Borders, Borders from Georgia and Garrett, Jackson from Mississippi and Colgate, Raymond Henderson from Virginia and Oberlin—they brought Athens and Jerusalem together. This is our responsibility. But, we must never lose the complexion that belongs to our exposition.

There's a story of a man who produced dog meat at a dog meat company. They were not selling well so he said to his sales force, "We're not doing well. Our dog meat has received the highest endorsement from the Veterinarian's

Association. But, it's not selling well. The advertising companies that give prizes for boxing, for packaging, that association has awarded one of its first prizes for packaging. The nutritionists have said that it's highly nutritious. But, it's not selling. Finally, I want to know why."

And one of the salesmen in the middle of the room replied: "The dogs don't like it!"

Now, if the dogs don't like it, you're not going to have a hearing.

Well, enough of that. When I started going to these New England schools, I found out that scholars never say that they left something out. They put an addendum which means, "I left it out. It needs to be added." So, I want to add something.

If you are interested in the history of preaching, you ought to see *The Concise Encyclopedia of Preaching* which has just been produced by Richard Lischer and William Willimon at Duke University. I forget who published it. One of the European companies I think. You'll want to get it. It is the most concise, the most complete. Now, Professor Duggan at Southern Baptist Seminary in the 1900s did two volumes—tremendous—on preaching. But, this is a concise volume, and on the types of preaching, and on some of the preachers who have gone down in history. I recommend it to you.

I want to talk with you today about something that really is a specimen out of my own experience. It is a biopsy of what I have passed through, a slice of my own experience.

All worthy preaching ought to in some sense be shielded autobiography, unless you are preaching at arm's length and reporting some far off, distant rumor. It ought to be something in which you have had some part. It is heart to heart work. This is the advantage we have in being human preachers. As was suggested in the earlier lecture today, not even God could get at us from a distance. Not the lyrics of Isaiah. Not the tears of Jeremiah. Not the heartbreak of Hosea. It was only when he made common cause with our humanity, got into the bruises and brokenness of our situation, took upon himself our likeness, came to know our heartbreak, felt our loneliness, was exposed to our cold, knew the meaning of being turned against, that God could say to us, "You cannot tell me that you don't know what I'm going through." So, I want to talk with you a bit on seeing our hurts, or, trying to see our hurts with God's eyes.

This conference ought not close without the name of Peter Forsyth being mentioned at least once. Forsyth said that "worthy preaching is coming at men from the Godward side." Our job as preachers and as believers is to try to see the hurts of life with the eyes of God.

Now, we cannot really do that because we see everything, as Tennyson said somewhere, in broken arcs. God sees and creates the whole round. But, we can attempt to see our hurts with God's eyes.

Now, I want to read a passage. I borrowed this Bible. I made a terrible mistake. I left my Bible that I carry with me at home. I am going to put a Bible now in every bag I use so that will never happen in this world again. Really, when I left my Bible, when I discovered that I didn't have the good word, I nearly said a bad word. So, I'm using Rudolf White's Bible here, print made for a young man.

From the Gospel of John, there are these words in the fifteenth chapter, at the second verse: "*Every branch that shall bear not fruit in my name, He taketh it away. And every branch that beareth fruit, He purgeth it that it may bear more fruit.*"

I've begun in my last years filing what the merchants call a caveat emptor [Latin: "Let the buyer beware"].

The things of Scripture are addressed to believers. Now, we ought not fade into some kind of vague universalism as if the promises of God belong to everybody, the great provisions of grace are just to be had for having. They belong to believers. I would want to emphasize that part of the passage which says "in me," because that's crucial.

You ought to read the start of the thirteenth chapter of John again. I know you've read it many times, but you ought to read it again. You ought to realize as you read it that you have come on awesome territory. There's a hush that will steal over your spirit.

If you read it aright, at the beginning of the thirteenth chapter, and awe will start to fill you. For Jesus is dealing with his disciples in the flesh for the last time. It is that fateful Thursday night. Soon, they will go out into the noisy violence of arrest, and his final sacrifice on Calvary.

They have finished the supper. Perhaps they are putting on their sandals and throwing their cloaks around them to go out into the chill of the spring night.

He sees a certain consternation in their faces and, rightly so, because he has told them, "I will not talk with you much more. I will send you someone, but I won't be with you."

Have you ever been in a gathering where you couldn't put your finger on it but, some dis-ease, some restlessness, some feeling of impending doom seemed to be in the air? He saw that in the disciples' eyes. They were about to leave. But, he turned to them again to try to fortify them for what was to happen, to try to get them ready for the violence, for the terror, for the dangers that lay ahead, and he says to them these words.

The Bible is not a strong book on "why." You don't find a great deal of "why"s answered. I think it's the first or second psalm. "Why do the heathen rage?" No answer. Then, one comes to one of the fortieth psalms, Psalm 42 or thereabout, and there comes the question, "Why dost thou stand afar off?" No answer.

There, on that darkest Friday, as the Earth shivers with the horror of it, and the Sun wraps itself in the cloaks of darkness, and angels gasp, and the music of heaven grows silent, there is that awful cry that shivers up out of the pain and loneliness of Calvary, "My God. My God. Why?"

The Bible is a strong book on "how." It tells us how to get from Earth to bright glory. It tells us how to stand the storm. It tells us how to face persecution and difficulty. It tells us how to die. But, very seldom does it speak of why. Here is one of the few instances. He says that "every branch in me that beareth not fruit, he taketh it away."

Our country ought to hear that. I could wish at this conference that we could hear more about the need of our corporate responsibility before God.

This is a greatly blessed nation. It has been ventilated by the cross-ventilation of two oceans and, therefore, has had its whole society blown free of the old shibboleths and claims of Europe and other parts of the world. It is a rich land. Its great fields are heavy with grain.

When the *Arabella* came close to these shores, John Winthrop, speaking one Sunday, said that unless we abridge ourselves of our superfluities—he put it in his quaint language—in order that the necessities of others might be met, we shall secure the wrath of God upon our venture.

Our nation needs to realize that; it needs to realize that we cannot be a nation of plenty in the midst of great poverty. Expository preaching needs to search the Scripture to find those places where that assertion is made clearly and unmistakably.

It is a sad fact that, since the Civil War, only two presidents have been elected from the Old South, the Old Confederacy. I'm not talking about Texas. I'm not talking about Missouri. I'm talking about the Old Confederate South. It is very interesting that the two people who have been elected have been very different in their outlook on many things. But, they have both been most despised in the region which gave them birth, and in the denomination whose children they are.

You will find many disparities between them, their makeups and their characters, but the one common line, the one common spirit in them, has been on the question of race. They have been despised. It says something that Christians ought to look at, particularly in this great Southern region of America.

"Every branch that beareth not fruit, He taketh it away." This nation is under God's judgment. If we do not straighten up in our attitudes toward each other, the God of history will veto the greatness of America.

"Every branch that beareth not fruit, He taketh it away." We Black people ought to recognize that. It is a sad fact. Let us take two poll stars of our whole journey in this land. Why is it that we are forever exalting W. E. B. DuBois, and rightly so, and forever downgrading Booker Washington? DuBois left us tremendous insights. But, Mr. Washington left us a school through which thousands upon thousands of young people have gone.

Why this dichotomy? Why this lowering and separating? Why can't we say both one and the other? If we are so fanciful that we follow symbols rather than substance, appearance rather than reality, and if our churches fail to be loyal to the gospel in dealing with its people's whole being, the whole counsel of God, he will take it away. "Every branch that beareth not fruit, He taketh it away."

But, then a strange thing is said here. "Every branch that beareth fruit, He purgeth it, slices it, brutalizes it, wrenches it loose, leaves it raw." Now, are you saying to me, "Preacher, if you try to do right . . .?" Yes, this is exactly the word. For God is not in the business of making us comfortable. He is in the business of making us worthy to be the sons and daughters of God. He is in the business of making us worthy to sit down with Abraham and Isaac and Jacob. He is in the business of making us worthy to carry on commerce with Paul and Silas. And, it takes some hurting to do that.

James Stewart, that marvelous Scottish preacher, has a wonderful word from a novel, I think, by George MacDonald, in which a woman who has come up on a sudden and shattering sorrow says, "I wish I had never been made." And her friend says, "But, my dear. You have not been made. You are being made."

And it takes a little crying. And it takes a little sighing. It takes a little trouble. Takes a little sorrow. Takes a little pain. It takes a little grief to make you. For God is in the business of making us.

Do you realize, my brothers and sisters, what he is making of us? Do you know that, one day, you standing beside Jesus, angels may look at you and look at Jesus, and nudge one another and ask, "Which one?" It is almost impossible to conceive. But, there the word stands in the New Testament. *"It does not yet appear what we shall be. But, this we know, that when He shall appear, we shall be like Him"* (1 John 3:2).

So, in your churches, when trouble comes upon you, and you do not know which way you're going to turn, you say again as before, *Have thine own way, Lord. Have thine own way. Thou art the potter. I am the clay. Mold me. Make me after thy will. While I'm waiting. Yielded and still.*

God is out to make something out of us. And it takes some crying, and it takes some sighing. It takes some mourning. It takes some grief. It takes some betrayal. It takes some loneliness. It takes some sleeplessness through the midnight hours for him to make us what he wants us to be.

But, "every branch that beareth fruit, he purgeth it." For what reason? That it might bear more. More fruit. Do you want that it in your life? More grace! More faith! More understanding! More compassion! More love! More power in prayer! More power in your preaching! More! More! More!

Let me bid you good day by saying this to you. It is hard for me to say because I have known great sorrow. I believe with all my heart, when I'm at my best moments, that one day, we shall thank God. When we are delivered into the fullness of our inheritance, in Jesus Christ, we shall thank him. Thank him for every sorrow. When we see, when we know as we are already known, and no longer see through a glass darkly, we shall thank him for every grief, thank him for every tear, thank him for every sorrow, thank him for every loneliness.

When we stand on the shores of eternal deliverance, our thankfulness will rise like anthems forever across the celestial plains and reverberate through the heavenly places.

Thank you! Thank you, Jesus! Praise God! Thank you! Thank him for every sorrow. Thank him for every tear. Thank him for every fear. Thank him for every loneliness. Thank him for every night when we watered our beds with our tears. Thank him! Thank him! Thank him!

Chapter 5

Henry H. Mitchell (1919–)

Living Legend 1999

The Preacher

Rev. Dr. Henry H. Mitchell (1919–) has served the academy and the church with distinction for more than seven decades. Born in 1919 in Columbus, Ohio, he went on to pursue academic degrees at Lincoln University, Pennsylvania (BA), Union Theological Seminary, New York (MDiv), California State University at Fresno (MA, linguistics), and Claremont School of Theology (PhD, Black church history and theology) at Claremont. He also holds honorary degrees from the American Baptist Seminary of the West, Lincoln University, and Christian Theological

Seminary. While at Union, he met his wife, Rev. Dr. Ella Pearson Mitchell, one of the first African American women to graduate from Union, a fantastic preacher, author, and leader in her own right. They married in 1944 and were married for sixty-four years until his wife preceded him in death in 2008. The parents of four children, they often ministered in tandem at churches and in academic settings.

Dr. Mitchell has led in a number of different capacities during his long and fruitful ministry. From 1945 to 1959, he served as a regional denominational leader for the American Baptist Church (ABC) in Fresno, California. He also served as pastor of Second Baptist Church of Fresno from 1959 to 1966 and pastor of Calvary Baptist Church in Santa Monica, California, from 1966 to 1969. Upon moving into more formal academic leadership, he became the first person to hold the Martin Luther King Jr. Professor of Black Church Studies at Crozer Divinity School from 1969 to 1974. In subsequent years, he served as a professor of Religion at California State, Northridge and as the founding director of the Ecumenical Center for Black Church Studies in Los Angeles. From 1982 to 1987, he served as academic dean and professor of History and Homiletics at Proctor School of Theology, Virginia Union University. From 1988 to 2000, he and his wife, Rev. Dr. Ella Mitchell served as visiting professors of Homiletics at the Interdenominational Theological Center (ITC) in Atlanta, Georgia. After twelve years teaching in Atlanta, they also served for a season as team teachers for the doctor of ministry program at United Theological Seminary in Dayton, Ohio.

Dr. Mitchell is the author of many essays, articles, and books. A list of his book publications includes *Black Preaching*, *The Recovery of Preaching*, *Celebration and Experience in Preaching*, *Black Church Beginnings*, and *A Word for All Seasons*. He also coauthored *Soul Theology* with Nicholas C. Cooper-Lewter, *Preaching for Black Self-Esteem* with Emil M. Thomas, as well as *Together for Good* and *Fire in the Well* with his wife.

He has devoted his life to teaching, preaching, writing, and service to the church. Moreover, his legacy in homiletics lives on through the many students he has trained over more than seven decades of service. In 2019, he celebrated his one hundredth birthday.

The Sermon

You've heard a lot already, but I don't suppose anybody has mentioned what in my experience has been a very outstanding characteristic of E. K. Bailey, namely, that he is persistently and graciously grateful. I don't know anybody in his position who is more grateful and not just routinely so, but very warmly and graciously so. And it warms my heart. I've known him since he was a freshman at Bishop and I was doing Religious Emphasis Week along with Bill Shaw. You remember, that for me, seventeen years ago, he and I shared the pulpit or the rostrum at a college in South Carolina. I was doing the lecturing and he was doing the preaching. I don't know if he remembers it or not, but he said to me one day, "That stuff will preach, won't it?" And I said, "Yeah, I reckon it will." I was doing a lot of things on Afro-American history. He invited me to Concord to preach the stuff that I had been lecturing on, and I have to say that, at that point, he joined my two dreams. He joined my dream of academic excellence and my dream of ministry in the church together, and it was very, very fruitful. All sorts of things have come out of that. On the bookshelves out there, you will see a book which I coauthored called *Preaching for Black Self-Esteem*. That book came directly out of the ministry which E. K. Bailey asked me to do on Black self-esteem at Concord years and years ago.

Tonight, I am assigned a critically important lecture. In his words, I have to say that "this stuff will preach." In the sense that it helps people focus and empowers sermon endings, it will preach or help preach. I'm grateful for the topic because it's at the heart of my research and writing. On the bookshelves out there, you will see this book, *Celebration and Experience in Preaching*. It was designated by The Academy of Parish Clergy as the top book on homiletics in the year 1991. It was one of the top ten and the only one on homiletics. So, I get a chance tonight to talk about the things that I have talked about in that book.

Now I want it understood that what this book says and what I have to say about preaching, however, is not something I made up. As E. K. has already said, really, it's something we were doing all along, but we hadn't really learned how to talk about it analytically. What I'm doing then is not at all my invention, it's just that I'm one of the people that started talking about this position and giving names for what was going on.

Both of my grandfathers were Baptist preachers; I guess I have to say Black Baptist preachers so you can be sure. I have trouble with that from time to time. I have a habit in many places I go. I let them know that old Dr. H. H. Mitchell, my grandfather, was one of the signatories when the National Baptist Convention was organized in 1895. That lets them know. Otherwise I might have serious problems. Both of these grandfathers were Baptist preachers; one of them was educated, one of them was not. Both of them were powerful preachers and both of them did what we call "coming on up" at the end of the sermon. They could come on up. But in all of my years around them, I never heard them discuss "coming up." I never heard them discuss what they were doing. They just did it.

And many of us, when we talk about preaching, don't ever get around to doing a serious piece of work on "coming on up." We have other words for it, we talk about moaning; we sometimes use the verb *tune*. We talk about gravy and, of course, you know, we talk about whooping. But we didn't talk about it as a component of a serious understanding of preaching. We didn't talk about it as an aspect of preaching competence.

Let me now offer a name for "coming on up." It's a little more dignified and perhaps a bit better descriptive. It's the word "celebration." What does it mean? If you look in the dictionary, the first thing it talks about is celebration as how one celebrates a mass in a Roman Catholic Church. I was quite fascinated by that because one day I did a lecture to four hundred seminarians in a Roman Catholic Church. They were learning how to celebrate the mass, and when I asked them all, "Do you really celebrate?" all of them said, albeit with some regret, "Well, they don't really celebrate it in the sense of celebrating, they just run through the routine, do the liturgy, pass out the elements."

There's another understanding of the word celebrate. Some of you may have heard of a small group of musicians called Kool & the Gang. Their most famous song, if I'm not mistaken, is "Celebration." Well, what are they celebrating? I really don't know. Sometimes, I watch them. Many years ago, when I was professor at Colgate Rochester Divinity School, they had a concert, and I went to the concert. They liked to celebrate us to death, and all I could figure out was a whole lot of people are smoking pot in the auditorium. In other words, celebration for them was "freaking out." We have celebration as in celebrating the Fourth of July or celebrating our birthdays.

I want to propose that we talk about celebration as celebrating Jesus' birthday, his death, his resurrection, and his coming again. Celebration in this sense is to be glad about something, to rejoice regarding something. It is this understanding of celebration that boils down to what might be called intentional, purposeful emotion—intentional, purposeful, emotion.

Listen carefully. "Coming on up" or celebration is potentially the greatest contribution to American culture that our ethnic group has given, greater than the spirituals and their contribution to the culture of worship. For if celebration were as widespread as the spirituals and jazz and all the rest of the things that have come from Black culture, we could have some hope of rescuing the church from its precipitous decline in our time. It could actually resurrect the pulpit of mainline Protestantism and Catholicism. It could in fact be the cause of the salvation of a nation once thought to be in the will of God. For this to happen, however, there are some costly conditions. And I want to talk about those conditions in the time that I have. It means that we are going to have to escape almost completely from the Western attitude toward emotion as such.

We need first of all to distinguish between high emotion and low emotion. Too many times we think only of low emotion. We need to actively affirm the higher emotion. You remember Paul said, *"Now abideth faith, hope, and love"*—these three—*"and the greatest of these is love."* Did it ever dawn on you that all three of them are emotions? Now they may have intuitive content—in fact, they do. But they are certainly not primarily anything more than emotion. And unless you have that emotion you haven't even got religion.

So, if we want to talk in a degrading way about emotion, we are already saying that we don't want to be fully and completely committed to the religion of our Lord and Savior Jesus Christ. You've heard somebody say, "Now don't get emotional on me. Now you're getting emotional." What they seem to be saying is that any time you get emotional you're getting irrational. You're getting out of hand. You're getting out of control. You're angry, or whatever it is, and emotion is something to be avoided when the truth of the matter is that love is an emotion, and I ain't ready to avoid it yet. We must understand that there are good emotions and other emotions.

There are high emotions and low emotions. We have to really be careful to be sure that we don't think all emotion is anger. Anger is just one of them but it has an opposite. Hatred is an emotion but it has an opposite. We preach the gospel of Jesus Christ which in every case is in fact the opposite.

We have to escape the influence of the Stoics on Western culture all the way back to Greece that put us into a dualistic worldview and made us associate emotion with the so-called flesh and thereby condemn it when, in fact, unless we have it, we have not life and we are not whole. But as people heavily conditioned in Western culture, we have to say then, one of the things you have to do is not make the mistake of leaving all feeling tones, all deep feeling in worship up to the Holy Ghost. You hear me?

I've heard people say, "If the Spirit moves them 'Glory,' but I refuse to tamper with people's feelings." Well, if you gonna preach the gospel, you better tamper with my feelings cause that's where my decisions are made; that's where the gospel has its most important effect. Unless I learn that preaching the gospel automatically involves some kind of purposeful emotion, it will never have any power. To be sure, if people are going to be moved, they must to be moved by the Holy Spirit. But, we have to do some planting and some watering. We have to make straight a way in the desert or whatever you want to call it. We have to do some preparing, and to the extent that we do it well and do it in the will of God, God can bless our ministry in a much greater way than often is the case now.

When people say they don't want to tamper with folks' feelings, that probably means that they haven't conquered their own fear of emotion. They have probably been afflicted with major cultural inhibition. And if this is the case, we need to work at it seriously because it cripples a preacher to be that inhibited. And I know because I had it for a long time. We have to open up and let our feelings be known because, unless they are known, we will not be known to be sincere in any serious way. We ought to be sure as we are deep in emotion, that we are in the will of God, and doing it to the glory of God. We must be sure that we're not just playing with emotions in order to push people and manipulate them, but once we are sure that we are in the will of God, then we ought to let it go. In order to do this, we need to quit leaving it up to the Holy Ghost and do a little planning towards celebration. We need to learn to be intentionally emotive because joy and gladness is emotion. We need to be ready to do whatever we can to pave the way for emotion, which is focused on the word and the will of God.

Why in the world should I be shy? Why should I be a little shaky? If I love the twenty-third psalm. One of the greatest celebrations in the Bible is the twenty-third psalm. I have to get to that point where I say, "Thou preparest a table before me in the presence of mine enemy; Thou anointest my head with oil, my cup runneth over." And I can't just say "Surely goodness and mercy shall follow me all the days of my life . . ." Surely! Oh, surely, goodness and mercy follow me all the days of my life. Surely, I shall dwell in the house of the Lord forever! I think we have to be aware that faith is more caught than taught, that it comes by contagion. Unless I let mine show a little bit, it may never be caught by anybody else. I thank God that there are some churches that have some lay people who are a bit contagious, too.

I'll never forget sister Caroline Perry when I was pastor thirty-five years ago at Fresno, California. Sister Perry had an amazing sensitivity to the movement of the Spirit. She could tell when the Lord was moving. She sensed it sooner than other folk, and when she sensed it, well, she got loose. Now most of those folk didn't shout like sister Caroline Perry. But don't you know it, every one of them was blessed by her shouts? And a whole lot of people undoubtedly came to Christ because of the contagion of her spirit. You can teach the background of faith and you can remove intellectual obstacles to faith, but the only way people are really going to get it is to catch it. When you celebrate it, it catches them.

Now, let us deal with people that aren't so problematically involved in Western culture. Let us deal with what giving our contribution of preaching to the world and to our own people will cost all of us. Let's talk frankly about some of the widespread habits that we will absolutely simply have to break. We do have some bad habits.

The first one, and the most prevalent one, and the hardest one to break could be called irrelevant endings. I used to call it irrelevant climax but I decided that was a word that had too many meanings. A twenty-first-century congregation is not going to put up with irrelevant, unrelated celebration. It just isn't going to be possible to continue the clichéd stock celebrations that we run out Sunday after Sunday. "Ain't God alright?" Or, we talk about lilies of the valley, and all of this, and we have some people for whom it's a button to push for celebration and fine, if it's a blessing to them. But just understand that, in the twenty-first century, altogether too many people are going to be completely sensitive to what you are doing. They will know that it is a form of manipulation, and they won't respond.

If our son were living he would be fifty. So, this must be forty-plus years ago. He was nine years old, and I had preached in Redwood City one Sunday. We were riding down the road having eaten dinner, and he looked over at me and said "You believe in that?" Well, I tried to play dumb. I wasn't dead sure what he was talking about, but I was pretty sure. I said "What do you mean?" "What that man did, that's what I mean." And I said "Well, they like it; they enjoy it." I had preached and I had gotten as far as I could go. I was celebrating full blast and I sat down, and this man got up behind me. He said about four of the pushbutton words, and the place was wrecked. And this nine-year-old boy said to me, "Do you think that's right?" And I said "Well, they think it's right." "But I didn't ask you what they think," he said. "I want to know, what do you think?" "You don't see me doing it, do you?" He said "But just tell me straight out." This was a nine-year-old boy.

There are all sorts of people in the Boomers and in the Busters and all these generations that Dr. Bailey talks about who are sensitive to the fact that we are in many cases celebrating but not celebrating where we started. If you celebrate something you did not preach about it's like putting an eraser on it because you remember: you are influenced by the things with which you are associated most deeply emotionally. Unless you can celebrate what you preached about, you will avoid the possibility or miss the possibility of ecstatically reinforcing the word and the will of God while you are busy helping people celebrate something else.

Well, I'm not going to say what I thought about all the messages I've heard here, but you may want to look at that. To the extent that you celebrate what you preached about, you make it unforgettable. And to the extent that you preach a beef sermon and drown it in chicken gravy, you made them forget all about the beef. Some of the greatest preachers in America are guilty of studying, working, praying, meditating, and giving a major message, and then pulling a cord. And nobody remembers what he preached about, but he sure did preach.

Let me suggest that another habit we will have to break is a habit of preaching without a specific behavioral purpose. And let me say I have been really thrilled at this conference to see all these people making my speech. It's even in the literature. Dr. Bailey had on there that it's got to have an influence on your action and your attitude. But if you don't know what action and what attitude, is there any chance they'll know either?

We need to have a specific behavioral purpose which, if we hew to that purpose, it will give the sermon focus. Now, mind you, I'm not prepared to say, and I heard somebody else say it since I've been at this conference, I'm not prepared to say that my purpose will be accomplished by the preaching of that purpose. I don't know what the Holy Spirit is liable to do with it. But this much I do know, unless I have one purpose, if I have many purposes I'll be like the fellow who got on his horse and rode off in all directions and didn't go anywhere. We desperately need to know why we're preaching this sermon. It's just that important. We need the focus.

Related to that, also, is preaching in broad, eloquent abstractions and generalities. We gotta quit that! You can do a lot of pretty language, you can have a lot of alliteration, you can do all of that. But if you do not have in that sermon some very specific images of how this text applies to your life, how this purpose flows out in action, people won't really know. Jesus could have said, "You ought to have compassion; everyone should be compassionate." He didn't do that. He said, "There was a man who went down the Jericho road," and he went on to talk about a fella we have come to know as the good Samaritan.

Incidentally, on the side, I'm a little happy about that Samaritan because, if you know that the original Canaanites were Black—as Black as any of us—that they were from the ethnic stock of Africa—then you know that the Samaritan who was probably part Jew and part Canaanite was a brother. While I'm on that theme, let me suggest that the fellow who wrote about it, his name is Luke. Luke is short for Lukas, and the only time he mentions his name, I believe, is the thirteenth chapter of Acts when he talks about who ordained Paul, Lukas of Cyrene. Guess where Cyrene is. So, a Black doctor named Luke remembered a story Jesus told about a brother named Sam the Samaritan. Jesus didn't leave it up to chance; he wanted to know what compassion was, and he spelled it out. Sometimes you may get some very vague and general text, and you have to add some specificity to it.

Paul is guilty on many occasions of just making a sweeping statement. If it's going to come alive, you're going to have to make it come alive. When he says, "In everything, give thanks, for this is the will of God in Christ Jesus concerning you," there are no pictures in there anywhere. So, I try to make it concrete. Make people see it. So I walk up to Paul, and I said, "Paul let's get real. You talking about being thankful in everything?" Paul told me and said, "Well, remember, I said in everything, I didn't say for everything." "But then," he said, "but I'm serious." "You being real serious?" "Yeah, check me out." So I checked him out, and I saw him standing in front of Agrippa and he said, "I am very happy, I feel very fortunate, and I'm privileged to speak concerning the things whereof I am accused." You know what he was thinking? He was thinking, "Lookie here. I got a king sitting here, and I'm going to get to preach to a King. Most people don't get to preach to no king. I may have some chains on me. I may be a prisoner, but, but, but, but, I'm preaching to a king. And unlike kings normally who can say, 'If you don't make me laugh, off goes your head,' he's got to listen to me because he's not only wearing the crown of a king, he's wearing the robe of a judge. The judge has to hear me cuz I am a citizen of Rome, and therefore, at this point I am privileged to testify, and I believe that's what I'll do. And I'm so glad."

Now after I check Paul out I say, "You know what, I believe he's right. He ain't joking." But it would mean almost nothing for me to say "in everything give thanks" and leave it there. It's got to be seen. It's got to be heard and smelled and tasted and touched, so that it becomes real and vivid, and becomes for me a specific kind of experience.

Let me say briefly that we need to spread some celebration throughout the sermon. And I was quite pleased to hear Warren Wiersbe say something to the same thing. But I think we're talking a little bit differently about reasons. He said you go up so far, and you rest, and you go on and you rest some more. Well, I said you go so far, and you nail it with a celebration. Then you go a little higher and nail it with another celebration. Then you go to the top one and then you sure enough nail it.

Finally, let me suggest what I consider to be the second greatest sin of our pulpits today. That's the sin of being overly negative in our preaching, the sin of using the pulpit for a whipping post. We need to be extremely careful about this. Somebody said though, "But, Reverend, my people demand it." Well that's true, there are people who are like children. You ever seen a child so badly abused that a whipping was the only attention he or she has ever got, and they feel neglected if you don't whip them? There are congregations like that, which are spiritually masochistic, and you may get called to one. But, if you get called to one, do not succumb to the temptation. Help them, help them please. Not overnight will they change but little by little, if you love them and help them to celebrate the goodness of God, they'll change a lot quicker. It's just a fact that people are not helped by being browbeaten.

People say, "Well, Reverend, you getting soft on sin, that's what you doing." No, I'm not getting soft on sin. I'm simply suggesting that the most effective warfare against sin is conducted at the moment of transformation when people in the highest emotion they have are met by the Holy Ghost and changed. That's when it happens.

Fear only works until a greater scare comes along. Negative words without empowerment do not really do much, for the truth of the matter is that most people are not sinning because they don't know it's wrong. They are sinning because they haven't got the strength or the power, the spiritual maturity to overcome it.

Most people are like that fella who came to Jesus with his son and when Jesus said, "Do you believe? Can you believe?" "Yes, I believe, but I don't believe enough." Jesus doesn't fuss with him for not believing. Jesus knew the man said what all of our congregations are saying far more than most of us realize. "Help, thou, my unbelief, help thou my wayward mind. Help, thou, my selfish disposition. Help my anger, Lord. I just want some help. I don't need to be fussed at. I fussed at myself enough. Just help me! Give me some help!" This is the greatest way to overcome sin.

If you keep fussing at folk without giving them empowerment, you keep the sin on their mind, and if they keep thinking about it, you know what's going to happen? They're going to do it. Fussing preaching is an advertisement for the sin it speaks against. Fussing prophecy is a way of enhancing the sin because it keeps people's minds on it; it doesn't give them a thing except for fear with which to combat it. Most people want to do right. They know what's right. They want some help.

Here is a soundly celebrated formula that'll work for most sermons. Start positively. Don't turn the people off right away. Start positively. If there is a sin which definitely must be confronted, if there's a sin that they don't know about or a sin that needs to be addressed confrontationally, do that in the second move or the second point as we call it. A move is a point made to come alive. In the third move, celebrate and empower and help folk to overcome it. A rule of thumb would be to never preach more than a third of your sermon giving folk a spanking. Don't start spanking and don't end spanking, and don't spank too long in the middle.

Let me conclude with a scan of a sample sermon. It's a sermon that appeared in a book I wrote many years ago called *The Recovery of Preaching*. It's a sermon about a preacher who was planning to blow the folk up. It's about a prophet who was planning to get 'em told. He was in the heat of his spirit, ready to bless them for forever. His name was Ezekiel and you read about him in the third chapter of the book of Ezekiel. The first eleven verses he talks about how evil, how mean, how wrong, how everything those people are, and then the Holy Ghost gets a hold of him.

In the twelfth to the fourteenth verse, he's carried away in his spirit and, for seven days, in the words of our text, he sat where they sat, identified with the people, sat there and saw that all sorts of things that he was going to fuss at them about needed to be understood. He needed to sit where they sat and realize that what was on his mind was on the hill at Mount Zion and it didn't apply down here. What he was fussing about was a society that was centered around the church, had its own tax-supported cathedral, and all the rest of it. Here were people who were a religious minority. They had no building at all. They had no support at all, and they gathered by a steamy canal referred to as the River of Chebar. In that hot steamy environment, they still remembered Zion so much that they said in one of the songs, "If I forget Zion let my hand be cut off." They said, "How can we sing the songs of Zion in a strange land?" because they had been taught by the priest that the only place to worship was in Zion.

When he saw all of that, he thought a little bit differently. It wasn't as bad as it looked. The very fact that they gathered with no building and no air conditioning, the fact that they had to get against the whole majority culture suggested that maybe they had much better religion than he thought. But he didn't see it until he sat where they sat. The results of his sitting there have tremendous historical significance. It is awesome to contemplate what he did as a result.

In the eighteenth chapter he says, "You've heard it said that our fathers have eaten sour grapes and the children's teeth are on edge." No more let this be said, as the soul of the father is my soul, also is the soul of the son, and the soul that sins, that one's gonna die. What this boils down to, in case you hadn't noticed, is that we are each of us individually accountable and this was not known until he sat where they sat. God saw fit to release them from the fear of being cursed by their parents.

Individual accountability has been taken too much to great extremes, but the truth of the matter is that we wouldn't have individual accountability at all, and that would be worse—except that he sat where they sat. Here was a dis-spirited, discouraged group of people who came down by the river anyhow, and he told them he had seen a vision.

Over later in the book, the vision was a valley of dry bones. When he got through talking about how those bones could come to life, they had hope. But the most interesting result is this: he says it, and I think it's in 36:34 or 24 that God says, "I'm going to put my Spirit in your heart." And that sounds easy enough. But, you know what's behind all that? Here are a group of people who thought they had to be in Jerusalem, and what he is saying is that God will be with you. God's Spirit will worship with you. God will go with you wherever you want to bow your knee and say a prayer. God is there. The whole movement of synagogues and all the rest of it, that have kept the faith alive in the diaspora which has covered all the four corners of the Earth, all of that comes from a vision which, mixed in with a lot of other negative prophecies, says, "God says, 'I will be worshipped, and my Spirit will be present with you wherever you are. I'll give you a new spirit in your heart.'" Jewish faith has survived in a far more significant way then it might ever have survived had not Ezekiel sat where they sat.

But I want you to notice this last move, because this is the part with the celebration. The application, of course, of this whole thing is quite clear. We have to sit where other people sit. We have to sit where other generations sit. We can't write off a whole generation of teenagers; we have to sit where they sit and find out how they think.

One of the things I love about the Concord Church is that they are studying these age groups and figuring out what's in their mind. You have to sit where the generations sit, you have to sit where all these other people sit. The homeless, you have to sit where dope addicts sit. You have to sit where AIDS patients sit. You have to sit where violent people sit. I hear somebody saying, "But, Reverend, that is entirely too much. No way in the world can we sit with all those people."

I know a church that feeds the homeless, and they like for their members to sit among the homeless. But instead of that on a Sunday morning, when they come for breakfast, they finally moved the homeless across the street. They let the Christians sit in the main building because they couldn't sit where the homeless sat. And they did away with 90 percent of their witness because they wouldn't sit.

But just in case, just in case, you think still that it's too much, let me just simply say that it wasn't too much for Jesus. It wasn't too much for Jesus. Paul said he thought it not robbery to have been equal with God and yet to come down and sit where we sit. I have that imagination that . . . [recording interrupted] . . . [believes that Jesus says] "I'll sit where they sit. If they get thirsty, I'll get thirsty." And on the cross, he cried, "I'm thirsty. If they get hungry, I'll get hungry," and in the wilderness, he went without bread for forty days. "If they get much too homeless, I'll be homeless," and somebody said he had not where to lay his head. "If they cry, I'll cry," and John says that Jesus wept. "If they sit anywhere I'll sit where they sit. If they feel betrayed by their friends, I'll feel betrayed." And I hear him look up one day and say, "Will you also go away?" "And if they feel abandoned by God, I'll feel abandoned by God," and on the cross, he sang a song from his childhood, "My God, my God, why hast thou forsaken me? Oh yes, I'll sit where they sit. I'll sit where they sit. And one day I'll come back, and I'll find the ones who sit where other folks sat, and I'll take 'em back with me, and they'll sit where I sit. Amen."

Chapter 6

Walter Kingsley (W. K.) Jackson (1914–2003)

Living Legend 2000

The Preacher

REV. DR. WALTER KINSLEY (W. K.) Jackson (1914–2003) served the people of St. John Missionary Baptist Church of Oklahoma City, Oklahoma, for close to fifty-eight years. Born in east central Oklahoma in 1914, he received his bachelor of arts degree from Bishop College in Marshall, Texas, his bachelor of theology degree from Oklahoma School of Religion, Langston, Oklahoma, and his doctor of divinity degrees from Morris-

Booker Memorial College of Dermont, Arkansas, and Oklahoma School of Religion, Langston, Oklahoma.

In 1945, he began his tenure at St. John Baptist in Oklahoma City. When Rev. John Wesley Johnson, the senior pastor, developed a series of health problems, he called Pastor Jackson to serve as his co-pastor, a role he held at the church for sixteen years (1945–1961). Over that time period, he partnered with Pastor Johnson in establishing the Johnson Memorial Bible Institute (JMBI) and presided over the construction of a three-story Christian education building.

Then, in 1961, after the death of Pastor Johnson, the church called him to be its senior pastor. He served in his role as senior pastor or senior pastor emeritus until he passed away forty-two years later (1961–2003). The church grew and prospered under his leadership. In 1979, the church built a new facility for its growing congregation, and, in subsequent years, it expanded that facility to include the W. K. Jackson Family Life Center and the Christian Heritage Academy. His autobiography, which is also a history of the church from 1919 to 1994, is titled, *I Let the Lord Do It.*

His church also became an important beacon for civil rights under his leadership. He led various protests in Oklahoma City such as in 1969 when he led a group of Black clergy to stand with and march with the city's mostly Black union of sanitation workers in a protest over unfair wages and working conditions. A personal friend to Martin Luther King Sr., every year, Dr. Jackson would also highlight and honor King Jr.'s life through a celebration and worship service around his birthday. According to a recent article in *The Oklahoman*, he "is credited with hosting a birthday celebration and service for the younger King that evolved across America as an annual worship service commemorating the slain leader's life and legacy on or around his January birthday."[1]

Dr. Jackson served in leadership with many organizations, including as one of the founding members of the Progressive National Baptist Convention, Inc. (PNBC) in 1961, as the president of the Baptist Ministers Union for twenty-three years, leader of East Zion District Congress and Association for twenty-two years, president of the Oklahoma Baptist State Convention, president of Progressive Oklahoma Baptist State Convention, president of the Coalition of Civic Leadership, as well as many other roles. He was the husband of the late Mrs. Eula Lee Jackson. They had one daughter. He was also the godfather to the late Rev. Dr. E. K. Bailey.

1. Hinton, "Fabric of Faith."

The Sermon

If you have your Bible, will you then kindly turn to 2 Chronicles, and chapter 18, and the context of the whole setting of what we want to look at is in these first five verses? Especially verse 5. And we're reading from the Living Bible (TLB):

> But rich, popular King Jehoshaphat of Judah made a marriage alliance for his son with the daughter of King Ahab of Israel. A few years later, he went down to Samaria to visit King Ahab, and King Ahab gave a great party for him and his aids, butchering great numbers of sheep and oxen for the feast. Then he asked King Jehoshaphat to join forces with him against Ramoth-Gilead. "Why, Of course," King Jehoshaphat replied. "I'm with you all the way. My troops are at your command! However, let's check with the Lord first."

Isn't that beautiful? Don't you see? Here is a literal situation faced by King Ahab, and he was in fellowship or even a banquet with King Jehoshaphat. Jehoshaphat was the king of Judah, and Ahab was the king of Israel. Ahab presided over ten tribes. Jehoshaphat was king of only two tribes. But they were all the same lineage; they were the descendants of Jacob, the descendants of Abraham, the father of the righteous.

So, then, King Jehoshaphat, when his son got ready to marry, he would marry one of his relatives of the same blood. To be sure that this was done, he arranged an agreement with King Ahab and went down to Samaria to the king's house. The king prepared a great feast but Ahab couldn't enjoy the fellowship or the food because his kingdom was threatened by the King of Syria. Do you hear me?

Even though this was a day of fellowship, even though this was a great fellowship, Ahab couldn't enjoy it because of the rage of the king of Syria. So, he said, even though he had ten tribes, a whole lot of people, he had been afraid to fight. The Lord had enabled him to win a lot of battles, but he was afraid to go up against a heathen king. Because he knew that he had not followed the Lord in everything. So, he asked Jehoshaphat, who had been a good, godly leader, "Join with me and help me fight my enemies."

Jehoshaphat said "Why, yes, we'll be happy, we'll enjoy working and fighting along with you. But before we do it, let's check with the Lord." Do you hear me?

A lot of us get in a whole lot of trouble. A lot of us find ourselves frustrated, indecisive, not sure about which way to go, because we have left the Lord out of all our doing.

Now, you may say, "Well, now, pastor, we don't have to follow the Lord about everything." Hmmm! Well, I've come to tell you that if you are frustrated today, if you are afraid today, if you are dejected today, you are living a negative life. The Lord wants you to be happy. Do you know that?

The Lord—it doesn't make a difference about how young you are, how old you are—the Lord wants you happy. And if you are not happy, it's not the Lord's fault. I know, I've said to a number of you in counseling that, when it comes to any situation, you ought to put everything you have in it. Don't go at anything half-hearted. Our parents used to say that anything that is worth doing is worth well-doing. Hmmm!

So, then, if you are not happy, if you're afraid to go to sleep because you may have bad dreams, it's your fault. If you are afraid to wake up the next morning because of what you're facing, it's your fault. The Lord wants you and wants me happy.

Didn't you hear him say in John 10:10, "I have come that you may have life, and may have it more abundantly"? And I have come to tell you that you don't know what living is until you let the Lord in on everything you do.

So Jehosphaphat, he says, "We'll be happy to join our forces with your forces, but before we do, let's check with the Lord." You don't have to wonder. The Lord will indeed let you know what to do and what not to do. Now that don't mean you just sit down and don't do a thing, and you think the Lord is going to fill your cupboard. If you're in school and don't study and do your homework, don't you think the Lord is going to give you the answers to those questions the next day. We're supposed to do everything we can do, that we know is right to do.

Like I have said a number of times, work at a thing as if the total outcome depends on what you do. A lot of folk are too lazy to be a child of God, [we] want the Lord to put food on our table. When the Lord said you will live by the sweat of your brow, he meant for you to work. Now it's alright to go to other folk if you can't get anything yourself.

But, in this day and time, too many folk are not trying to do anything about their situation. But the Lord wants you to get up in the morning and go to work, and when he gives you money, don't throw it away. Pay your bills. But, in paying your bills, pay the Lord first. I told you one time about this matter of tithing, the Lord said, "Will a man rob God?" He said "Yea, you have robbed me in tithes and offerings."

Thirty years ago, somebody broke in to Capitol Hill Baptist Church, and took the safe and all the money. And the paper announced about the church being robbed, and the late Pastor Buffer, he was pastor, and he announced on that weekend, "All the members be at church, for in the morning, I'm going to tell you who robbed Capitol Hill Baptist Church."

And then the members who hadn't been at church, they said, "I would just like to know who had the nerve to break in our church, and break in the safe and take all of our money." And Pastor Buffer said, "I'm going to tell you so you can really catch him and put your hand on him." That Sunday morning, he got up and read the Scripture in Malachi, *"Will a man rob God?"* And then the prophet answered, *"Yea wherein have we robbed him?"* And the Lord said, *"In tithes and in the offerings."* And then Pastor Buffer said, "All of you out there who have not paid the Lord the tithe are robbers. Now if you want to get the fella, get yourself first!" Hmm!

The Lord wants us to be honest; he wants us to be fair with everything that he blesses us with. When you have done that, then you are praying and trusting him as if everything depends on God. If you do that, then, you will enjoy life. That is special!

Jehoshaphat said, "Yeah, yeah, we will go with you, Ahab, but before we do, let's check with the Lord." Don't you know that there ain't no use of you doing anything and expecting to win without the Lord. You have your health. You have your strength. You got up this morning, but you wouldn't have been able to get up had it not been for the Lord.

You're sitting in this seat, and I'm standing here, but you couldn't do that, I couldn't do this without the Lord. Just suppose all of us would check with the Lord. If things are not going like you want them to go, check with the Lord. There's no use fussing and raising a fault.

The Lord has the whole world in his hands. He knows how to make your enemies your friends. Stick with him. If that husband isn't doing right, if that wife isn't doing what she ought to, check with the Lord. Because the Earth belongs to him, you know that don't you?

The world . . . belongs to the Lord. Check with him. Well, I tell you the reason. Because at our very best, we are limited.

Maybe you didn't get that; I said the reason why we ought to check with him because, at our very best, we are limited . . . . Don't you know that? That's why we ought to check with him. You don't know what the next minute has for you, and I don't know either.

When I've done my best, the Bible says it is no more than filthy rags in the sight of God. How much have you got in an automobile? Honey, you may go out there, and it won't even start or the devil will fool you because you have a little make up on. But don't you know? Before you get to the bank, it could go broke? Before. We are just limited. We can't do this, the Bible says. Hmm! Except with him! Hmm!

Paul said after he had met the Lord, "Only the master's rule." He had been sure enough saved. He wanted to live only for the Lord. Do you want to do that? Paul discovered that he was so inadequate until he said, "Every time I try to do good, evil is present."

Paul said, "I would like to be the kind of preacher the Lord would have me be. But, anytime I make it up in my mind and know for a certainty what I ought to do, I find myself doing the opposite." That's the reason you ain't got no grounds to be criticizing somebody else. Don't you know it takes all of your time?

Try your best to do what the Lord would have you do. When you hear folk always talking about somebody else, and the mistakes of other folks, they aren't doing a thing but showing how upset they are. Hmm! You know the devil is trying to make us be fanatical, giving the impression nobody else is right but me—hmmm—when you know and I know that we fall short every day.

You'll find in Romans chapter 7 and 8 that Paul put forth every time to do right every time. But he said, "Every time I try, I miss it."

That's why we need to come here and enjoy the fellowship of one another. I need you, and you need me. You look at the television and think you can't do any better. Oh, but every time you look at the television ministry, they're making mistakes and are at one another's throat. Hmm!

You don't have to be bothered about Oral Roberts and about Schuller . . . . You know yourself. You make a mistake yourself. One who knows the Lord ought never to say anything short about anyone else. You know that, don't you?

Paul became so concerned with the Lord and asked ask the Lord to "fix me up so I won't make this mistake again." The Lord said, "I'm not going to do that. You'll get beside yourself. But if you'll keep on preaching, keep on fighting in My Name, I'll give you grace." Huh!

It's official! You don't worry about tomorrow, what you ought to do today, day to day. Right now is the accepted time. Hmm! So that's why you ought to check with the Lord, you can't do it yourself. You know that. No need to be hard-headed. No use trying to fool somebody else. Nobody knows any better than you how far off you are. Now that's the first reason we ought to check with him because, at our best, we are inadequate, and we are limited.

Even here in worship, you can't enjoy this if you don't let the Lord in, sitting up, trying to be sophisticated at it. I don't care what kind of degree you have. If it hadn't been for the Lord, you never would have gotten that degree. Nothing wrong about the AB, the MA and the TH, but the one you need first is the BA, being born, born again! Hmm!

If you have him, you will enjoy the song, *"He is all over me, keeping me alive. He is the one make me clap my hands."* Hmmm!

Do you ever feel the Spirit? Hmm! Do you ever stop and think about how good the Lord is? Check with the Lord. Since you know you are limited, since you are inadequate, check with the Lord. The God I'm talking about has all knowledge and all power. I can't stop you but he can. I may not know, but he does. Hmm!

The Lord knows from whence you came. He knows where you are. He knows how long you're going to be here and that nothing is impossible with the Lord.

Abraham, his wife Sarah was beyond years of reproduction, but they wanted a son. Sarah got so anxious she wanted to help the Lord out telling Abraham to go and sleep with the maid.

God doesn't need your help. Hmmm! The Lord knows everything, and He has all power in his own hand. He can fertilize. He can reproduce. The Lord, if he needs to, can stop the sun and he can make the clouds sad. Don't you know that?

Anything he shall meet. All you have to do is just speak the word. Lord, you are so good! You brought me through dangers seen and unseen. Lord, I've been rising, and I've been falling. I'm honest about it.

I've made a lot of mistakes, but you know my heart. You know how you picked me up, and put my feet on a solid rock. Lord, I feel you right now moving all over me.

Lord, cold chills roll through my very veins. The Lord has brought us a mighty long way. He knows just what I can take, and he knows when I need his help. Not only should I check with him because he knows, but I ought to check with the Lord because he always comes out victoriously.

Well, if you don't believe that, ask Moses and the twelve tribes. They'll say, "Yes, he brought us out of Egypt and carried us across the desert, and when we got to the Red Sea, we weren't able to cross over. But we just stopped and talked with him, and he called the waters to backup and made a highway in the sea."

If you don't believe he can win the battle, just ask Daniel. And Daniel said, "When you turn it over the Lord, the lions can't eat you. The Lord went down in a den of lions and locked their jaws and made them a pillow for me all night long."

Well, if you don't know what to do, you ask Shadrach, Meshach, and Abednego. They'll tell you he can take heat out of the fire and air-condition a furnace and let you walk around free all day and night.

Well, if you don't know what the Lord can do, look out yonder on Calvary's Hill when they marched him from judgment hall to judgment hall, and placed the cross on his shoulder, and made him go up to Calvary. Somebody said, "Who is that? Why don't he come down and save himself?"

But Jesus kept on dying on the cross, and let them take his body down and place it in Joseph's new tomb.

Well, early, early, early Sunday morning, before the birds started singing in trees, before the sun started casting its ray, early Sunday morning, Jesus got up out of the grave and pulled his grave clothes off. He . . . said, "All power. All power. All power. Not some power but *all* power. Death can't do me no harm. The grave isn't able to hold me. All power." Invitation for membership in the Lord's church.

If you are here now, check with the Lord. He will do for you what no other can do. You may come as a candidate for baptism. A vital statement as a Christian or by letter. Whatever it is, check with him first. Hmm! Will you come? Will you come?

Chapter 7

Stephen F. Olford (1918–2004)

Living Legend 2001

The Preacher

Rev. Dr. Stephen F. Olford (1918–2004) believed that "the expository preaching of God's infallible Word, in the power of the Holy Spirit, concerning Jesus Christ as Savior and Lord, is the ultimate hope for humanity's deepest need, national righteousness, and social justice in the world."[1]

    Born to Plymouth Brethren Christian missionaries in Zambia 1918 and raised in Angola, Dr. Olford went to university in the United Kingdom with the desire to become an engineer. During his college years, he entered into a

---

1. https://stephenolford.org/lifeline-projects/.

season in which he turned away from God. He also had a near-death experience after being involved in a motorcycle accident. While lying in bed after contracting pneumonia and with a grim diagnosis, he received a letter from his father, a missionary, with an oft-quoted line inside used by missionaries and other Christian leaders: "Only one life, twill soon be past. Only what's done for Christ will last." Upon reading his father's letter, he recommitted his life to Christ and experienced a dramatic call to ministry. As his biographer and friend John Phillips puts it, "When Stephen Olford dragged himself off his deathbed, dropped on his knees, and cried to God for mercy, longing for the Lord Jesus to be made real in his life, God met him."[2]

During World War II, he served as an Army Scripture reader and also spoke to soldiers on the need for Christian faith shortly before their deployment for battle. He pursued theological studies in London, where he came under the tutelage of his mentor in expository preaching, the Scottish expositor W. Graham Scroggie, a man whom he quoted from often when he would deliver lectures on preaching.

In 1953, he began his years of pastoral ministry, first as the senior pastor at the Duke Street Baptist Church (1953–1959) in Richmond, Surrey, England, and later on at Calvary Baptist Church (1959–1973) in New York City. He traveled all over the world preaching for crusades, conventions, and learning centers. As a preaching pastor, itinerant preacher, and trainer, he influenced a generation of preachers such as Billy Graham, who was a close friend and confidant, Charles Stanley, Adrian Rogers, the missionary Jim Elliot, and many others. He founded Stephen Olford Ministries in 1976, the Institute for Biblical Preaching in 1980, and in 1988, he opened the Stephen F. Olford Center for Biblical Preaching in Memphis, Tennessee, a ministry which is now owned and operated by the Global Ministries Foundation (GMF). The Center's mission is to train pastors and Christian leaders in expository preaching and pastoral leadership and to develop resources in order to equip, empower, and train churches.

Dr. Olford received his doctorate of theology degree from Luther Rice Seminary in Jacksonville, Florida, and he received honorary doctorate of divinity degrees from Wheaton College, Houghton College, and Richmond College. He was also the author of at least ten books and contributed to leading periodicals. He was the husband to Mrs. Heather (Brown) Olford for fifty-six years, and the father to Jonathan and David. His two sons along with Dr. Ted Rendell continue his legacy not only at the Center's campus but through its work at various locations across the U.S. and around the world.

---

2. Phillips, *Only One Life*, 38.

The Sermon

Why have a conference on expository preaching? Is preaching really necessary? Why sweat it out—preaching? Is it all that important? I would like to answer that question under the title of "The Vision of Our Vocation." Turn with me to Ezekiel chapter 37.

Now, I know that there isn't a single preacher here who hasn't preached on this, but this is authentic this time. [Laughter] Alright, Ezekiel 37. Let's stand to honor the word of God. I will be reading from the New King James Version. It's Ezekiel 37, verses 1–7.

> The hand of the Lord came upon me and brought me out in the Spirit of the Lord, and set me down in the midst of the valley; and it was full of bones. Then He caused me to pass by them all around, and behold, there were very many in the open valley; and, indeed, they were very dry. And He said to me, "Son of man, can these bones live?" So I answered, "O Lord God, You know." Again He said to me, "Prophesy to these bones, and say to them, 'O dry bones, hear the word of the Lord! Thus says the Lord God to these bones: "Surely I will cause breath to enter into you, and you shall live. I will put sinews on you and bring flesh upon you, cover you with skin and put breath in you; and you shall live. Then you shall know that I am the Lord."'" So I prophesied as I was commanded; and as I prophesied, there was a noise, and suddenly a rattling; and the bones came together, bone to bone.

At that point, I asked Brother Armstrong to sing his song. The foot bone to the leg bone and all that. *"Indeed, as I looked, the sinews and the flesh came upon them, and the skin covered them over; but there was no breath in them. Also He said to me, 'Prophesy to the breath, prophesy, son of man, and say to the breath,'"* that word can be translated as wind and can be understood as spirit. *"Prophesy to the breath, prophesy, son of man, and say to the breath, 'Thus says the Lord God: "Come from the four winds, O breath, and breathe on these slain, that they may live."'" So I prophesied as He commanded me, and breath came into them, and they lived, and stood upon their feet, an exceedingly great army."* Interpretation. *"Then, He said to me, 'Son of man, these bones are the whole house of Israel. They indeed say, "Our bones are dry, our hope is lost, and we ourselves are cut off!" Therefore, prophesy and say to them, "Thus says the Lord God: 'Behold, O My people, I will open your graves and cause you to come up from your graves, and bring you into the land of Israel. Then you shall know that I am the Lord, when I have opened your graves, O My people, and brought you up from your graves. I will put My Spirit in you, and*

you shall live, and I will place you in your own land. Then you shall know that
I, the Lord, have spoken it and performed it,' says the Lord."

Lord, this is your infallible word. Bless us as we open it up and bless the message to our beating hearts as we seek to know your word. Let us be seated.

The vision of our vocation. Why are we here at this conference? We see from this passage that preaching and the power of the Holy Spirit is the vision of our vocation. I was privileged to be at Amsterdam One, Amsterdam Two, and Amsterdam Three. I had the privilege to preach at each occasion at the invitation of my beloved friend of fifty years, Billy Graham. In 2000, he couldn't come, but there were some wonderful speakers there. Amongst them was Dr. John Stott, who's a very dear friend. He said something I knew technically, I knew biblically, I knew in a sense personally, but I'd never heard it put quite the same. He looked upon that vast congregation of ten thousand people from all over the world who had come for a conference on evangelism—and it just happened that Amsterdam 2000 was technology at its best—the screens, the flashers, the PowerPoints, all of it was amazing. I was absolutely brought to silence. I'd never seen anything like it. It was technology at its best. I thought of all those people who'll never ever have a computer, who'll never have a microphone, who'll never have the facilities that were represented in that great conference, and my heart went out to them.

John Stott got up. He said, "I want to make a statement here, and I hope you want to listen to me. There are only two great weapons that God has given us to destroy the kingdom of Satan and build the kingdom of God. One is authority. The other is power. Now, let me explain that," he said. "These parts are similar but they're not identical." He went into the New Testament to show that authority stands for the word of God and power stands for the Spirit of God.

Looking out on that vast congregation, he said, "All you need is the commission of God, of course, the calling of God, the preparing of God's spirit on your life, but the two great weapons you need are the word of God and the spirit of God. Go preach."

I don't know anything in Scripture that illustrates this quite like this vision. We'll look at these together. First of all, Ezekiel was a young priest whose name means "the strength of God," who was taken into captivity in Babylon and situated on the River Chebar, in the city of Tel-Abib, it used to be, but today Tel-Aviv. For twenty-two years, he faithfully prophesied concerning the vision and revelations that God had given him to his people there in captivity. Of all great visions he was given, the one that we're going to consider tonight is the vision of the valley of dry bones.

I want to speak to each one of us here because I believe there's a message in this passage for you and for me, all afresh in this conference on expository preaching. And the three ways in which I want to take it is the vision of a general situation, the vision of a personal obligation, the vision of a spiritual visitation.

Number 1: the vision of a general situation. "The hand of the Lord was upon me and set me down in the midst of the valley full of bones and, lo, they were very," I add, "very dry," as the original shows. If you and I are going to sense the urgency of preaching the gospel to the world of our day, our contemporary day, we've got to catch this vision here tonight in a mighty way.

The vision that Ezekiel saw was the vision of a valley full of dry and scattered bones. The primary application, of course, is in verse 11–14. It refers to the house of Israel. God is saying of the house of Israel that it is a scene of absolute shame. No Jew, no Jew would want bones; they were always buried! But there they were in the open. A vision of spiritual and national disaster. But it is a vision also of a day that's coming, where this prophecy would be fulfilled to the very "t," to the very letter, as Paul delineates it in Romans 9, 10, and 11.

A day is coming that the nation of Israel will see him, every eye will see him, and they will see him whom they pierced. They will mourn because of him, and a nation will be born in a day. The peace road we hear about so often on the news will be irrelevant because God will put his people in the right place at the right time, and at the right moment.

In the meantime, I believe that the vision for the house of Israel doesn't exhaust the teaching of this passage. There is an application for you and for me right here. It's special to my heart because I've been living with this now for several days, and I believe it's going to stir us to action, to realize how important our task is as expositors of God's word in the power of the Holy Spirit.

In the world today, we have a general situation, and it's of men and women who are spiritually lifeless. Men and women who are spiritually lifeless. The valley was full of bones. Now bones denote death! Death!

Although we live in Dallas or New York or Memphis, where we come from now, people around us are charming, intellectual, reasonable, emphatically okay, the actual fact is that they're dead in their trespasses and their sins. If they haven't experienced the regenerating power of the Holy Spirit, I repeat they are dead in their trespasses and their sins. I don't care if it's a three-PhD professor at Harvard or some simple soul you meet in the street. If they've never been born again, they're dead. Paul says they're dead in trespasses and sins. Jot it down, Ephesians 2:1.

As I've crisscrossed this country and talked to thousands of pastors, I am more and more convinced that our churches are full of dead men and women. Despite the fact that they all claim, "Oh, I came forward, I'm a Christian. I was baptized." Yes, you can be baptized a dead sinner, and come up a wet sinner.

I long for another George Whitefield. Some of you may not know who George Whitefield is. You look at the bookstore. There's a new biography that's come out on George Whitefield. He's my favorite evangelist-prophet-preacher of the ages. He was a little man, he had an ailing heart, angina, as you call it here, angina, and he was a man who very often had to lie flat on his back in the preacher's office before he came to preach because of the pain on his chest. He had a squint in his eye; he was an Oxford man. Highly intellectual. He'd swallowed up the word of God. But, the fire of the Bible burned in him, and we owe so much for the great revival of this country under his ministry alongside his American comrades. Here was a man who in Philadelphia was studied scientifically as he preached night after night in the open air downwind and could be heard for three miles, though not at stupid things like this.

There are preachers who walk and run with lollipops in their mouths. Lollipops, and crooners and singers, nothing can be done now without amplification. Here is a man that could be heard for three miles without a microphone. I want to tell you something. He absolutely tore this country to pieces on dead religion. He didn't preach on the text they would have expected him to across the country: "If my people who call my name shall humble themselves and pray, turn from their sins, and seek my face, then will I hear from heaven, rid their sins and cleanse their land."

No, he preached on one text practically everywhere he went. "You must be born again." He saw more conversions a month, people in the church, in the church pews, than he ever even saw outside. But, you see that impact of religious people getting saved and then breaking loose created what we call revival followed by spiritual awakening.

With one church, when he had been invited, he spoke on "You must be born again," on Sunday, Monday, Tuesday, Wednesday, Thursday, Friday, Saturday. The crowds grew so that he had to preach loud enough for people to be heard outside as well with the open windows and doors. A bunch of deacons at that church came up to him and said, "Mr. Whitefield, you've been preaching on nothing else than 'You must be born again, you must be born again, you must be born again.' Don't you have another message?" His classic reply, I'll never forget: "You see, I'm preaching, 'You must be born again' because YOU must be born again!"

One of my very dear pastor friends said to me the other day, with a choking voice, he said, "Stephen, brother, you know something? I believe that, if the Holy Spirit were to withdraw from many of our so-called evangelical churches, nobody would tell the difference." You know, that pained my heart, but I'm afraid it's true.

I want to ask you, pastors. Are people in your church, or in membership—I'm not talking about the strangers who come in, all those who are brought in—are they born again? Are they born again?

We talk about reaching the lost, but what about our churches? What about our churches? I remember catching up with Duncan Campbell, the Rev. Duncan Campbell. Some of you may not know his name, but God used him mightily in the North of Scotland in the Hebrides Revival. I asked him a whole lot of questions, and one of them was a stupid question really. I said, "With many of these people getting converted, night after night, day after day, what do you do to follow up? Do you have a pamphlet? Do you have literature?" He looked at me and said, "What do you mean? Follow up what?" I said, "Please explain what you mean." And he said, "Listen, unless and until so-called converts turn up at the prayer meeting, they're not born again."

One of the great religious characters of the New Testament, an enemy of the church of Jesus Christ, was Saul of Tarsus. God transformed his life as he traveled on that Damascus Road, and a light shone above the brightness of the brilliant sun. He kissed the dust in repentance and said, "Who are you?" and heard, "I am Jesus whom you persecuted."

He learned the doctrine of the church in one second. The head was feeling the blows that he was administering to the body. Then, God came down to Ananias and said, "Ananias, I want you to follow up on this man, Saul of Tarsus." He said, "Lord, you know what kind of man he is? He's our enemy! He's our enemy." And do you know what the answer from heaven was? "Behold, he's praying." That brilliant mind of the first century, the apostle Paul, had prayed thousands of times, but he'd never prayed.

There's a little chorus we used to sing as kids. "I often say my prayers, but do I really pray?" There are lifeless people all around us, spiritually lifeless people. The second that you notice, all around this general situation are spiritually useless people. Not only lifeless but useless. The bones were very dry. There is a place for bones. You can use bones in some ways, but when they're bleached—and the Hebrew emphasizes, "very, very dry"—they're useless! They're useless! I didn't say worthless. Jesus died for all of us. Every blood, every drop of blood he shed was for people of worth—you and me.

But, listen carefully. There's a difference between being full of worth and being of no use. Remember what Paul says in the Epistle to the Romans.

"There is none that does good, no, not a single one." They are all going out of the way and together have become what? Unprofitable, useless.

Yes, I'm afraid there are a lot of people in our churches today that are there because they are celebrities. Oh, we've got to get him in. He's a doctor. But, are they really born again? If they're not truly born again, ultimately, they're useless because God does not bless the works of the flesh. He does not bless the works of the flesh. In fact, the works of the flesh and the works of the spirit are indemnity.

These bones not only speak of spiritually useless people, spiritually lifeless people, but there is a third one, spiritually hopeless people. Look again at verse 11. "Our bones are dried and our hope is lost."

The Scriptures speak of the unregenerate men and women as having no hope, without God in the world. Unless men are begotten into that living hope in our Lord Jesus Christ, they are actually hopeless. Bind them to the wall, and you'll find they are hopeless.

We have two sons, one Jonathan and the other David. God only gave us two, and we love them. They are both in Christian service. Jonathan served the Lord for eight years as a missionary in Kenya. He saw such strife with missionary kids who were never prayed for at prayer meeting. Missionary kids who are like any other kids but are expected to live like angels. What a burden to his heart. Many times, he saved guys in a school known as Rift Valley Academy from being sent home with a blacklist. He had such a burden for them that he came home and said, "Dad, I'm going to hit the books again. He's now a Doctor of Clinical Psychology, and morning, noon, and night, he's counseling missionaries, missionary kids, and pastors alike.

But, the Billy Graham movement has caught up with him and said, "Jonathan, we need you." He has done a study to show that we are in the most hopeless condition of our history in America. He has been to all the five boroughs of New York lecturing to so-called counselors who are suffering from compassion fatigue! Eighty percent of all New Yorkers, and that's almost typical of the country, are depressed as never before, especially since 9/11. That is where he's been counseling.

He was recently in Boston at the scene of that terrible fire and explosion, again counseling people depressed lying out in the streets as if they were mad from sheer depression. Now, I could tell you that spirit of hopelessness with this continuing war that doesn't end in Iraq and all the other problems—economic problems, financial problems and so on—could make us go out of our minds if we didn't have the hope of Jesus. Indeed, in my forty years of ministry in this country, I don't think I've ever met a group of people who are more depressed than right today.

But, you know, you carry with you a message of hope if you're truly alive in Jesus. Well, if that doesn't make you want to preach, my friends, I don't know if you're a real preacher.

Here's our general situation: a world of lifeless people, a world of useless people, a world of hopeless people, and they need Jesus. Which brings us to our second movement in this vision. The vision of personal obligation.

Let me read. The prophet was told, *"Prophesy unto these bones, and say to these bones, 'Hear the word of the Lord.' And also prophesy and say to the wind, come from the four winds, oh breath, and breathe upon these slaves that they may live."* In each case, he prophesied as he was commanded. Now there's a twofold obligation we have, and you churchgoers know that from your beloved pastors, but I want to speak to the preachers for just a moment. There are two obligations we have.

Number 1: you have an obligation to preach prophetically. There must be prophetical preaching. *"Prophesy upon these bones, and say to them, 'Hear the word of the Lord.'"* Now listen carefully here so I'm not misunderstood. In both the Old and the New Testament, in a sense, the word "prophesy" can mean two things: foretelling—that's predicting the future—and forthtelling—that's what's being used here. What's being used here is forthtelling, and the definition here, it denotes forthtelling with urgency, the specific human condition. That's preaching prophetically.

We could stand up here and give great sermons of objective truth which are very, very wonderful, and unfold the Scripture and so on while people are snoring or sleeping or gossiping and it isn't addressing the urgent issues of today. We were hearing about that relational preaching the other day. Yes, preaching prophetically, and I want to just expand on that for a moment.

"Son of man, can these bones live?" And the answer was, "Lord, you know." We can almost imagine the hesitancy of Ezekiel who, by the way, was spirited into that valley. There's a strong verb there, brought into there like Philip being spirited away to another city. That man was put into that valley of dry bones almost by force. And there he saw all those dry bones, and he was told to preach to a valley of dry bones.

How do you preach? I want to tell you. It's a very difficult thing to confront a world of lifeless, useless, difficult people with anything else but the word of God. That's why that occurs again and again. This is the word of the Lord. I want to say something very important.

People tell me we ought to make the Bible relevant. Did you know that makes me mad? That's why I'm bald, pulling out my hair. Making this book relevant? I tell you it's relevant. In a million years, it's still relevant. We heard it from my beloved brother Dr. Wiersbe. It's a living book. It's relevant! We've got to catch up with it! I want to tell you something. If you don't believe that, I wonder if you really believe in inerrancy. We talk about the infallibility of the word of God, it's trustworthiness, but I want to go a bit deeper and talk about its inerrancy. If you believe in inerrancy, that absolutely proves this book is alive for all ages. There's never a time when that book isn't alive.

I want to say something important here. I want you to hear me. If you hear a man say, "Make this relevant" and he's talking about the language and making it understandable, well, that's the whole purpose of preaching: exposing, unfolding, explaining what the word of God means. Don't turn around and say, "Forget the Bible, and listen to me." This is the incorruptible seed of the word.

I want to remind you of that glorious word in Isaiah 55:11. Write it down and put it on your desk. Put it in your wallet. *"So shall my word be that goes forth out of my mouth. It shall not return unto the void, but it shall accomplish that which I please, and shall prosper the thing what unto I have sent."*

This book is alive. The word of God is alive. It's adequate. Even to the dividing asunder of heart, soul, and spirit, this book is alive. This book is alive. I remember my friend Alan whom I succeeded at Duke Street Baptist Church going into the open air to preach. Alan had a great idea. He took his little Bible that he kept in his pocket and put it under a hat, a hat that was absolutely ridiculous. He stood there on the street corner and said, "There's something living under that hat." A huge crowd grew, and his friend Roy said, "What's alive?" And Alan picked it up and said, "The word of God," and began to preach.

There's a wonderful theologian pastor by the name of Dr. Robert Gayle, who wrote one of the greatest works on the atonement. He wrote massive sermons, and they were published. Dr. Campbell Morgan went up to see him. "Dr. Gayle, did you preach this to your people?" He said, "Yes." He said, "How could they take it? It's deep stuff." And he said, "I never asked them. I just preached it." It's alive!

Listen, I was born and brought up on the mission field, and I've seen my blood-father preach the word to people who didn't even know what a book was like. Never heard the name of Jesus. Now, I knew it because I learned the language: Yesu. He preached the word.

I sat by the fireside while we were trekking into the villages with a big tent behind us. Father insisted a fire be built there, and we had our wash bins which were a canvas basin. Then, there was an outer court with some logs around, and there was an inner chamber, and a Holy of Holies with a partition where mother and father slept. We boys used to see that and use that as the tabernacle—he taught the tabernacle to people who couldn't read even!

I saw with my eyes men and women saved, and it became the nucleus of the strongest church in any village that I ever saw in Africa. No silly gimmicks or silly stories. It was solid preaching from the tabernacle.

I can never think about that without hearing Paul. Here's this mighty apostle, this great intellect of the first century. He has planted churches. He has written theology, blazed trails, languished in prison for his faith. Now, he is going to glory. They'll stand for his arrival in heaven. And he says, "Timothy, you're going to follow me, you're my successor. I'm giving it all to you. I've got one last word to say to you: Preach the word! Preach the word! Preach the word! Be instant in season, out of season; reprove, rebuke, exhort with all long suffering and doctrine, do the work of an evangelist."

That's precisely what Peter did. On the day of Pentecost, the mighty Spirit of God came upon him. You remember he expounded the book of Joel. He brought two signs to back up what he said. It was a God-conceived sermon, and Christ-centered sermon, a Spirit-controlled sermon.

He began to preach, and when he came to that tremendous note, he said, "*Jesus, whom you crucified, and God named Lord and Christ.*" Suddenly, there was a cry of anguish, then: "*Brethren, what shall we do?*" Stabbed through the heart. Then, what does he say? "*Repent and be baptized, everyone, in the name of Jesus Christ. And ye shall receive the gift of the Holy Spirit.' And they that had received the word were baptized.*" What did he do? Preach the word. Preach the word.

But, we must not forget the other side of the equation. Not only must our preaching be prophetic, it must be dynamic. Listen. "Breathe upon these bones that they may live." With the preaching there may be a noise, a shaking, a coming together of bone to bone, even the appearance of skin to skin, but the word says there was no breath in them. With the word of preaching, there must be the power of preaching, hence, preaching dynamically.

Through preaching, people may be convicted of sin, of righteousness, of judgment. They may be guilty of conscience and the rest of it, but they can go out from your congregation still without breath in them—breath of the Spirit.

There is a need of the Spirit upon that preaching to bring about the miracle of rejuvenation and renewal. This calls for complete dependence upon the Holy Spirit. Paul said, "I came to you in Corinth. I was weak. I was trembling. I was fearful, but I came to preach Christ and him crucified in demonstration of the Spirit and of power." He said the same thing to the church in Thessalonica.

Preacher, do you know the anointing of the Holy Spirit upon your preaching? Preacher, do you know the anointing of the Holy Spirit upon your preaching? Don't leave this conference without finding the answer. Jesus said,

"If you, then, be evil and know how to give good gifts to your children, how much more will your Heavenly Father give the Holy Spirit to them that ask him?" That statement is preceded by the words "ask, seek, knock," all in the present tense. Go on asking. Go on seeking. Go on knocking.

Matthew talks about the good gifts of God, but my good friend dear Brother Wiersbe has put this together—the gifts of the Spirit. We receive the Holy Spirit once and for all when Jesus comes into our lives. There's no second baptism. Not in my Bible.

We're baptized by one Spirit into one body, Paul says, by one baptism, and that's it. It is symbolized in water baptism but there are not two baptisms. But, with the baptism of the Spirt there is the fullness of the Spirit. Ephesians 5:18: "Be filled." And if you're not filled with the Spirit why, this is disobedience. This is a command not a suggestion. Instead of the imperative, it's the passive voice. You yield to the Holy Spirit; this is for daily living, in singing and praying and exhorting one another.

We should be living the Spirit-filled life as a lifestyle day by day. But, I'm talking about something else. I'm talking about being human with the Spirit, that holy anointing. Jesus said, "Don't you dare put out a tract. Don't you preach on the street corner. Don't you get going winning souls for me until you are filled with the power." That's what it means to be clothed. You're not clothed. You're naked. Naked to all the attacks of the world, of the flesh, of the devil.

I believe there's an anointing as my precious savior was anointed on the banks of the Jordan. He was filled with the Holy Spirit from his mother's birth. There was never a time when he wasn't filled with the Spirit but, on the banks of the Jordan, he received that anointing. With that he went out to preach the gospel.

You need the anointing of the Spirit to preach dynamically. This is still God's method today. Yes, preaching prophetically. Dynamically. We mustn't be satisfied with anything less than pouring ourselves into our preaching. This world of lifeless, useless, hopeless men and women will not be impacted without prophetic and dynamic preaching.

Now, we come to our last point, the vision of the spiritual visitation. The breath came upon them, and they lived and they stood on their feet an exceeding great army. When God breaks through from heaven, there are at least four miracles that take place. When the Holy Spirit, through the preaching, hits a world of lifeless, useless, and hopeless people, these four things happen. Men and women are vitalized. We read that they lived. These corpses were reanimated, revitalized, brought back to life. The same thing happens today when we preach the gospel in the power of the Holy Spirit. It's the Holy Spirit who makes alive. Without giving an invitation, people have actually come alive in our pews. They came in dead. They go out living. They came forward to tell me they were alive. "I can't explain it, but I know I am different," and they were discipled later to show that they were alive. That was the date of their birth.

Not only were people vitalized, but men and women were energized. They stood up on their feet. Paul prayed that this would happen to his congregants. Notice in Ephesians 3:14–17: *"I bow my knees to the Father of our Lord Jesus Christ, from whom the whole family in heaven and earth is named, that He would grant you, according to the riches of His glory, to be strengthened with might through His Spirit in the inner man, that Christ may dwell in your hearts through faith; that you, being rooted and grounded in love,"* one of my favorite texts. That prayer!

One of the biggest accusations in the church is the lack of disciples. "As you go." That's the participle there. The imperative verb is "make disciples." Not make decisions. Now, I'm not foolish. I know a decision is involved, but Jesus told us to make disciples. And my task, and your task, pastor, is to follow the language of the apostle Paul in Colossians chapter 1, where he says, "I am a minister and my task is to warn every man teaching, every man, until I present every man perfect in Christ." That's all-around mature. Fifty-three thousand people leave the church in the evangelical community in this country every single week, and don't return. Why? No discipling.

Yes, they were vitalized, energized, and by energy, I mean they were brought into energetic discipleship with Jesus Christ. Thirdly, notice that they were mobilized, an exceedingly great army. It's the work of the Holy Spirit to bring individual units into your home. The apostle informs us that by one Spirit, we're baptized into one body as I referred to a moment ago. Furthermore, we're exhorted to keep the unity of the Spirit in the bond of peace.

I'm glad that Charles Colson has come out with a new book. One was on the body, now a new book. You ought to read it, *Belonging to the Body.* Emphasis on belonging. We are a body and our Lord Jesus Christ, by his Holy Spirit, through the love of his Father is bringing together a body here on earth. Guess what? You're my sister whether you like it or not. You're my brother whether you like it or not. We're in the body. But, unfortunately, the body life is not working. Why? Because we refuse to be mobilized as the Scriptures teach. And I'm glad to see that this concept is coming back again, to emphasize the body. The church needs mobilization. But I want to say that's not enough as we go that far.

The church must be utilized. He shall put his Spirit into you, and you shall live. You'll be placed into your own land. The ministry of the Holy Spirit is not only revitalized, not only energized, not only mobilized, but utilized!

Now, I will give you something to think about, preachers. We talk about expository preaching. I want you to study the form of Ephesians very carefully. I've been drawn to this very recently. Our task is not over in just getting people to make decisions, or even discipling them, but having discipled them, we're to mobilize them.

I'm studying Ephesians from the commentary by John Stott on that very subject. He gave this story of an experience he had in Boston where he went to an Episcopalian church. He's an Anglican. He's an Episcopalian, and he preached at that church. But, as he came to the little gate that led into the church, he saw the little board announcing that Dr. so-and-so was the senior pastor. That's fair enough. The Rev. so-and-so was head pastor, the ministers of the church—"the membership." Did you get me? The membership. Where'd he get that from?

God in Christ gave gifts to the church. The foundational gifts, yes, the evangelist. The pastor teaches. Why? For the edification of the saints, and for the work of serving. Every single person in the church should be in a slot of service for Jesus Christ. In my ministry, before discipleship classes were over, we found out the gifts of everyone in that class and found places for them, before they were even given the right hand of fellowship. If you have no job at the church, then something is very wrong. This church, Concord— that's a beautiful word that means "harmony"—is one of the great examples of this. What I saw last night, that was church-sponsored.

The whole ministry in the past years, in this conference of expository preaching, is almost carried entirely by the volunteers of this blessed church. I want to tell you. I don't think we've really reached the lost until that happens.

At Calvary Baptist Church, I used to close the Sunday morning service having given the invitation and people would go downstairs for coffee and cold drinks, and a roll call was called to find how many nations we represented. The minimum was always forty, but it usually got up to around one hundred different countries in one service. I really wish I could have enjoyed that, and sometimes I was ready to do so, but my task was to come down to the communion table and stand there, because I wanted to shake hands with thirty, forty, fifty, sometimes over a hundred, one time nearly two hundred people who'd been led to Christ by the membership of our church that week. They had never seen me or heard me before but they brought them. They brought these converts to hear me for the first time and wanted to introduce them to their pastor. I knew every one of those would be followed up, discipled, brought to the class, and put into their slot. They came up the aisle. That wasn't because I gave the invitation. They were saved already! That's mobilizing your church!

As far as I'm concerned, there is only one concern in the heart of my Heavenly Father, through his Son, by the Holy Spirit. That's the primacy of the church, the universal church represented by the local church gathered here today.

I want to tell you something. When the last soul is saved, according to my understanding of prophecy, whether it's in Dallas or Afghanistan, I want to tell you, we'll hear the shout of the voice of the archangel of God. We'll be called up to meet the Lord in the air. It's all over down here except for judgment and a cleaning up game.

That's why Jesus died. He loved the church and gave himself for it. And in that church should be people who are not only vitalized and energized and mobilized, but I want to tell you something, the time is coming when they're going to be totally changed. Operation liftoff will take place. And they'll become just like the Lord Jesus himself.

Not only is that the primacy of the church, but it's the mission of the church. It's the victory of the church! I want to tell you something. Even though we're divided, even though there are factions, even though there are splinters in the church, Jesus said, "I will build my church, and the gates of Hell shall not prevail against it."

One of these days, when that shout comes, and we have been judged at the judgment seat of Christ, and all is said, we are going to be a body—listen carefully—"without spot or wrinkle or any such thing." A perfect church. That's his interest. Until that moment, here's my last word to you. All slumbering saints should wake up. All lukewarm saints should fire up. All dishonest saints should own up. All disgruntled saints should sweeten up. All discouraged saints should cheer up. All depressed saints should look up. All gossiping saints should shut up. All dry-bones saints should stand up. Jesus is coming again.

Chapter 8

Edward Victor (E. V.) Hill Sr. (1933–2003)

Living Legend 2002

The Preacher

Rev. Dr. Edward Victor (E. V.) Hill Sr. (1933–2003) served as the senior pastor of the Mount Zion Missionary Baptist Church of Los Angeles, California, a church that he led from 1961 until his death on February 4, 2003. He endured significant challenges early in life as one of five children born into poverty to a single mother in rural Texas during the Great Depression and Jim Crow era segregation. At one point, his mother sent him to live in a log cabin with one of the mothers of the church so that he could have a better chance and a brighter future.

Dr. Hill answered the call to preach in 1951, establishing himself immediately as a gifted pulpiteer and mentor to younger preachers. According to some estimates, he mentored "more than one thousand preachers" during his lifetime.[1] Soon after coming to Mount Zion Baptist in 1961, he transformed it into a major hub of compassion and justice ministry. On top of his pastoral responsibilities, he also served as the senior policy advisor to the mayor of Los Angeles, the president and director of the World Christian Training Center, and the president of E. Victor Villa, Inc., a senior-citizen housing project. In the national political arena, he offered an inaugural prayer for President Nixon and, on two occasions, led the Clergy for Reagan Committee. Hill was also a lifelong member of the NAACP and the National Baptist Convention, USA, Inc. He published two books: *A Savior Worth Having* and *Victory in Jesus: Running the Race You Are Meant to Win*. He was married to Mrs. LaDean Hill, and they were the proud parents to three children.

The Sermon

Now, I want to talk for about fifteen to twenty minutes about something that happened to me my first year as a preacher. Generally, I would always leave service on Sunday night with my message for next Sunday in my mind. Robert L. Rowe who used to pastor at Munger Avenue here got me in on that. He told me, "Young preacher, you ought to practice making a list of your preaching responsibilities and have a ninety-day schedule." I'm preaching now on a six-month schedule. I'll be preaching the life of Christ chronologically for six months step by step.

I preached on hell for a whole year. It is one of my greatest desires that nobody I have ever come in contact with or pastored should end up in hell. But I warn them that "if you don't hear me and get ready, don't try to stop me at the gate."

"Pastor, we're having a little problem but we told them you'd straighten it out."

"I ain't straightening nothing out; I'm going on over. I'm doing all the straightening out right now. If you don't pick it up now, I'm going on over and you can go to hell if you want to, but I'm going over."

---

1. Simmons and Thomas, *Preaching with Sacred Fire*, 700. Thomas and Simmons are also the source for information on Hill's involvement in the Nixon inauguration and the Clergy for Reagan Committee (p. 701).

But that Sunday night—and generally my sermon always was about something that I forgot to say that day, something I forgot about or somebody said something to me that disturbed me some kind of way and I made a note. My wife would always say, "I saw when you wrote your sermon for next Sunday." But I left that night, and I was blank. How many of you have ever been blank? Yeah, yeah, yeah, yeah, don't practice that. You'll be tempted to go out and buy one. At the National Baptist Convention, they'll even tell you where to whoop.

It's like the old man in Houston whose daughter typed his sermons in great big typed letters. She would sometimes make a mistake and just wouldn't do it. She would just draw a line through it, and she wouldn't tell him. The old man would be preaching, and he'd say, "And Jesus went up to Calvary and omitted it." And she would put a little parenthesis—"Now, daddy, kinda lift your voice here"—and he would say, "Now, daddy lift your voice."

I was blank. Monday morning, I went to church, prayed, read—nothing. So, Monday night I concluded that the Lord for some reason (and I had several in mind) had fired me. I didn't have to wonder why. I knew what he fired me for, and you know it, too. But in those days—they don't do it too much now—the old preachers used to come and sit out near the church under a tree or open their study door for the purpose of young men that might come by for a little advice.

So, I went by and, lo and behold, there was Dr. B. H. Roberts. How many of you remember Dr. B. H. Roberts of Shiloh in Houston? My God, you missed a privilege. B. H. Roberts had no beauty to behold. But he was he was a preacher-and-a-half. Down in San Francisco, for the National Congress, B. H. Roberts preached on the subject: "An Insane Man on an Insane Mountain." And he talked about that sinner who tried to tell Jesus, "Save us, come down." Said, "He's crazy." He talked about that crazy man giving up heaven just to save us. He said, "The whole mountain was insane." And then he talked about amidst this insanity came a sane voice: "Master when you come in the kingdom, remember me." There are folk living today who still swear that they saw a halo standing over B. H.'s head as he talked about a sane voice on an insane mountain.

So, I pull over, and I talk with him. "Yep, yep, young man, how ya doing?"

"I'm fine, doing fine."

"That's good, that's good. I hear of you down there at Mount Gray. You're doing all right, doing all right."

Deacons come by. That's one thing about it, the deacons would always go by those old sainted preacher's houses, tell 'em what their pastors preached about.

"Deacons mighty proud of you son, you're doing fine."

I said "Well, Dr. Roberts, I'm in trouble."

"Well now, I've been in a lot of it too." He said, "What's your trouble?"

I said, "Dr. Roberts, the Lord has fired me."

He said, "Well, since he knew everything about you before you hired you, I doubt whether he's fired you." He said, "It's not as if he has run into any new material. Now why do you think he's fired you? Are you mixed up morally?"

I said, "No, I just don't have a word to preach about Sunday." He said, "Oh, that ain't no sign that he's fired you. It is a sign that the days are running out and you got to get up, that's what's bothering you." He said, "Now, that tells me three things about you and it tells me three things about those who raised your hand."

He said, "First of all, it tells me that you have not been walking among your flock much." He said, "If you, if you get among Negroes, you'll have something to preach about. And you won't have no hard job finding no text neither." He said, "So, you've been busy"—and I was busy in politics and with Martin, Martin Luther King and others in Civil Rights—and he said, "I've been reading in the paper you been running for office and everything. Now maybe, maybe you oughta kind of mingle, mingle among your people, among the sheep. The sheep might even have a suggestion as to what you ought to talk about. Sometimes if you get close enough to your sheep, they'll tell you what they're hurting and how they're hurting. And you can get a whole series of sermons out of just how are your sheep. They out there lying and going on, talk about lying some."

So, my first point in my lecture tonight is *don't get too far from the sheep*. Talk among 'em, talk among 'em. I'm confessing that's one of my weakest points. I'm confessing that when I look at my calendar and my secretary tells me what I am faced with the next day there's very little room in there just to fellowship and go among my sheep. I'm confessing that emergencies such as last night—I had to rush to the hospital at eleven o'clock before trying to get ready to come in, 11 o'clock, almost midnight, I had to rush to the hospital—those are the kinds of situations—the other boy got shot and all that, the other boy that police beat up—I had to rush out there to keep that from developing into a riot. Those are the kind of relationships that I have, and I confess that's wrong.

You ought to just mingle among the sheep. Let them touch you, and don't be afraid of them learning about you being a man and you being a natural woman. Some of you are scared to get close to folk because they may smell something. Well, that's one of the reasons they are staying away from you. They don't want you to smell nothing neither. You have to mingle. Get close.

Dr. Roberts told me, he said, "Son, I know one thing without you telling me anything else, you're not mixing among your folk enough. You're not going around and just being available."

Manuel Scott talks about the power of a casual visit to your choir rehearsal, casual visit to the ushers' meeting, and all the other clubs, not on official business, but just kind of go in there. You'll find something that you need to preach about.

And [Dr. Roberts] said, "Now, the next thing that tells me is that you haven't been looking at the book too much this week. You been reading newspapers and whatever but you haven't been reading that Bible too much. Because," he said, "that Bible"—and he had very sharp teeth and red gums— "that Bible is pregnated, and it, it'll catch you. Stuff you read twenty years ago will come alive." He said, "You ain't been in that Bible. Y'all talking about getting your civil rights, and better housing and all that, but you better try Jeremiah and Isaiah."

That's impossible to put your head in that book often, not hunting for a sermon. And I might add also, studying it and not just reading it. Study it.

I was coming back from Kennedy Airport in New York flying back to Los Angeles, and I had six hours. And I decided, I said, "Boy, I got six hours, I'm gonna read me, I'm gonna read my Bible for six hours. I'll tell you what I'm going to do. I'm gonna read some psalms." I got over to the book of Psalms, and I opened it, and it fell through, and I did just like your members do, they say that the way the Holy Spirit does—you just open the Bible and, whatever it falls on, that's what he wants you to read. Now, I ask my members, "Has it ever fallen on, 'Bring ye all the tithes?'" You got this selective falling here.

It fell on the twenty-third psalm. And I said, "That's where I'm gonna start right there at the twenty-third psalm. I'm gonna read this psalm after psalm. I might read thirty-five to forty psalms." And I started off, before we took off: "The Lord." Hold it, hold it, hold it, hold it, hold it. "The Lord": the eternal, all wise, everlasting, the Alpha and Omega.

"The Lord—is." And my English teacher majored in agriculture. I don't know where Pat gets all of this explanation he gets at times; he didn't get it from me. "The Lord is." Right now. Present tense. Don't have to say "Lord, one day." Don't have to be like Deacon Rainey: "Lord when I've done all I can do and can't do no more, save me." The Lord is! And you know, our pews are filled with people unconscious of the is-ness of God. The Lord is right now. And they came over the telephone and said, "We just passed over New Jersey." And I said "I got to get started here. I'm gonna read twenty-something psalms."

And I said it again. "The Lord is—my." Hold up! My. That's mine. Mine. My. Mine. Mine. That settles it. He's mine. The Lord is mine. Now, you don't have to read no further than that to get a sermon out of that. The Lord is mine. Oh, what joy! Oh, what assurance! Jesus is mine!

Since I'm a farm boy, the next word hit me: "shepherd." Guiding and directing and leading me, and stirring me, and holding me, and fighting for me. The Lord is my shepherd. I'm not out here by myself. I have a shepherd. You better not mess with me. He knows how to use that rod and that staff. The Lord is mine.

I said, "Well, let's move on quickly then. 'I shall not want.'" And I had a list of things in my Bible I was in need of, and this tells me "I shall not want." Mama had been trying to tell me all along that it works that way. Mama said, "Not going out then, California boy, you'll be alright." Mama called him a Midnight Rider. My Midnight Rider will come by. I slept on the floor. I didn't know nothing about no Posturepedic mattress. I slept on the floor. We just had two rooms in the log cabin and Mama and Papa slept in the bed. I slept on the floor. And Mama wouldn't pray until around twelve o'clock because she'd think I'd be sleeping. But the way she would pray would wake me up. She said, "Oh, Midnight Rider! We done run out of food, and we ain't got no money. And the boy is hungry. Midnight Rider!" The next morning at six o'clock, Anthony, Anthony, Budd Anthony drops by a sack full of groceries. She didn't order him, she didn't make no contact with him. She just said, "Midnight Rider." Drop that: "My shepherd."

I said, "Well, 'He maketh me to lie down.'" Praise the Lord! Now young preachers, get that now. And don't always have the Lord to have to make you. Your members got sense enough to take rest. On big Sundays they take rest.

I used to be at my church, and my sons, they can tell you, Pat can tell you and all of them, I used to be at my church every Sunday morning at 8:30 a.m. sharp. On your knees. Blue joined my church, Blue and Henry, and they were preachers. And they come walking down the hall one Sunday morning about 10:45. "Where should we sit?"

"Anywhere you want. Why don't you try the balcony?"

"Well, we, we just want to know where, where do the preachers sit here, in the pulpit or the balcony?"

I said, "Try the balcony." I said, "Everybody that sits in the pulpit, they have to be here early enough to get their assignment, and I give out assignments at 8:30, and we pray over it at 8:45. I wouldn't know where you sit because you wasn't on."

And before Henry died, I was over at his church, and he was explaining to his deacons, "Now, I don't give out assignments at ten o'clock." So, I told Blue "Try the balcony."

Next morning, old Blue is there at eight o'clock. I used to be there at 8:30. Eight o'clock. I stand outside and teachers and superintendents be running and ushers be running. And I'm watching my watch. Now I can't do it, can't get up that well now. I don't get to church now until 12:00. I don't bother about it. I've taught 'em for forty-one years. If they ain't got no sense by now, can't open, can't, don't know we sing, "All Hail the Power of Jesus Name" by now, if I put in forty-one years at this, I have to rest now. I've stood on 'em long enough. So, I can't do what I used to do even though I'm not all that old. I started early.

And I kept on reading here, "He leadeth me. He's my shepherd, I shall not want. He maketh me to lie down." And he had to do that to me. But, thank God. I was watching y'all coming in the lobby of the hotel. Negro preachers, this is our week to show the goodness of the people of God to us. I watched your suits, and some of you change three times a day. We got off the plane at 5:00, and we got to the hotel at 6:00, and the man said I really do have to wait on you because you're due there at 7:00.

And my wife said, "Edward, you need a shower, and you can't preach in that suit you flew in, that suit."

I said, "I've preached at Concord in overalls." There's some things you got to make your people understand don't make no difference. A White man came to my church once, and my favorite garment, if I don't have an occasion where I should have a suit on, is overalls, coveralls. I like those with the suspenders and even the shirt that matches, the blue shirt.

White man came up and said, "Is Dr. Hill here?"

I said, "Yes, he's, he's, he's here."

"Could I see him?"

I said, "Yes, follow me." And I took him into my office and had him sit down, and I said "Now, can I help you?"

And he said, "Go get Dr. Hill."

I said, "Oh, you want to see Dr. Hill, okay."

I intentionally just stayed out for about ten minutes. I came back and got behind the desk and said, "Now, may I help you?"

He said, "We been waiting on Dr. Hill."

"I am Dr. Hill."

"You, you, you, you Dr. Hill in overalls?"

"I'm Dr. Hill in my shorts. I'm Dr. Hill in my shorts. And if you just really want to know something, I'm Dr. Hill in the shower without no shorts on. And uh, if you need any more information ask my wife. I'm Dr. Hill!"

Don't, don't become self-impressed, and don't let people get you in debt by forcing you into all of these suits.

My wife, my wife, about four months ago, starts talking about St. John. I said, "Well, she's really into it. She's in the word." St. John's, St. John's. and I said "So, you, you, you really like St. John's?"

She said, "Oh yes, yes! St. John's. St. John's."

I said, "Now, did you read Matthew?"

She said, "Oh no, Edward. There, there, there ain't no Scripture. St. John is a suit."

I said, "Now what have they done now? St. John is a book in the Bible; it ain't no suit." And then I get this bill from St. John, and she had gone out and bought two. And the bill is $1,600." I said, "I'll be damned if that's so. This is going back! This thing is going back!"

"We gonna stick with St. John's. That's what's gonna happen here."

And then the lady came over, the, the captain came over the intercom and said, "We have just now entered the state of Illinois." I'm gonna read twenty chapters, I'm on two verses and have flown over three states.

And then, this really got me: "He restoreth." Ain't that wonderful? Oh, pastoring people drains you, and pulls every bit of life out of you, and robs you of your blood. And, if they see you getting joyful, they'll do something to kill that. He's a Restorer. And I began to cry a little bit. The lady said, "Is there something wrong?" She said, "Well I noticed you were crying a little bit. Anything happen, anything wrong?"

I said "No," I said, "you wouldn't understand."

She said, "What?" I said, "I'm, I'm reading some Scripture and, uh, that one touched me because in these fifty-seven years, he restoreth my soul."

And Bailey—keep on believing. I see him working. Keep on believing. You keep on believing. Let's folks, I want everyone, keep on believing: he restoreth my soul.

I said, "I was just reading but you, you wouldn't understand."

She said, "I'm born again. I'll understand."

I said, "Well then, come on in here then. Come on in here. You don't have to be waiting on these people. Let's read this Scripture here." And we went way down, and I was way out over Nebraska when I got down, "Surely goodness and mercy shall follow me."

And old man Roberts said, "Son, you're dry because you haven't been in the word." He said, "Now I didn't say you haven't been in words, but you haven't been in the word."

And you who are younger, you who are younger, you're not even as old as I have been preaching. Y'all are getting too impressed with words and not the word. Now, there is a difference. Words can leave you looking for a dictionary, but the word can send you looking for a place to pray. Oh yeah, oh yeah, oh yeah!

The word can send you to your office and you'll get so much to preach about. Have you ever done this? Have you ever been in your office until one thirty, two o'clock just getting stuff, and you're tired? And have you ever said "Spirit, would you please let me go to sleep?" . . . .[recording interrupted] . . . .When you get up and catch that plane at five o'clock in the morning, when you get into the word.

"Boy, you haven't been in the word." And then Dr. Roberts, he said, "Finally," and that will be my finally, "it tells me is a sign that it tells me that you haven't been talking to God much." He said, "Because anyone who talks with God, anyway you talk with him; you want to sit silently and just let him go on. If you want to talk with him out loud, go ahead."

A woman in my church used to say, "Amen, well, and help him now" after every word so I had to call in. I said, "Now I appreciate your Amens but not after every word. I mean, kinda let me get a point and then say, 'Amen.'"

She said, "No, Reverend, it don't work that way." She says, "When you tell the truth I don't have to wait on no point, I say 'Amen.'" And she said "Now, and when you mess up and make a mistake I say, "Well." And when you fumble around and mess around now and telling jokes and then I know you don't know where you're going I say, "Help him Jesus. Help him, help him, he doesn't know where he's going."

Old man B. H. Roberts—at a time when I pastored the prestigious Mount Corinth Church where Pat pastors now, Patterson (I recommended him for that church, recommended one or two others. They got rid of them), he's been there thirty-seven years, they're scared to get rid of Pat, because Pat, Pat can throw that Greek on them and Hebrew, and they don't know whether he's sending them to heaven or hell. So, they're scared. They say, "We better keep him here and find out what he's saying."

He [Dr. Roberts] said, "Hill, three things." And I say to you tonight young preachers, older preachers, experienced preachers: if you hit a drought, accept responsibility. You haven't been among your people. You haven't been visiting enough sick. It's been years since you called on a delinquent member. Y'all got this book that they print them about. When you don't hear from them in ninety days, drop 'em.

Old man N. C. Crane decided to do that in Houston. Told his secretary "Get the names of all those who haven't paid nothing in ninety days, and Wednesday night we're gonna drop 'em." So, she brought the list out, two or three hundred. She read 'em off. "Brother pastor, I move you that every last one of those slothful and negligent folk be dropped from the roll of the St. John's church. Get rid of that trash. We've been carrying on without 'em and we can do without 'em." "Second the motion. Second the motion" All over the building: "Second the motion."

He got home. Telephone rings. "Dr. Crane?"

"Yeah?"

"I hear you dropped grandma from the church rolls. Now, you know she used to be your nurse but you know she's a double amputee now. She can't get to you no more but Pastor Crane, should you have dropped her? Or maybe it's your time to get to her now."

He said, "Oh, oh, oh, we didn't mean her, we didn't mean her, we'll put her back on. That was just an accident. It was an oversight on my part. Tell mama everything's alright." Hung the phone up.

Ring. "Dr. Crane, ain't no need of you dropping my daughter, she died two years ago. She's already in heaven. You were out of town, we couldn't find you. We got another preacher and had a funeral."

Said, "Oh Sugar, I'm so sorry, you know we didn't mean that either."

She said, "It don't make no difference."

"We will add her to the roll."

"No, no, she's all right." Hung up.

Ring. "Dr. Crane?"

"Yeah?"

"I don't know what my boy fighting over there in Vietnam in the fox-hole is gonna feel when he hears that his church has dropped him when y'all should have been praying for him."

And said, "Well, we didn't know that, and you didn't . . . but we want to add him back."

Ring. "Dr. Crane?"

"Yeah?"

"I hear you dropped my wife from your roll. I've been trying to get her off a that roll a long time; I want to thank you for helping me cause she's cussing you out louder than I am now." Hung it back up. Ring.

"Dr. Crane?" Ring. "Dr. Crane?"

He took the phone off the hook. He came out that Sunday and said, "I just need one motion and that is that we put every name we dropped back on that roll, and that all of you deacons here will select three people a piece and go from house to house and find those people."

And he said: "Hill, that's what brought revival to St. John's." He said, "Because people came in saying, 'I didn't know you even thought about me. I didn't even know you cared. Jehovah's Witness comes every day; we could join one of them.'"

I never seen no Baptist, well, here tonight, let's vote. How many of you here tonight have ever had a Jehovah's Witness knock on your door?

Look at that, look at that, raise 'em high. I don't think I've missed a hand. Hands down. How many of you have had a Baptist knock on your door, to talk with you about church, or Jesus Christ? Raise your hand. One, two, three, four, five, six, seven, eight, nine, ten, eleven. Eleven to one thousand. Is that saying anything to us tonight? Is that saying that maybe we ought not to spend so much time practicing our whoop as much as we ought to be mingling with the sheep?

A boy had missed my church. He was married to one of the sweet girls at our church, wonderful children. But he had missed the church. She called me and she said, "Pastor, I'm having to get out of the house today because he got the rifle last night and said he was going to kill us all."

I said, "Where is he?"

Says, "At work."

"Thrifters?"

"Yes."

"Okay, stay home."

She said, "I'm leaving now; I ain't gonna be shot." I said, "Stay home."

I went into Thrifters and he saw me. He said, "Pastor Hill, what do you want?"

"Chocolate ice cream."

And he gave it to me, and said, "That's alright, you don't have to pay for it."

"No, I'm gonna pay for it. I just want chocolate ice cream," and I walked out. And he went back and apologized to his wife and his children. Sunday morning, he led 'em into church and wrote me a note and said, "One day I want to give you a chocolate ice cream in gold because I know you didn't come to buy no chocolate ice cream. You came for me." And he said, "I needed it in my life at that time somebody to come for me. I was tied up and tangled up with the wires and the muck and mires of life, and living, and I didn't know what to do next. I needed somebody to come for me and when you walked in the store, something in my heart said, 'There's your pastor, let him come on in.'"

You're dry because you don't mix and mingle with the folk. Now, I don't mean that you ought to play with their foolishness. I'm not with this gang of young preachers who play dominoes and cards with their trustees. You better take another look at that. They want to bring us to that level; bring 'em on up to Matthew, don't throw no jack on 'em. Bring 'em on up to Matthew. You haven't been in that book much and you haven't been talking with him much. Oh, when you talk with him, he'll talk back to you! I said, he'll talk back to you! I said: he'll talk back to you!

"And finally," and let me put this finally, he said, "now, what I want you to do Sunday," old man B. H. Roberts said (old preachers never left you without a recommendation), he said, "I want you to go to your study and get a sermon." He said, "I hope you're writing all your sermons."

I said, "I do."

Said, "Well, get your sermon and get one that you flunked in. Get one that nobody heard. Ain't nobody going to run and say, 'I heard that one before.' Get one that nobody didn't hear that morning. Get one that you wish you could have just crawled out of." He said, "And go through it, and get you a better text and get you some more Scripture in there. Take out all the lies."

Hey man. Had a young preacher preach for me while I was, last year, I thought I'd go abroad. Franklin, and he's talking about going abroad, and the farthest he's ever gone is Watts, California.

So old man Roberts says, "Take all the lies out. Pray over it, and preach it Sunday.

And I said, "Oh no, Dr. Roberts, no, no, no, no. I promised God that if He give me a church I would never repeat a sermon."

He said, "Well, thank God that God is wise enough not to hear all we say."

I went and got a sermon that even my wife, baby, and you know baby would encourage me, even baby said, "Edward, I think you can do better." And I got that sermon, and I reworked it. I put in some of my own self-experiences of failures that I was talking about, and I preached that morning after prayer, and all the devils and everything shouted. The roof looked like it came in, and they came up and said, "Lord, what has happened to you, pastor? We ain't never heard a sermon like that before in all of our lives."

Get among the folk. Get in the word, and talk to him. He has not sent you on a mission—You know these telephones you got now, Pat has one, where you dial and it says the owner refuses to answer this unidentified number? I hear he used to be in my balcony, and he comes up identified number. I called him, "Who the devil do you think you are? I licensed you. I'll take my license back." Unidentified number—God has not refused to accept our call. I got a boy in jail who calls me about four times a week, and sometimes, I just don't accept it. But God has not refused to accept our call. He'll hear us, and so will Sunday. Between now and Sunday, go on back home and mingle with your folk. Saturday evening, call ten of them that you haven't seen in two years. Mingle with 'em, on the telephone, anything. Get in the word and get on your knees and tell the ushers to be ready because it's gonna rain. It's gonna rain! God bless you!

Chapter 9

A. Louis Patterson Jr. (1933–2014)

Living Legend 2004

The Preacher

Born in Granger, Texas, Rev. Dr. A. Louis Patterson Jr. (1933–2014) "made the conscious decision to accept Christ" at the age of nine at the St. Love All Baptist Church.[1] He knew at a very early age that he would be a preacher, practicing his technique while he was still a preteen. In a 2014 interview with Dr. H. B. Charles Jr., he told him that the first congregation to hear him preach was a congregation of corncobs.

1. Sections of this short biography have been adapted from the tribute found in Goode, "Rev. Dr. A. Louis Patterson, Jr. Dies."

Like many preachers before him, he ran from his call, avoiding it for at least eleven years before surrendering to God. Influenced by mentors such as the late Revs. O. S. Davis and E. V. Hill Sr., he developed a deep passion for teaching and preaching God's word. Starting his journey at Mt. Zion Baptist Church in California, he later accepted a call to become the senior pastor at Mt. Corinth Missionary Baptist Church in Houston, Texas, where he served for over forty-four years. One of his mentors, Rev. Dr. E. V. Hill, recommended him.

While still a young man, he married the love of his life, Mrs. Melba Beverly Lorraine Simmons Patterson, whom he first met at church in the Sunday school class at Mt. Zion. They remained married for forty-eight years. Together, they had three children: Albert Louis (deceased), Alan Lamar, and Alette Lorraine. He also had a third son named Anthony.

Dr. Patterson's preaching ministry spanned more than "four decades, numerous states, and international waters."[2] Many of his contemporaries considered him the "Godfather of Expository Preaching." He lectured, taught, or preached at countless conferences, all four National Baptist Conventions, and fourteen state conventions, and he conducted forty-eight citywide revivals in twenty-five cities. He preached over one hundred and fifty sermons to the National Baptist Convention alone.[3] He also received numerous honors and awards such as being recognized five times as a legend by his peers, serving regularly as a speaker at the National Baptist Congress of Christian Education of the National Baptist Convention, USA, being inducted into the Morehouse College Hall of Fame, and being listed on the honor roll by *Ebony* as one of America's greatest Black preachers in 1993.[4] He conducted revivals throughout Europe, Asia, Africa, and the Caribbean, and he authored three books: *Prerequisites for a Good Journey, Joy for the Journey,* and *Wisdom in Strange Places.*[5]

The Sermon

First Corinthians, chapter 15, and verse 1. When you have it, will you say "Amen?" King James Version reads on this order—1 Corinthians 15:1:

2. Goode, "Rev. Dr. A. Louis Patterson, Jr. Dies."

3. For more specifics on Dr. Patterson's preaching, lecturing, awards, and distinctions, see his obituary published in *The Houston Chronicle* on April 16, 2014.

3. See "15 Greatest Black Preachers."

5. No publication information could be found for Dr. Patterson's final publication, *Wisdom in Strange Places.*

> *Moreover, brethren, I declare unto you the gospel which I preached unto you, which also ye have received, and wherein ye stand; By which also ye are saved, if ye keep in memory what I preached unto you, unless ye have believed in vain. For I delivered unto you first of all that which I also received, how that Christ died for our sins according to the Scriptures; And that he was buried, and that he rose again the third day according to the scriptures.*

Amen! Can somebody say "Amen"? You may be seated. Amen!

Let me rush to deal just briefly with this text tonight. I wanted to do this in memory of the one who spent his life [Dr. E. K. Bailey] doing this, recognizing that not all of us are gifted with his keen intellect and supernatural gifs, so he organized this particular conference so that we could be better equipped to preach the gospel.

I wanted to talk for just a few minutes tonight about the full gospel—the full gospel—with a particular emphasis on the fact that where you stand determines really how you see things.

Paul declares in this text, he said, "Now this gospel is the means by which you are saved." You know, God saves, but he uses an instrument, a humanly designated instrument. He says, "I received this gospel. I responded to this gospel. Now, I'm releasing this gospel. Now if you hold onto it, and keep it in the memory, then it will not be in vain." That's what he said. Then, he focuses in verse 1 on "standing in this gospel." I was trying to suggest that where one stands determines one's viewpoint.

As an example, I see Brother Taylor here on the front seat. I could say to him even now, "I'll give you a $100 bill if you'll tell me the color of the tie of the man that's right behind you." I'd have him stand and do that. But he could not tell me unless he looked around because he's standing with his view in this direction.

Now, that's one of the reasons we have some problems today if it is based on our viewpoint, our standpoint. Sometimes our emphasis is in the wrong direction.

But, he says, "according to the Scriptures" in our text, "He was buried, raised again, died, according to the Scriptures," and then the preposition, the connective element: "for our sins."

Now, that's where I want to launch. I'll give you the outline in case I don't make it there. Amen! I stand tonight in the gospel. I stand amazed. I stand amazed at his choice to save me. I stand amazed that he gave me the charge to preach the gospel. I stand amazed that he made me into what I am. The tenth verse of this same chapter says, "I am what I am by the grace of God."

So, our outline tonight. *I stand amazed at his choice.* Not only do I stand amazed at his choice, but *I stand assured at his conquering.* The chapter ends with a conquering celebrative note. I'll refer to it in just a moment. But, *I'm also standing in anticipation of his coming,* either in death to receive me or for his church.

Let me say just a word about each one of these and I'll be through for tonight. When we talk about standing in the gospel and being saved from sin, the thing that amazes me is what happens to us because of Jesus Christ and our sin.

See the context, the larger context tonight. Paul has been dealing with domestic bitterness, moral impurities, and temporal values because this church at Corinth is an unusual church. It's a church noted for its suing saints with the disease of division, and sordid, sexual, sinful activity. He's been dealing with all of that, and he comes to this text, and he says, "Now, what you need is the gospel. What you need is Jesus Christ." That's in the first verse. He said, "I'm not debating with you; I'm not discussing." It's a declaration.

He said, "I declare unto you the gospel, the *euangelion* and the *euangeletsomai.*" He said, "The *euangelion* is the good news of Jesus Christ, dying on a hill called Calvary, buried and rose again. The *euangeletzo* is the preaching, and Jesus is both. He's the message and the messenger." Everywhere he ever went, I don't care what the problem was—the condition, the culture, the circumstances, the complaints—he said, "What you need is Jesus." For all people, for all places, for all problems, for all purposes, he would say, "What you need is Jesus."

He learned one time trying to discuss poetically with the skilled scholars of that day. He had gone on up beyond the Acropolis, on up beyond the Areopagus in dealing with all of them, and climbing the mountaintop of intellectuality, and surveying the heights of academic splendor, and he was not very effective. When he came back down, this text tonight in the fifteenth chapter overflows into the second chapter of 2 Corinthians. He talks there about, *"I have determined from this point on to know nothing among you save Jesus Christ and him crucified."* What am I trying to suggest tonight? The problem according to the text is sin.

I listened to Dr. Bailey in the clip tonight, one of the few times you'll hear sin mentioned in a video graphic form. In other words, when we listen to television today we don't hear anymore about sin—we hear about silver.

But Matthew 1:21 says, "His name shall be called Jesus and he shall save His people from their sin." John 1:29 says, "Behold the Lamb of God who taketh away the sins of the world." So obviously, then, the person is in the text—that's the Lamb of God. The problem is in the text—that's sin—and the place of the problem is in this world. It's not necessarily socioeconomic deprivation. It's not necessarily that the problem relates to a political participation in order to have a participatory democracy. The major problem may not be cultural-ethnic deliverance.

If the book is right, it's probably sin. I know something about sin and you do, too. Sin is ugly. Sin is destructive. Sin is disruptive. Sin is disgusting. We are all sinners without exception and, if we remain sinners, we're sinners without excuse. For he died for our sins.

Look what happened when he died for our sin. According to Isaiah, the thirty-eighth chapter and the seventeenth verse, it says very clearly what he has done with our sins. He has taken our sins and cast them behind his back. Jeremiah the fiftieth chapter, and the twentieth verse, says that he has taken our sins and that they are remembered no more. Job the fourteenth chapter, the seventeenth verse, says that he has taken my sins, placed them in a bag, and then sewed up the bag so that they can no longer escape. Micah, the seventh chapter, nineteenth verse, says that he took my sins and cast them into the depths of the sea. My grandmother said to me one time, "Boy, don't you know that he placed a sign out there that said, 'No Fishing Allowed'?"

If y'all don't go to sleep on me, do I have a witness in the house? Colossians 2:13 says that he took my sins out on a hill called Calvary. The next verse says that, if you get quiet enough, you'll hear the hammer ringing because he nailed those sins to that tree. Ah! Hebrews, the tenth chapter and the seventeenth verse. If I had a little time, I'd catalogue and chronicle all of these references.

It's such a relief to me to know that I don't have to walk around with a guilt-ridden complex simply because I said things I wish I hadn't said, and I've done things I wish I hadn't done, and I've gone places I wish I hadn't gone. But I'm free because he died.

You know, did you all know that I was a Baptist preacher? So, at the risk of doing violence homiletically, I've got to tell you he died! *He died* until the grave got sick of the stomach and started vomiting up its dead. *He died* till the elements of nature started suffering fits of cosmic epilepsy. *He died* until the dead in Christ got up on the first Easter morning and staged a protest march down the streets of Jerusalem. *He died* until there was a *"fountain filled with blood drawn from Emmanuel's veins; sinners plunged beneath that flood lose all their guilty stains."* He died until the Centurion said, "Surely, ain't, ain't no doubt about it. Surely, he must be the Son of God!" He died! You know I ought to say, "Didn't he die?" But, he died for our sins.

I see some of my dear friends here from the other culture tonight. Seriously, I had a problem with that for some years because I was denied access to the library in my hometown. You'll help me here. And, then, I met Christ.

I'm convinced that if any man bows at the cross and gets up with color on his mind he ought to bow again. For Christ takes care of that. I'm trying to help somebody here tonight on the full gospel. I ought to tell you that it didn't start fifteen years ago. You can dust off the biblical pages of history and rethread your way back across the vast wilderness of time and stand on the dusty shores of Jerusalem, and you'll hear the gospel, the good news that he died. Ah, but I don't want to stay there too long.

I'm amazed that he saved, I'm amazed that he made, and I'm amazed that he gave. In other words, he gave the Holy Spirit to accomplish his pre-designed plan before the foundation of the world. He has all of that in mind.

But, there is a second emphasis in this text as we keep reading paragraphically right on down. It says that, if we stand in amazement at his choice to save us, then we stand, by the grace of God, assured of his conquering. Listen. Listen to what the verse says down around the fiftieth verse of this same chapter. He says, "Now, when this mortal shall have put on immortality, and this corruptible shall have put on incorruption, then it says this, "O death, where is your sting? O grave, where is your victory? For the sting of death is sin," and so forth and so on. But, then it says, "Thanks be to God." Now, that's the conquest! That's the victory! Thanks be to God who "giveth us the victory."

So then, what am I to do in the meantime? I was about to say whenever I preach the gospel by the grace of God, when I sit down, I'm the most amazed man in the house. I don't even understand how God does it. But every now and then, he'll clear up my mind and give me a story to tell, and when I sit down, I say to the Lord, "You did it again."

That verse says, 58, of the same chapter, "Now brethren." It's in there. "Brethren." What does it say? "Be, therefore, steadfast, unmovable, always abounding in the work of the Lord, inasmuch as you know that your labor is not empty." Your labor is not useless. Your labor is not wasted because whenever you preach the gospel . . .

I wish I had time just to walk about this text. He opens in the larger context. You remember 1 Corinthians 1:18–21? *"For the preaching of the gospel is unto them that perish foolishness, but unto us who are being saved it is the very power of God."*

Now, what he's trying to say to me and to you is that preaching is the key. Listen! For the *preaching* of the gospel. Where is this power located that he uses to get things done? The power is located in a word about the cross. You've got to preach the cross!

Not only is the power located in a word concerning the cross, but the power is activated when we preach. For the preaching, participle, you've gotta keep on doing it, when it is done, things happen. May not be sensational. May not be flamboyant, but God is at work. Whenever the preaching of the gospel takes place, the *Logos* is being presented. It is divine intelligence. It is divine revelation. It is divine order, and it is divine communication.

Back up through that, and I've got diametrically the opposite on my hand. If I do not yield to the preaching of the gospel because of the communication, then there will be no order in my life. The reason why there is no order is because I have rejected the intelligence of God. The intelligence of God has been made available to me because of his revelation.

That's what happens when we preach. Seems like somebody's gone to sleep on me. It is located in the word. It is activated in preaching, but how is it demonstrated? The verse says, "We are being saved." It will be demonstrated in the lives of the ones who hear it and mix it with faith.

I sure wish I had some time here tonight because that conquest is what keeps us going. Here's the point—it's a gift. If somebody were agreeing with me tonight. I cannot vouch for you, but I know who I am. I am what I am by the grace of God.

You know what grace is? I'm glad you asked. Grace is unlimited. Grace is unknown. Grace is unimaginable. Grace is unexplained. Certainly, grace is unmerited. It is not only God's attitude toward us but is his activity in us. Then, it is his ambition for us. Grace. Grace is God's assigned gift to us predetermined from his own sovereign will so that we could be gripped by grace even when we don't deserve it. Oh yeah! I could name the greatest gift to you tonight. I'm gripped by grace because I'm walking in the word. Another word for that is "controlled by the word of God."

Whenever that happens, it will be evidenced, demonstrated in our lives because we will have inner peace independent of circumstances, companions, and conditions. But, the inner peace will overflow into a relaxed mental attitude. I will not always be walking around tight, tense, and touchy. Because of that, then, God can work through me to love the unlovable. Because I'm loving the unlovable through the grace of God, then I start mastering the common details of life because of the indwelling presence of the life-giver king.

That's what this gospel is all about. It doesn't have too much to do and yet it's a byproduct oftentimes. Cars, cash, clothes, commodities, creaturely comforts, Caribbean cruises, and cottages in the country may not be the emphasis of the One from Galilee. Because there comes a time when cars, and cash and clothes and commodities, they don't administer comfort at the graveside. They are not often called upon in ICU.

We have to have something on the inside that time will not erase nor ages destroy, and it is all in the Spirit. We conquer from the inside. It is unlike this sickly secular society, and this crumbling and collapsing culture.

One of the reasons Jesus rose . . . you know, he did rise. I was sharing today that when he said, "And I, if I be lifted up." You know, at resurrection time, Easter Sunday, we all focus on, "If I be lifted up." Have you ever reflected on the idea that, when Isaiah talked about it seven hundred years or so before it happened, syntactically, it gives us a real reason for reflection? It says this: "I saw Him high and lifted up." Now, under normal conditions it would have to be, "I saw him lifted up, then high." Somebody's not hearing me. But, he put "high" first. The reason is, when Isaiah looked up, he saw the undiminished deity. God, he was already there. Then, when he was lifted up, that was his perfect humanity. Don't y'all lose me.

You see, he was not only lifted up, John 12:32, from the Earth. He was lifted up on Earth. Are you hearing me? Then, he died and stayed in the grave three days. Then, he was lifted up out of the grave. Then, out on that mount, Acts 1:5, he was lifted up from the earth. You can't separate what God has joined together. He was lifted up on Earth. He was lifted up out of the grave. He was lifted up from the Earth.

Now is the session: the resurrection, the ascension, and then the session. He's at the right hand of God the Father making intercession for you and for me.

That's not the only reason he was raised. Let me tell you one other additional reason is why I rejoice tonight with the conquest. He was raised not only to go out and occupy what we now call outer space but also so that he would occupy the inner space. That's where the victory is: inner space. Christ lives in me! I better get a little closer to y'all. I said inner space is what he occupies now.

Dr. Arturo told us on Monday night about the hypostatic union. That alone messes up a lot of our doctrinal conclusions. I heard a fellow on television the other day. He was talking about cars and cash, and he said, "You are a little god." Let me throw in something parenthetically on that. The theology of preposition tells us this. You know: in Christ, through Christ, for Christ, under Christ, with Christ. In other words, in Christ: union and communion with him. Through Christ: his mediatorial ministry. Everything God is going to do for us, he does it for us through Christ. Anything we do ought to be unto him or, for Christ, and we can't do it unless it is with Christ.

But here's my point. [We are] on our way to one day being like him, not being like him as God, in his undiminished deity, but like him in his perfect humanity, because we will be stripped of our old sin nature so that we can then worship him—somebody ought to help me here—without that old sin nature invading the worship experience.

See, I can't worship him the way I ought to right now. Because I've got a messed up mind, and it has to be renewed day by day. That's why it is *being* saved. See, I have been saved, I am being saved, and I will be saved.

Every time I ever hear the gospel, I ought to be saved from something. Somebody here tonight needs to be saved from anger. Somebody else here tonight needs to be saved from bitterness. Somebody else here tonight ought to be saved from a critical spirit. Somebody else ought to be saved from a divisive attitude. All kinds of saved!

That word "saved" is a technical term for the delivering activity of God. Only the context reveals what the word "saved" means. Sometimes it's deliverance. Sometimes it's development. Sometimes it's direction. Sometimes it's change. Sometimes it's conversion. Sometimes it's challenge. Sometimes it's initial salvation. Sometimes it's sanctification. Sometimes it's glorification. Only the context.

I'm through now, but I got one more. Amen! I'm living in anticipation of his coming. See, that same Christ that you see going up is coming back. I'm at that stage now where I've stopped listening; I've stopped looking for the signs. You know, they say, "Everybody, look for the signs of his coming." I've stopped looking for the signs. It's so close now that I'm listening for the sound. You all ought to help me here.

Is there anybody here who knows him? Let me close out by telling you who he is. Christ. C-H-R-I-S-T. He died for our sins, and he's coming back again. C. He's the one who came. As the old preacher used to say, "Down through forty-two generations." But, when he came he ended up hanging on a tree.

You see, if you don't believe he ended up hanging on a tree, listen to the gospel for the first time under the leadership of the Holy Spirit, after the ascension of the risen Savior, and the descension of the Holy Spirit. In other words, the first gospel sermon ever preached with the anointing of the Holy Spirit is in Acts, the second chapter, commencing in the twenty-first verse. It says, *"Ye men of Israel, hear these words. This Jesus of Nazareth, a man approved of God among you by miracles, signs, and wonders, whereof he did it all in the midst of you as ye yourselves also know, by the determinate counsel and foreknowledge of God, ye by wicked hands have crucified and slain, whom God has raised up, having loosed the pangs of death, because he should not be holden of it, and David said 'And I keep him always before my face.'"* But the point is the twenty-third verse. *"By wicked hands, they took and crucified him."*

In verse 22, we have the actions of Jesus Christ: miracles, signs, and wonders. In the twenty-third verse, we have the reaction of men to the action of Jesus. Wicked hands! They took him and slew him. But in the twenty-fourth verse, we have the reaction of God to the reaction of man to the reaction of Jesus, which means that God always has the last word.

So, he ended up hanging on a tree. But, he didn't stay there. He is risen! Didn't he rise? So not only did he come, not only did he end up hanging on a tree, but he rose. And he rose, listen carefully, so that he could indwell me.

When he walked around in Jerusalem, he was limited to that little small geographic area. And one of the things about it, I went over there [Israel]. It's smaller than I thought. You take me from Houston to Austin, north to south, and you take it from Houston to Galveston, east to west. That's it. He never moved beyond that area except when he was a child down in Egypt.

But, now, he indwells each of us on the wheat fields of Kansas, the swamplands of Louisiana, the Appalachian areas of Pennsylvania, the Golden Coast of California, the rugged plains of Texas. I ought to have somebody in the house. He's all over, and he's everywhere because he's indwelling. But, he's indwelling for a reason, and that is to strengthen us for the task. Do you know him? Have you ever tried him? I can never talk about it without remembering what he has done for me.

I used to walk across streets, and I was so empty. I didn't even know I'd walked across them. I used to sit down to read a book and could not concentrate. I used to miss a signal light, and it was too long to wait.

Then, I heard about the man who was down at the river giving sight to the blind. That's why he doesn't have to quiet the storm on the Sea of Galilee anymore for me because he quieted the storm in my own heart. He doesn't have to turn water to wine anymore for me because he's given me an internalized joy that time will not erase nor ages destroy.

My own testimony is: I know I am a child of God, and I know my name is in the Lamb's Book of Life. Oh, I know, my record is on high, and if I were E. K. Bailey tonight, I'd say, "Oh, I ought to have a witness somewhere in the building."

Do you know him? He's an answer for my agony. He's a balm for my bruises. He's a cure for my calamities. He's a deliverer for my distress. He's an eraser of my error. He's a fixer of my faults. He's a healer of my hurts. Oh, if you know him, then, let the redeemed of the Lord say so. If you've got good religion, then show some sign. Oh! Oh! Oh!

Chapter 10

Clarence Booker Taliaferro (C. B. T.) Smith (1916–2009)

Living Legend 2005

The Preacher

BORN IN THE SMALL community of LaVernia, Texas, the Rev. Dr. Clarence Booker Taliaferro (C. B. T.) Smith (1916–2009) grew up in humble circumstances. His father was a sharecropper, his family picked cotton to supplement their income, and he was the ninth child of fourteen. He attended elementary school in LaVernia, high school in San Antonio, and college at St. Phillips Junior College, also in San Antonio. While in high school, he met the love of his life, Mrs. Rosie Lee (Hartfield) Smith, whom he dated for eight years. They were married on January 2, 1943. Despite his plan for a two-week honeymoon, he was deployed one day later for active military service in the Army during World War II. They were married for sixty-five years until she preceded him in death in 2008.

God called him to preach in a vision in the middle of the night, one in which he woke up in a cold sweat with an undeniable sense that God had called him to pastor and preach. His vision led him to enroll at Bishop College in Marshall, Texas, and later, Southwestern Theological Seminary in Fort Worth, Texas. Dr. Smith preached his first sermon in 1946 at the New Light Baptist Church, San Antonio, Texas. In the late 1940s and early 1950s, he pastored four churches at the same time in St. Augustine, Marshall, Longview, and Waxahachie.

In June 1952, the congregation of Golden Gate Missionary Baptist Church called him to become only their fourth senior pastor. Under his leadership, the church grew numerically, financially, and spiritually. It cleared its debt, purchased property, and served the Dallas community through its vibrant ministry. He served as the senior pastor at Golden Gate for forty-five years until his retirement in 1997. Over that same time period, he developed a stellar reputation as a preacher, pastor, leader, and person of character in Dallas, throughout Texas, and across the nation. Two years before his retirement, in 1995, he was featured on billboards and posters throughout the Dallas Metropolitan area as a *Legend of the Clergy* during Black History Month. Even after his retirement, he continued in active ministry, traveling widely to lecture, preach, and lead revivals until his death at the age of ninety-three. After he passed in 2009, the city of Dallas renamed the street on which the church is located, Sabine Street, in Dr. Smith's honor. The church's address is 1101 Reverend C. B. T. Smith St., Dallas, Texas.

The Sermon

The text that I have here is found in the fourth chapter of the book of Acts of the apostles. I'm going to read a few verses.

The late Dr. Manuel Scott said, "If you don't think you're going to do too much in preaching, read a lot of Scripture." At least they can say, "He sure did read." So, I want to do that. I want to begin with the fourteenth verse in the fourth chapter and read through verse 20, or probably verse 21. Acts 4:

> And beholding the man which was healed standing with them, they could say nothing against it. But when they had command-ed them to go aside out of the council, they conferred among themselves, saying, What shall we do to these men? for that

indeed a notable miracle hath been done by them is manifest to all them that dwell in Jerusalem; and we cannot deny it. But that it spread no further among the people, let us straitly threaten them, that they speak henceforth to no man in this name. And they called them, and commanded them not to speak at all nor teach in the name of Jesus. But Peter and John answered and said unto them, Whether it be right in the sight of God to hearken unto you more than unto God, judge ye. For we cannot but speak the things which we have seen and heard. So when they had further threatened them, they let them go, finding nothing how they might punish them, because of the people: for all men glorified God for that which was done.

"We cannot but speak the words of what we've seen and heard." I'm going to talk about it if you'll help me a little bit.

I want to talk about *the imperative of the gospel.* "We cannot but speak the things which we've seen and heard." These were bold and courageous men. The words that Peter and John spoke followed in the wake of a man being healed at a gate called Beautiful, and it upset the city and the city fathers. They spoke with a bold sense of divine compulsion; it was accompanied by a boldness that does not count the cost. It might be death for them, but they spoke just the same. They did not stop speaking and calling the name Jesus.

The experience they had with Christ was so overwhelming that it impelled them to speak in the name of Jesus Christ of Nazareth. Without being endowed with divine urgency, they could not have penetrated that hard shell, religious traditionalism of that day.

The priests and the captains and the Sadducees were all grieved because of what had happened. People had gone after these two men and they were very grieved about it. When they saw them, they laid hands on them, and they kept them overnight. The next day they brought them before the Sanhedrin council to speak there.

Now, Peter and John gave praises to God. The council was trying to get down to the real root of the matter. It was a crisis in the city. They were trying to get down to the root of it. They were trying to find out what really happened here. What happened? We know that they found this man who was at the gate called Beautiful. They had never seen him in the temple, and now he was leaping and shouting for God.

They said, "We want to get to the root and once we can get to the root, we will understand what's going on. Then, we'll know who we're looking at and whether we ought to let 'em stay here or whether we ought to send them out of town."

When listening to the boldness and the fearlessness of the two men, it convices us that there yields an imperative truth in the gospel. If Jesus Christ is there, you just can't help but tell it. It's something that moves you. It's there. You just can't say, "Well, we ought to let it go." There's an urgency that moves within you that'll keep you from holding your peace.

They got there. I looked at it, and look at the authoritative, masterful—look at the commanding. Look at the urgency. It says that they just would not let go. You will be given over to these words that you speak.

It's like Paul who said, "Woe is me if I preach not the gospel. Something will happen to me if I preach not the gospel."

One man came to me, and he said, "Well, I heard you gave up the gospel."

I said, "No, sir. Now, wait just a minute. I didn't give it up because the gospel won't give me up. I retired from pastoring, but I can't retire from the gospel." I gotta do that. If I can't find somebody to preach to, I'll get in my car, go out, and stop at a tree and have a good sermon with a tree because I can't help but do it. Am I right about it?

You've got to tell it! You can't keep from telling it. That's the reason Peter and John said, "But, we cannot but speak. We don't have no other alternative. We don't have no other way. We've gotta speak the things that we have seen and heard. That's on our hearts. We can't do it." In other words, "We've already talked that over. We had a two-man conference. We got together, and we decided that death and whatever may come into our lives, whatever you want to do that's up to you all, go ahead and make your decision. We've already made our decision. We cannot but speak the things that we've seen and heard."

It's good when you can see some things and hear some things with your faith. Am I right about it? Faith has eyes to let you see in. Faith has ears to let you hear in. And if you see enough and hear enough in faith, you'll be just like these two men. "We cannot speak but the things we have seen and heard." Help me, Lord Jesus.

Now, we see several things here. Help me, Lord! That's what these young preachers of today, they taught me that. They taught me, "You've got to have several things here." [Laughter] So, if I want to stay in the mix, I've got to get with it.

Now, there were several things here. They gave themselves to the preaching of the gospel. You know, if you're going to preach for change, there must be a yielding to God's word. You have to yield to God's word if you're preaching for change.

When I looked at that, and I saw it in this verse, verses 7–12, it says here, first of all, they witnessed the gospel's resources. The council asked them, "By what power, and by what name did you do this? What is the source, where did you get all of this from? This man is walking, he came down here with a cup, he dropped his cup and picked up a cry. And I want to know, what is it? From what source, by what power, and by what name did you do something like this?"

Peter was filled with the Holy Ghost! You know, sometimes, we don't like to talk about the Holy Ghost. For a long time, Baptists were scared of the Holy Ghost. But, if you don't have the Holy Ghost, you don't have no ghost at all! You've got to have it!

And, he was filled with the Holy Ghost. You know, over in the second chapter, they passed by Pentecost, and Peter gave the theme sermon. Didn't he give it?

In the third chapter, he and John said, "We better go up to the temple, to the prayer meeting." That's where they met that man. It says, "He was filled with the Holy Ghost," and it looked like he said, "I'm glad you asked me that."

He said, "Behold, the man that you crucified, you put him in the grave, and you thought you was through with him. *That* man is the reason why *this* man is standing here."

That's the source! Help me, Lord Jesus! "It is in the name of Jesus Christ of Nazareth, that's the reason why that man is standing here. So, if you want to know the source, here it is right here. If you want to know why we have power, I'm giving it to you right now. You know, it is by the name of Jesus Christ of Nazareth whom you crucified, but now he's resurrected."

Even by his name, this was the stone that was set at north, but now it has become the head of the corner.

This name is the source of power and of gospel. This name transforms the pioneers of the gospel. This name transforms prisoners' bars and makes a pulpit out of it. This name from which the gospel sermon is preached. This name is the source by which we operate. We can't help ourselves. We're operating from this power.

I'm glad you asked me. We did not take up the calling as a matter of self-directed course, but by the obedience of the impulse of consciousness.

This is an irresistible gospel. You see, children, through Paul, he said, "Through all I preach, I have nothing to glory of for necessity has been laid on me."

I looked at that and found out he was saying, "The gospel is necessary and, out of necessity, I preach." So, I'm not here just playing around. What I'm saying is necessary. I've been necessitated to tell you that God is able. I'm here tonight to tell you that we can't quit doing it. I'm here to tell you that it's an imperative. It's got to be, it must be, it shall be preached. Somebody's got to do it.

As an old man, I'm so glad to see all of these young men coming to the ministry. I go all around this country, and they're doing great jobs. I wish I could wake up some of them old fellas that went on before me, because I know that some of the ones that went on before me asked me what this world would look like when we've gone on. Now, I can tell them that it's good. God is able.

You can't kill the gospel. God's got a plan. I understand that, and I'm so glad about it. I just can't help myself. I can't evade it. I can't avoid it. Am I right about it? I must preach the gospel of Jesus Christ. I can't help but do it. So, therefore, they found that the source was the name Jesus.

Then, secondly, it looks to me, not only was it the source, but they also witnessed the relationship. They had a relationship. At verse 13, when the council saw such boldness in Peter and John, they perceived that they were ignorant and unlearned, uninstructed into Jewish schools. "They took knowledge and marveled that they had been with Jesus." They were not excited about them being unlearned and ignorant. They didn't get excited over that. But they got excited over the fact that they had a current relationship going on with Jesus.

Brothers and sisters, let me tell you that we've got to have a current relationship, and they've got to be able to see that relationship between us and the man we're representing. They saw that relationship, and they were worried over that relationship. That's what caused the excitement and the surprise and the amazement, that they saw that they had a relationship with that teacher Jesus.

The Sanhedrin really believed that Jesus was finished at the crucifixion. They thought it was over; he was buried. But, behold, they discovered that Jesus reappeared in Peter and John. That really got them going when they looked and saw that he had reappeared in them. For some of the things Jesus was doing when he was on Earth they saw coming out in those preachers, and they got excited. They had trouble with him when he was on Earth, and they said, "Do you really mean that, now, we're still gonna have trouble?"

I say that you're gonna have worse trouble now! They could see it. When they could see him going on and having relationship with his believers, they all felt that he was finished. But at the cross, he didn't say he was finished. He said, "It is finished!" Am I right about it?

Jesus was talking about the plan of salvation; it was already set up. The plan was through, and he said, "Father, I'm coming home!" That's what he was talking about; they thought they were finished with him.

I'm going to say something here. Now, I'm just passing through, you know. To me—I want you to get this—it seems to me that the satanic forces of the world today are trying to buy partnership in the church programs. I'm just talking about what I'm seeing. It looks like they're trying their best to buy partnership with church programs. They're doing so by trying to convince the church of a living Christ to just keep downloading your programs with meaningful things. Help me, Lord Jesus. Meaningful things. Not kingdom, but thing-doms. Thing-doms. Not kingdom. Thing-doms. They're meaning-ful. Help me, Lord Jesus. They're trying to fill up the church program so that there's less preaching about Christ. I know it'll never happen, but it seems to me that, if something like that were to keep going, then churches would turn out to be grand entertainment centers.

We've got to keep the name Jesus. Keep the gospel in there. They didn't say to Peter and John, "Y'all can't preach no more!" They didn't say, "Y'all can't have no more worship services. Go ahead. Have all the worship you want. Preach good sermons and stuff and all like that, but just don't mention the name Jesus."

"Go ahead. Do all the preaching you want. Do all the preaching you want. You can preach about anybody. Aristotle. That's good. Preach about him. Plato. Preach about him. Talk good about your governors. Say some things about your mayor of the city. Just don't mention that name Jesus! For they tell me that name, going around giving sight to blind, that name, giving the lame to walk, that name is raising the dead, and that's what's messing up the city fathers. We can't have that. Go ahead and have a good service. Clap your hands and praise him. But, leave the name Jesus out of the question." Help me, Lord Jesus.

I'm afraid they're trying to water it down. I look at a lot of things on TV. It gives me an opportunity to let me know what's going on. I don't know if you see something else creeping in. Some of these late-night programs re-ally get down after it. Then, when you take a break, a church comes on with an announcement. Then, it goes right back off, and they go back on again. Trying to water it down. Well, I just said that. Y'all pick over it, and see what y'all get out of it.

They told them, "Don't mention the name. This name is why the city is so tore up, this name that's got us meeting with you today. We just want to know if this name will make believers shout. Look at the folk following you now. Look at them hollering, 'Glory to God.' There's something about that name."

"The name Jesus," they said, "Let it be off limits." They pushed them to answer the Sanhedrin. They had to do it because the preachers found out where their resources were. Then, they found out about the relationship with Jesus. Now, lastly, they found out about the resurrection. They said, "We cannot but speak the things that we have seen and heard."

You saw a lot of things, and they heard a lot of things, but allow me to mention two things. These two things get me to see the imperative of the gospel. Peter and John got a good look at the resurrection. They weren't there, but the women came because the angel had told them to go tell them, "He is risen."

They got there, and John outran Peter. I guess he came back to Peter. But, I'll tell you. He saw something that really moved him. He saw that the napkin and the headpiece were folded neatly, everything laying just like it ought to be. He knew that somebody dead couldn't get up like that. A live man had to get up like that.

I heard my grandma, she used to say, "Children, he's a dying bed maker. He can make up your dying bed." I heard one of the daughters say that, "Daddy taught us how to die." But, E. K. got back and let him make up his dying bed.

Peter saw that. He had been following afar off. In fact, he went fishing when he was crucified, but when he saw that, he was moved by it. The last thing that helps me to know that there is an imperative in the gospel, they saw that it is inescapable, unavoidable, commanded, necessary, authoritative. It is powerful.

Peter said to John when they came up. I don't know what the conversation was. But, soon they got to that gate when they saw that man lying up against a beautiful gate.

Preachers, let me tell you. Ugly and beauty meet every Sunday at the beautiful gates of the church. I'm talking about ugly attitudes and bad tempers and all of that. All the bad gossip; it finds itself at the church. Am I right about it? You don't find beauty and ugly getting together easily nowhere else. I've never heard of an ugly contest. I've heard of a beauty contest. They can't get applicants if they set up for an ugly contest. Nobody wants to be called ugly. Am I right about it?

But, here at the church, ugly and good, ugly and beautiful find their place at the church on Sunday morning. But, I'm glad to know that the gospel can separate them. Am I right, children? Help me, Lord!

Peter looked at John and said to him, "Well." It looked like he might have said to him, "Sometimes, it's hard for me to preach without me making some assumption as to what I feel that might be going on." Maybe they were on their way walking when they saw that man . . . . help me, Lord Jesus, Peter said to him, "You know John, I've been following afar off. You know, he's been trying his best to get me to follow him. And, you know, when they were trying him, I was standing out on the porch, and I warmed myself by the fire." Am I right about it? He said, "I turned down him for them."

He said, "But, John, since I had a look at the resurrection and saw how he was raised from the dead—I'll tell you right now—I'm not gonna mess up my chances now. I've got a chance to do something for him. I'm not gonna give that man any money." Am I right, children?

I want you to excuse me now. This is the way they done it when I came along. "I'm not going to let them have it . . ." Help me, Lord Jesus.

Oh Lord, I'm gonna tell it! I'm gonna use Jesus at a time like this. You know, children, there's a time when you've got to use him. Am I right, children? The storm may rage. Thunder may come. Well, you've gotta use him!

I'm going to hold myself. I'm just trying to hold myself. Help me, Lord, but I can't help it. Help me, Lord! I've been doing it so long till somebody told me, "It's alright!" Oh, help me, Lord Jesus!

Do you know him, children? Do you know him? He's alright! I heard him say when he got there, he said, "Look on us!" Now, I love that! Really, when you've been saved—am I right, children?—you develop an "us" philosophy.

He'd been talking about me and mine. I remember when he wanted to come to the water, to Jesus, he said, "Lord, if it be you, I want you to let me come." He didn't even mention those other fellas that were back there on that boat. "Let *me* walk to you."

Now, he has changed his philosophy. He said, "Look on us!" Am I right, children? Then, he said, "Silver and gold have I none. You might as well drop your cup because we don't have it. But such as I have, I'm gonna give it to you. But, in the name, in the name, in the name, in the name of Jesus, rise up and walk a little bit!"

He rose up. He went skipping and jumping on up in the temple. Am I right about it? They decided that they're gonna let him go because they didn't have nothing they could sentence him about.

I'm so glad that they can't sentence me from talking about the resurrection of Jesus Christ. You see, he paid the price. Now, you can't sentence a man for one price that's already been paid.

I'm free, I'm free, Oh yes, I'm free to talk about Jesus! Am I right, children? Tell it! Tell it on Sunday morning! Tell it everywhere you go. Tell it! Am I right about it? Tell it! He got up! Tell it! He was crucified. Tell it! Then, they buried him. Tell it! Early, early, early Sunday morning, he got out of that grave. Aren't you glad? Aren't you glad? Thank you, Jesus!

That's the imperative in the gospel. I can't quit it! I can't avoid it! I've got to tell it!

Chapter 11

William J. Shaw (1934–)

Living Legend 2006

The Preacher

Rev. Dr. William J. Shaw (1934–) was born in Marshall, Texas, the youngest of six children, in 1934.[1] At a young age, he dedicated his life to serving God. He was baptized at age seven and preached his trial sermon by age eleven. He served as supply pastor at his home church at fifteen and was ordained as senior pastor of the Oak Hill Baptist Church in Harrison County, Texas, at seventeen.

1. Several paragraphs from this biographical profile have been adapted from the "About Us" webpage profile on the White Rock Baptist Church website. See http://www.whiterockbaptist.org/about-us/church-leadership.

Dr. Shaw has maintained a love of learning throughout his life. He was valedictorian of his high school class at sixteen. He attended Bishop College, graduating summa cum laude at age nineteen with a major in philosophy and religion and a minor in world history. Then, he received his bachelor of divinity degree (now known as the master of divinity) from Union Theological Seminary in New York in 1957. Later, in 1975, he earned a doctor of ministry degree from Colgate Rochester Divinity School in Rochester, New York, with an emphasis on biblical interpretation from the Black perspective. A doctor of humane letters was conferred upon him from Barber-Scotia College in Concord, North Carolina, in the year 2000.

He has served with distinction as the senior pastor of the White Rock Baptist Church in Philadelphia since 1956. The church celebrated his sixtieth year of service in 2016. He considers his work as pastor his highest calling. He has led White Rock through a period of strong growth with the establishment of several outreach ministries including a science and math after-school program and a substance abuse recovery ministry.

Dr. Shaw has also served as a religious leader at the local, state, and national levels. He has served as president of numerous organizations such as the Pennsylvania Baptist State Convention, Inc., the Baptist Ministers Conference of Philadelphia and Vicinity, the Metropolitan Christian Council of Philadelphia, and the Union Theological Seminary National Alumni Association. From 1981 through 1994, he served as director of the Ministers Division of the National Congress of Christian Education. He has received numerous awards such as the Unitas Award given by the Alumni Association of the Union Theological Seminary and the T. B. Maston Foundation Christian Ethics Award from the Southwestern Baptist Theological Seminary.

On September 9, 1999, Dr. Shaw was elected as the sixteenth president of the National Baptist Convention, USA, Inc. With his focus on Vision, Integrity, Structure, and Accountability (VISA), the convention reached several milestones including burning the mortgage on the Baptist World Center, paying more than $1.125 million dollars of inherited debt, implementing a retirement plan for pastors and church workers, establishing fiscal accountability, and increasing the role of technology. He was reelected to the Convention presidency in September 2004.

Dr. Shaw is married to Mrs. Camellia L. Shaw. They are the parents of one son, Timothy, and the grandparents of two granddaughters, Lillian and Brittany.

The Sermon

I want to focus on a passage that is in the Old Testament. The book of 2 Chronicles, chapter 18, and the parallel passages in 1 Kings, chapter 22. I read several verses to refresh the memories of Bible students who are here. I don't have to read the whole story, but I have to read enough that it will open your memories, and you'll be able to go along with me. 2 Chronicles 18:

> Now Jehoshaphat had riches and honor in abundance and joined affinity with Ahab. And after several years he went down with Ahab to Samaria, and Ahab killed sheep and oxen for him in abundance and for the people that he had with him and persuaded him to go up with him to Ramoth Gilead. And Ahab king of Israel said to Jehoshaphat king of Judah, "Will thou go with me to Ramoth Gilead?" He answered him, "I am as thou art, and my people as thy people. We will be with thee in the war." And Jehoshaphat said unto the king of Israel, "Enquire, I pray thee, at the word of the Lord today." Therefore the king of Israel gathered together of prophets, four hundred men, and said unto them, "Shall we go to Ramoth Gilead to battle, or shall I forbear?" And they said, "Go up; for God will deliver it into the king's hand." But Jehoshaphat said, "Is there not here a prophet of the Lord besides, that we might enquire of him?" And the king of Israel said unto Jehoshaphat, "There is yet one man, by whom we may enquire of the Lord: but I hate him; for he never prophesied good unto me, but always evil: the same is Micaiah the son of Imla." And Jehoshaphat said, "Let not the king say so." And the king of Israel called for one of his officers, and said, "Fetch quickly Micaiah the son of Imla." And the king of Israel and Jehoshaphat king of Judah sat either of them on his throne, clothed in their robes, and they sat in a void place at the entering in of the gate of Samaria; and all the prophets prophesied before them. And Zedekiah the son of Chenaanah had made him horns of iron, and said, "Thus saith the Lord, 'With these thou shalt push Syria until they be consumed.'" And all the prophets prophesied so, saying, "Go up to Ramoth Gilead, and prosper: for the Lord shall deliver it into the hand of the king." And the messenger that went to call Micaiah spake to him, saying, "Behold, the words of the prophets declare good to the king with one assent; let thy word therefore, I pray thee, be like one of theirs, and speak thou good." And Micaiah said, "As the Lord liveth, even what my God saith, that will I speak." (KJV)

I will cease reading here, and you will read the rest of it. I will stay here in Chronicles, chapter 18, and its other recording in 1 Kings 22.

I want to focus on key points in the story, verses 6 and 13. Jehoshaphat said, "Is there none here a prophet of the Lord besides, that we might enquire of him?" Micaiah said, "Even what my God saith, that will I speak." Question: Who is in the house? "Is there not here a prophet of the Lord besides, that we might enquire of him?"

The setting is of a state visit made by Jehoshaphat king of Judah to Ahab king of Israel. An alliance was in force between them. The son of Jehoshaphat had married the daughter of Ahab, not a courtship, but a state arrangement, signaling their alliance. So, Jehoshaphat makes a state visit.

Ahab gives him a royal reception. He takes the occasion of the royal reception to raise a question that might not have been anticipated by Jehoshaphat. For he asked him, "Will you go to war with me against Syria?" Ahab had brooded over an unkept promise by Ben Hadad of Syria who promised a prior settlement of war to return Ramoth Gilead to Ahab. Ramoth Gilead was a strategic city, a trade route to Damascus.

But the promise had not been kept, and this was brooding in Ahab. He had said to his own counselors, "Look, Ramoth Gilead is ours and we're not doing anything about taking it back."

When Jehoshaphat arrives, Ahab invites him to become a part of a coalition of the willing, if you will. "Will you go to war with me?" There is a pact between them already so there was a willing response. Jehoshaphat said to Ahab, "My people are your people. My armaments are yours, the bottom line is." But he said this with hesitation, So, he asked of Ahab, "Let us enquire of the Lord today."

There are at least two premises, and I say this before moving further into the story. There are at least two premises at the base of this biblical story, and indeed of the Bible from beginning to end—at least these two. One. There is just one absolute center-possessor of absolute power—that's God. All other powerholders have derivative power, not absolute power.

Second, there is one absolute point of ownership. The earth is the Lord's, and the fullness thereof, the world and they that dwell therein. If there is just one absolute point of ownership, then every other claim of ownership is an entrustment or stewardship.

Now, with these premises, you can proceed with the story. You can read the Bible and understand the issue of sin. Without these premises, sin is moot. Prophecy, prophetic declarations are unwarranted intrusions. But, if you accept these premises, then you can see the legitimacy of the prophetic roles.

Here are two kings, two holders of power, and they are about to go to war. It is their decision. Ahab had decided he was going to fight against Syria and reclaim Ramoth Gilead. He asked Jehoshaphat. Because Jehoshaphat was king, he didn't have to hold a counsel. He simply said, "My people are your people. My armaments are your armaments, I'll go with you."

Here are two power holders. But, one has hesitation about war, and he says to the other, "We'll go, but let's enquire of the Lord." More accurately, as the King James reads it, "Let's enquire at the word of the Lord."

There's a striking suggestion here because two kings were possessors of power about to do something; they're power holders; if they have it absolutely, they have to do.

Power tends not to be answerable or accountable to anybody. Religious power is dangerous because holders of religious power can tend not to be answerable to anybody, not even to God. Political power is dangerous because those who hold it tend not to want to be answerable to anybody.

We live in a time now when we're supposed to be in a democracy, and democracy says rulers are accountable. But, we are seeing played out in the scene now that holders of power don't want to be answerable and therefore will act as if they are not accountable. If you are not a religious leader or a political leader, but you grew up in the Black family tradition, you still know what that is, that holders of power tend to be absolute in their view.

There was a time when children, they wouldn't dare to ask Mama and Daddy, "Why?" And the answer was not with an answer. The answer was, "Because I said so," and that settled it. If you ever had a question, you didn't raise it anymore. If you did, you went outside and you talked about it, but you didn't deal with it anymore there because power tends to be not answerable to anybody.

Here is a striking thing that two holders of power would dare to do a thing that only one of them thought about doing. "Let's enquire of the Lord." The move was a prudent move because war should never be a cavalier act. You don't rush into war. You shouldn't rush into war for frivolous reasons. You shouldn't lie about it.

So, Jehoshaphat says to Ahab, "Let's enquire at the word of the Lord." Now, that's a challenge. For whenever holders of power feel the need to ask somebody else to convey what they're doing, you're dealing with an ego challenge. There's an inherit confession here, that there is a higher judgment than that which belongs to heads of state. They have already decided they're going to go to war, but Jehoshaphat says, "Let's enquire at the word of the Lord." That's always a challenge.

It's a dangerous thing, quite frankly, to ask something of God. It's dangerous period to ask a question. But, surely, you don't ask God questions if you don't expect or you're not ready for an answer. So, what you're asking is hollow; it is a courtesy to the Divine.

We pray, but we don't really pray. We do it because we want to be courteous to God, but we're not seeking answers. We are looking for acquiescence. You hear that in much of prayer life in congregations. You hear it often times in those of us who are part of the religious structure.

Here in this political game, it is clearly an instance where one of the askers at least was not looking for an answer. He simply wanted acquiescence. "Enquire at the word of the Lord."

The problem is, though, where do you go if you want to enquire at the word of the Lord? I know I'm pushing a translation here that may be faulty, but it does open up some windows for us.

Where do you enquire at the word of the Lord? Is the word of the Lord at a place? Is it resident in a person? Does it have objective existence unto itself? "At the word of the Lord."

It may be each of these but, more centrally, if you're dealing with the word of the Lord, you need to look at a person. Look to persons because God has chosen to relate to us in persons. We've got the Bible! The Bible was inspired of the Spirit of God, but it was penned by persons. The ultimate truth says, "In the beginning was the Word, and the Word was with God, and everything was made by the Word, and the Word became flesh and dwelt among us."

So, they said, "Let's enquire at the word of the Lord," and Ahab thought he had the ready answer. He summoned four hundred prophets and asked them, "Shall I go or should I refrain?" and with one voice, they said, "Go up!"

They counseled and said, "This is the way you're going to scatter them, that you're going to annihilate them." Four hundred prophets said, "Go up," but Jehoshaphat was uneasy so he raises a question that is striking and disturbing for the four hundred had spoken.

He asks Ahab, "Is there not here a prophet of the Lord besides?" Four hundred prophets, but he had not discerned in that massive gathering that there was a prophet of the Lord.

Ahab answered, "There is one man." Now, some troubling insights follow as the story proceeds. Four hundred prophets and not one prophet of the Lord? Does this not suggest to us, more than suggest to us, does it not *declare* to us that prophets of the Lord are not in large supply?

Plenty of pulpits, but prophets are not in large supply. Plenty of spokespersons for religious centers of power, but not many prophets of the Lord. Plenty of spokespersons for political centers of power, but not many prophets of the Lord. Prophets of the Lord speak on behalf of God.

Prophets of religious centers speak on behalf of religious centers. Political spokespersons speak on behalf of political centers of power. But, the prophet of the Lord speaks on behalf of God to religious power centers, to secular power centers, even to people of the land. And if the prophet speaks, he does not speak about trivialities. He speaks about national issues, speaks about war-based implications.

This is a matter of war! Now, when the wars were fought, it would have been alright if Ahab and Jehoshaphat had fought Ben Hadad. But, instead, all of Israel was involved. If the leaders did the fighting, that could be restricted some. But, here families and systems are involved. Here's a national issue.

Pulpits that don't deal with national issues, pulpits that don't deal with national power centers, pulpits that don't deal with national social issues and moral issues are not speaking always for the Lord. Many times, we deal with trivialities instead of the stuff that really matters.

Not many prophets, and there may be a reason for that. For the second revelation is that it's dangerous to be a prophet of the Lord. It's dangerous to be a prophet before authority.

Listen as Ahab responds to Jehoshaphat, "There is one, but I hate him. I hate him because he does not let me define moral and spiritual issues. He does not speak good of me." The Lord doesn't speak evil. Now, Ahab equated good with his own desires and equated evil with any challenge to his desires. He equated the good with his own self-interests as king, and it is evil to speak otherwise.

That's the way that most power centers work. If it's in my interests, then it's good. If it's in my perceived interests, it's good. If it's not, it's evil. That's why children look at parents like they've done the worst thing in the world when they don't let them do what they want to do. The parents are evil to the children because good for them is acquiescing with their desires. So many times, we raise that with the Lord, and surely in larger settings, that's a danger.

Here is Micaiah running the risk of danger because Micaiah was already disliked by Ahab. The fact is, as the story unfolds, he was already in confinement. It's always dangerous to be an object or a subject of dislike by power.

Power has a way of striking at you. It has a way of undermining you. So long as you confirm and affirm, then you'll be alright. But you better not get outside of that confirming, affirming thing because you are subject to all kinds of untold actions, subject to all kinds of retribution. For power does not like to be challenged.

"I don't like him. The fact is I hate him because he does not speak well of me." But, Jehoshaphat persists and says, "Don't talk like that. Send for him." So, Ahab begrudgingly sent for Micaiah.

You see Micaiah on his way back, and you discover that, if you go to be a prophet, if you're called to be a prophet, it's going to take some courage. It's going to take the courage of your conviction to stand in the prophetic role. For it takes courage to go against the tide.

Four hundred prophets have served Ahab well and while Micaiah is on his way back to the whole assembly, the messenger says to him, "Now, here's what has happened. Four hundred men have spoken with one voice. Now don't you break ranks. When you go up there, you say what they have said. Don't go against the tide."

That's always the term. It's dangerous, and it takes courage to stand against the tide. If everyone and everything is going one way, and there's something in you saying, "Don't do it," it takes a whole lot of willpower and fortitude and strength to stand against the whole tide.

So, Micaiah answers in a way that is most challenging to us. Micaiah said, "Whatever the Lord tells me, that's what I'm going to say." Now, the messenger didn't like it. The prophets didn't like it. Surely, Ahab wouldn't like it. But, that was the role of the prophet.

The prophet's message is not self-generated. It isn't a matter of what you like or what you want. You may feel otherwise, but the Lord may rest upon you a word that is different from your own desire. When your desires and divine direction collide, you have to be ready to decide where you're going to stand. It takes courage sometimes to stand with the word of the Lord against the flow of the tide.

So here they are. They come back and Ahab and Jehoshaphat play a psychological game on Micaiah. When he gets there, they are situated as in a royal court, each one of them sitting on his throne, each one royally garbed, each with his attendants around him, and four hundred prophets all around blessing the presence there. Now, here is this one man, standing in the presence of not just one king but two kings. They are in court already. And, the courts of power can be awesome in places.

It's a striking something to go sit in the board room of the president of a giant corporation. Board rooms of corporations look differently from the street. I was in New York City once, in the board room of the Chase Manhattan Bank, and I said, "My God, New York looks a lot different from the board room view than from the street view."

There's something awesome about being in a great big room with mahogany chairs, long, impressive tables, no food on the table, no paper on the table. Just a chair that presides over the table. There's something awesome about that.

There's something awesome about being in the Oval Office where the President sits. I've been there, and some of you have been there waiting for the President. He doesn't wait on you. You are in there when he comes in, and you're seated, and he walks in with his entourage. It's an awesome thing to be in the presence of that power. It can be intimidating to do anything other than acquiesce.

So, Ahab says, "Shall we go to war?" Now, I don't know if Micaiah was intimidated or playing games with Ahab because the first answer Micaiah gives is, "Go. Go up, and you will win."

Was he working on him psychologically or was he working on him speaking sarcastically? The authors say he was speaking sarcastically. I'm not sure. He may have been intimidated.

But, Ahab recognized that there was something false about what he had said. "This man has never said anything good about me." He said, "Don't play with me."

If Micaiah had been intimated, then the godliness in him had been awakened. For he stood up and said, "Well, let me tell you what I really saw. I saw the Lord sitting on his throne, and I saw all of Israel scattered as sheep without a shepherd."

Ahab got the message right away. "You see! I told you that he never said anything good about me." Now, when Micaiah saw smoke, Zedekiah struck him. You run the risk of the wrath of the prophets of the courts and the court has ways of striking. Sometimes, it's physical. Sometimes, it's not physical. Sometimes, it can be undermining. Sometimes, it can be repu-tation assassination. Sometimes, it can be rumor. Sometimes, it can be a counteroffensive of lies that are meant to look like truth because they hold the weapons of communication in their hands.

It's a dangerous thing. You may be struck if you go be a prophet of the Lord. The fact is that, after he was struck, Ahab said, "Take him back to prison and make his lot worse than what it was before."

In the face of that, what in the world would make a man stand up and speak prophetically? How do you stand with integrity, with conviction, in that kind of setting?

I suggest two or three things. Then, I'll take my seat. First of all, he who is prophet recognizes that the prophet is not a volunteer. So, you don't have the luxury of opting in or opting out. The prophet is drafted. The Lord lays hands on and, if the Lord lays hands on you, then you are not under your control. You are under his control.

Read the record. Real prophets were not submitting resumes to the Lord and saying, "I understand you have some prophetic vacancies, and I'd like to be a prophet in your court." No! No! Prophets are not volunteers; they are drafted.

Even when the Lord lays hands on, the prophet tries to back out of it. "Moses, I want you to go down into Egypt," and Moses says "No, Lord you don't know how I got out of Egypt. You don't want me to go down there." The Lord lays hands on Jeremiah, and Jeremiah says, "No. No, Lord. You don't want me. You need a more seasoned prophet. I'm too young to go down." A prophet is not a volunteer.

But, one can dare stand even before the coalition of the majestic if one has had a vision of another sovereignty. I started off saying that none of this makes sense unless you have the premise that there is one absolute sovereign, one absolute center of power, one absolute possessor, absolute owner of everything that is.

Listen to why and how Micaiah was able to stand before the kings and speak as he did. They were in royal garbs. They had their hosts around them.

But, Micaiah said, "I've had a vision of the Lord of Hosts. I saw another throne, and his throne was bigger than these thrones. I see your army around you, but I saw the hosts of the Lord around him. The Lord's army is a mightier army than any army of Earth. Earthly sovereigns pale before divine sovereignty and his majesty.

We can shine as humans, but the Lord's majesty dazzles and even blinds so that everything else pales in its significance. Earthly sovereignty can't prevail against God.

The Lord told Micaiah what to say. Micaiah said it. Ahab didn't believe him, not fully. It haunted him, but he went on in defiance anyhow. But, he went in disguise. Here's this mighty man doing what he wanted to do. But, he said to Jehoshaphat, "I'm not going to dress up in my uniform, but you dress up in yours. I'm going to go as a commoner and go out to battle." And Jehoshaphat went along with it.

It's amazing how the Lord does things when you're stupid. Ahab went out in defiance and in disguise. But Ben Hadad said to his army, "I don't want you to go after anybody but Ahab. Don't bother any other sovereign. I know there's a leader's army over there, but don't mess with Jehoshaphat. I want you to go after Ahab."

Now, there was a marksman in Ben Hadad's army. He let loose a volley, and an arrow pierced the armor right between the points of protection. He couldn't have done it better if he had been standing over him though he fired from a distance because the Lord was involved. An arrow strategically struck Ahab, and he was felled in the battle.

Jehoshaphat inclined towards God. Though disobedient, he was delivered. The Lord helped him. That's one of the assurances, one of the blessings of grace. Even when I'm defiant, if my inclination is towards him, then the Lord can help me.

There's something about divine grace; there's something about divine mercy that prevails even in my rebellion against him. The Lord helped Jehoshaphat even though he didn't know it because the Lord got in another man's army and said, "I don't want you to bother anybody but Ahab." The Lord has a way of putting walls around you so that your enemy will not lay hands on you even though you are in the enemy's territory. The Lord helped him, and he returned home safely.

What's the final observation about this, then, this whole business of prophecy and prophetic preaching, and serving and working with the Lord? It is a recognition, ultimately, that this faith thing, this battle that we have on the Earth, is really a matter of collisions of sovereignties, collisions of kings.

I hear the New Testament writer saying, "*We wrestle not against flesh and blood. We wrestle against principalities and powers, against the authorities of this age.*" Our battle is a matter of collisions of kingdoms, the sovereignty of God and the sovereignties of the Earth.

Now, when you look at the battle in that light, you have to decide which is going to prevail. This story says that the Lord prevailed, but it was in human form.

You're going to leave here and go to the ultimate battle. This happened over at Ramoth Gilead, but there was an ultimate battle, a collision of kingdoms, that happened just outside of Jerusalem on a hill called Calvary. It was posed there. Pilate wrote over a crucified man, "Jesus of Nazareth: King." He had it right. He thought that this king was challenging Caesar. He had the designation right, but he didn't recognize the fullness of the kingdom. Not just King of the Jews, this is the King of kings and Lord of lords. The Sovereign over all the Earth, he's the master of everything there is.

I hear him say at one point, "If you talk about battling, if I want to battle like this king wants to battle, I've got legions of angels that could come down. Just one angel of the Lord could deal with all this itty-bitty crowd down here. But, I'm not fighting on that level. For it is a battle of sovereignties."

So the king of heaven comes down, engaged in battle, not just with Pilate and Caesar, but with the ultimate challenge to divine sovereignty, located in one we call Satan, the Evil One, however you want to characterize it, that thing which separates us from God ultimately and finally. Who really has control?

Jesus was crucified, put in a tomb, and the folk looked at it and said, "Jesus lost." They didn't know what a battlefield was. Tradition has it that when he died, instead of just laying in the grave, he went down in the precincts of hell and preached the gospel of redemption even there.

The record says that he moved among the dead, and the dead heard, so much so that the dead were released from their graves when he died. He wrestled with death and took away death's sting. Ultimately, he was raised by God from the grave with the power and the victory over the grave in his hands.

Listen to what he says now. "I am he who was dead. But, behold, I am now alive, and I'm alive forevermore. And I've got all the power, all the power in my hand! Augustus doesn't have authority in his hand—it's in my hand. Pilate doesn't have authority—it's in my hand. The United States doesn't have authority—it's in my hands. I've got all the power."

"Now, I want you to go, those of you who are mine, and deal with this matter of kingdoms and powers and make clear that all power is in my hand. Ultimately, all stand before me in judgment." *"It's appointed for all men once to die."* But, it ain't over then, after that, the judgment.

Now, and I'm finished. Let me say this. The challenge of the pulpit today is to dare to yield to the power of the Lord in the face of prevailing tides in religion that are popular but not based in the book. Pop psychology. Pop feel good. No cross. No redemption. Just name it and claim it. No Calvary. There is no salvation outside of him who was crucified, dead, buried, and raised as victor. Not victim, but victor. Everybody who sides with the powers of this age are prophets of the court. But, there's a difference between prophets of the court and being a prophet of the Lord. Let me go back to the question with which I began. Who is in this house tonight?

Chapter 12

James Earl Massey (1930–2018)

Living Legend 2007

The Preacher

REV. DR. JAMES EARL Massey (1930–2018) spent more than seven decades preaching, teaching, and serving in churches, seminaries, and universities across the nation and around the world. Nicknamed the "Prince of Preachers" by the Church of God movement (Anderson, Indiana), Dr. Massey established himself as a brilliant preacher, scholar, leader, and person both inside and outside the movement of which he was a part. In 2006, *Christianity Today* named him one of the twenty-five most influential preachers of the past fifty years.[1] He was also a classically trained pianist and a military veteran, having served as a chaplain's assistant.

In his autobiography *Aspects of My Pilgrimage*, he recounts the moment that God called him to preach when he was only sixteen years old despite his plans to become a concert pianist. He writes: "The Voice that called me was so clear, and its bidding, though gentle, bore the unmistakable authority of a higher realm. Since that time of encounter during worship, I have known the work to which my head, heart, and hands were to be devoted."[2]

Dr. Massey's academic journey started at William Tyndale College where he received his bachelor's degree, followed by a master's degree from Oberlin School of Theology, and a doctorate of philosophy degree from Asbury Theological Seminary. His journey in church ministry officially began when he was ordained in the Church of God movement in 1951. A few years later, at the age of twenty-four, he became the senior pastor of Metropolitan Church of God in Detroit, Michigan, where he served for twenty-two years (1954–1976). From 1977 to 1982, he attracted a broader national following as *the* speaker of speakers—also the first African American—on the Church of God radio broadcast known as *The Christian Brotherhood Hour* radio program (later called *Christians Broadcasting Hope* (*CBH*). His contributions to theological education included serving as principal of the Jamaica School of Theology (1963–1966), a professor, campus minister, and dean of Anderson School of Theology (1969–1995), and a professor and dean of Tuskegee University (1984–1989). From 1978 to 1992, he provided leadership as a trustee of Asbury Theological Seminary, the same institution that granted him an honorary degree in 1972. He published eighteen books, which included three books on preaching, and he served as an editor for *Christianity Today* and the New Interpreter's Bible. He was also a devoted husband of more than sixty years to his wife, Mrs. Gwendolyn Inez Kilpatrick-Massey.

In 2009, nine years before his death, an interviewer asked him what biblical text he would choose if he could preach one last sermon. His answer was that he would choose 1 Timothy 1:12–17: "*I thank Christ Jesus our Lord, who has given me strength, that he considered me trustworthy, appointing me to his service.*" He said, "That is the text I would use because Christ is first and foremost and last in my life. I wouldn't have been in the ministry if it hadn't been for him."[3]

---

1. See "25 Most Influential Preachers."
2. Massey, *Aspects of My Pilgrimage*, 53.
3. See obituary in Shellnutt, "Died: James Earl Massey."

The Sermon

I want to call your attention now to the passage that has gripped my heart: 1 Timothy, chapter 1. I want to read verses 12 through 17. The apostle Paul is addressing a younger pastor by the name of Timothy and he is giving a personal statement to him about his ministry:

> *I am grateful to Christ Jesus our Lord who has strengthened me because He judged me faithful and appointed me to His service, even though I was formally a blasphemer, a persecutor, and a man of violence. But I received mercy because I acted ignorantly in unbelief and the grace of our Lord overflowed for me with the faith and love that are in Christ Jesus. The saying is sure and worthy of full acceptance that Christ came into the world to save sinners, of whom I am the foremost, but for that very reason I received mercy. So that in me, as the foremost, Jesus Christ might display the upmost patience, making me an example to those who would come to believe in him for eternal life.*

Parenthetically, at that point he's about to shout, so he says in verse 17, *"To the King of the ages, immortal, invisible, the only God, be honor and glory forever and ever. Amen."* Please be seated. A Grand Word about a Great Savior.

For some years now, my wife and I have been living in the nation's Bible Belt, over in Alabama. In my coming and going, I am accustomed to the large lighted signs that churches use to draw attention to their services. Some signs even sport a concise message, sometimes a kind of saying to prod thought and to promote faith. I saw one sign that said, "Satan subtracts and divides. God adds and multiplies." Another sign I saw warned, "Forbidden fruit creates many jams." Another sign I saw on the church property: "God answers knee-mail." Still another one I saw: "Read the Bible. Prevent truth decay."

What a worthy word when so many unbiblical notions are steadily promoted in our syncretistic and religiously muddled society. There needs to be more reading of the Bible because society is religiously muddled. In my text is a saying, and Paul commends it as sure and worthy of full acceptance, a little longer in the wording, but still the saying. It's a saying that the early Christians joyously voiced whenever they worshiped, and they used it as a word of witness when they evangelized. Here it is: "Christ Jesus came into the world to save sinners."

As I was driving along on the way from Tuscaloosa home the other day, I noticed this sign on some property there, and I said to myself, "It must be a sign that I am supposed to preach this sermon as I planned." It was there on the lawn: "Christ Jesus came into the world to save sinners."

Now, we're all familiar with sayings, aren't we? If I were to ask any of you, you could stand or even sit and spout some maxim that you learned as a child, something given by our adult wisdom, learned by trial and error to teach us how to live. The saying of the text is not a trial-and-error truth. It's a revealed truth. It isn't something from below. It's something from above. You will remember the angel's confirming word to Joseph, not only confirming but informing: "Your wife Mary will bear a son, and you must call him Yeshua, Jesus, because He is going to save His people from their sins." That's a revealed word. It's from above. We hear enough from below.

Remember also what Jesus said to Zacchaeus as he visited him at his home: "*The Son of Man came to seek out and to save that which was lost.*" Notice the emphasis is still on salvation. Jesus did not come to make us feel good. He came to bring us salvation. The prophet Isaiah tells why: "*All we like sheep have gone astray. We have turned everyone to his own way, and the Lord God laid on him the iniquity of us all.*" No wonder he died asking, "Why? Why has Thou forsaken me?" He knew why, but he was quoting Psalm 22. All that he said on the cross was from the Scriptures because he was straightening himself with words from above. I find that's the only way to get straight.

Well, what about this salvation? It rescues us from two life-threatening realities. The first reality is God's wrath. Wrath: God's indignant anger against sin. I don't care what color the sin is. Some call sin black. Some call sin white. I don't know what color it is, but I do know that God hates it—any kind of sin and sin for any kind of reason, and it brings God's wrath on us whenever we sin.

God hates sin because it violates his righteousness. God hates sin, he's indignant against it, because it spurns his wisdom. God hates sin because it causes sad consequences to result. Now some of those consequences are sad, here-and-now outcomes from selfish choices we make—consequences and happenings for which we have sayings. "You reap what you sow." "You can't do wrong and get by." We learn that by trial and error because wrath was dogging our steps.

No one can do wrong and get by. No one, no one, no one. No exceptions. Because there is always a connection between sinful choices and sad outcomes. There is always a connection between sowing and reaping. There is always a connection between disobedience and disorder. Sin never brings positive results; they are always negative.

But God's wrath includes not only sad here-and-now outcomes, but a life of sinning invites eternal consequences as well, consequences the Bible refers to as "the wrath to come." Now, we haven't experienced that yet, and I don't want to experience that. The only way to know what that is would be to defy what Jesus came to do.

He took all of that on himself when he stood in our place on the cross. I say, "stood in our place on the cross." He was hanging there, but he was in our place. He took the wrath of God upon his own heart, and he died because of our sins. Jesus warned that whoever disobeys the Son will not see life, but must endure God's wrath.

John, chapter 3, verse 36: "Wrath must be endured." You can't, you can't dismiss it. You got to be saved from it. You can't wish it away. It doesn't go like that. Only one way.

"What can wash away my sins? Nothing but the blood. What can make me whole again? Nothing but the blood." A lot of religion in the United States, but not enough blood. I respect other beliefs and the persons who share those beliefs, but only the blood can take away sin. Truth is truth.

Well, he came to save us not only from the wrath of God, but from the waywardness that makes us worthy of that wrath. I speak of waywardness because that's the best word to describe the conditioning selfishness that sin induces in us, and that word, "waywardness," embraces the total gamut of deliberate human failures. Waywardness includes all wrongdoing. Scripture, according to 1 John, chapter 5, verse 17, tells us that "all wrongdoing *is* sin." Waywardness.

Now the passage I read to you reports Paul's testimony on how he came to experience this salvation, and there are four words which stand out quite boldly in his testimony about what issued from Christ to save him from his sins. He speaks about mercy. He speaks about grace. He speaks about faith and love as these being issued from Jesus.

Ever thought about Jesus having faith in the one to whom he speaks? He trusts you enough to share a word with you so that you can get out of sin. He has faith that you have the ability to choose. Paul says, "the faith and the love which are in Christ Jesus." They are toward us. And when he loves us enough to call our name, only a fool will spurn that call. And only fools go to hell.

Well, like every other human, this man, who's writing this testimony, years after the experience had initially touched his life, this man, like every other human, had a sinful past that needed to be remedied and a personality that needed to be changed, a flawed personality that needed to be corrected.

I'm not okay until he makes me okay. You are not okay until he makes you okay. You know, there was that saying years ago in books. You know, the philosophers and the psychologists were trying their best to make people feel important and give them a sense of self-regard. But, I don't care what they say. We are not okay until God works on us.

Here is this man—well-educated, the equivalent of a PhD in his time, highly gifted, tough-minded, tremendous energy figure, personally force-ful in his character. It all made him feel noticed, and it all made him feel valued. He dedicated himself to the service of a religious system, and they rewarded him by putting him over certain activities. But, although well-educated, although highly gifted, although tough-minded, although per-sonally forceful, although intensely religious, he was a sinner. He needed to be saved from his sins. He needed to be saved from himself. And he tells us in this passage how it happened.

Looking back on his life before his conversion, remembering how he had slanderously spoken against Jesus, he confessed, "I was formally a blas-phemer." Remembering how he had zealously sought out and arrested those who were followers of Jesus, he admitted, "I was a persecutor." Remember-ing how he had ordered the torture of Christians and had superintended and supervised the death of Stephen, he lamented, "I was a man of violence." It's all right there.

I don't know whether you ever tell what you used to be. I don't know whether you even want it known what you used to be. But here's a man who doesn't mind telling it because it's in the past. And what he's telling is to glo-rify God for having done it for him. "I was a blasphemer. I was a persecutor. I was a man of violence." But, it's been years since that happened as he writes this. He's now an old man. Although he's beyond the past, he mentions here, despite the incredibly active and fruitful life he lived since his conversion, he's still felt the stinging shame of the past—a shame so deep that he looked upon himself as the chief of sinners not because he was still sinning, but because he remembered the shame of having been a sinner. Because of the kinds of sins for which he was guilty, he remembered himself as at the head of everybody who ever sinned.

Let me make it plainer. You find the conversion story in three places in the book of Acts: chapter 9, chapter 22, and chapter 26. In every place, he's telling what he used to be. In chapter 9, it tells whom the Lord sent to talk to him about what had happened to him on the road to Damascus. Then, he confesses in chapter 26, the kind of mindset that he had as he was on his way to Damascus to scare, to scold, or even to slay believers. When the Lord speaks to Ananias in chapter 9 and tells him, "Get up and go to this street called Straight. There is a man named Saul. I'm working with him," Ananias says, "Lord, I know you heard what I heard. Do you really want me to go and deal with him when he's been dealing out death?" And then the Lord says to him, "At this moment, he's praying, and he has seen in a vision . . ."

Well, you know there is something about prayer. When you go beyond ritual and experience the reality of prayer, you see things. And, the Lord tells Ananias, "He is praying and, in his vision, he has seen you coming to help him out." When we pray, I'm not talking about saying words, when we pray, we see visions. At this moment, he's praying. From Paul's side, prayer was questioning, "Lord, what would you have me do?" From the Lord's side, he's being answered. From Paul's side, he was questioning. From the Lord's side, he was being supplied. From Paul's side, prayer meant seeking under-standing. From the Lord's side, prayer meant receiving wisdom. "*If anyone lacks wisdom, let him ask of God who gives to all men liberally.*" Not just in tidbits—liberally. Why are we so dumb?

We do not learn how to pastor nor do we learn how to preach merely by taking classes in school. We might learn methods. We might even learn theology, but the truth that grips the soul comes when we study Scripture and pray. And the wisdom needed to guide a congregation's life does not come from classes. It comes from kneeling down, asking like Saul did, "What would you have me do?"

You recall the prayer of Solomon, "I'm not wise enough to go in and out among your people. You'll have to give me wisdom." And that's a king talking. Who are you? Who am I?

Well, I said he was feeling the stinging shame of what he had been. So deeply did he lament the past that even the Lord honoring him by summon-ing him to be an apostle doesn't make him feel worthy yet. There's no way when the Lord touches your life, when you really understand how it happens, you don't get top-heavy. Here's a man witnessing across the empire world about Jesus as savior because he knew it firsthand—Jesus can save.

One of the lessons I learned entering the ministry under a noted pastor, he told us in one of the sessions we had with him, "Never preach beyond your experience." If we're not saved, how can we preach salvation? If we don't know what it means to be delivered, how can we talk about deliverance? Oh, we can talk about it, but when we've experienced it, there is a plus-element to it, there is a convincement that comes when we talk about it.

When Paul says, "I *was* . . . but mercy was shown me," ah, there's some-thing that rises up out of the text, and you begin to feel it then. Twice in this testimony Paul says, "I received mercy." Look at verse 13: "I received mercy." Due to God's mercy, that triadic magnitude of his sinfulness as a blasphemer, as a persecutor, and as a man of violence had been matched by what he found in Jesus Christ. As for that grace that came from Jesus, that favor, that attitude of accepting Paul in spite of what he had been, that's what grace is all about—an attitude of acceptance and regard "in spite of." He speaks of it now as an abundant quality of favor.

Notice what he says: "The grace of our Lord," verse 14, "overflowed for me." *Overflowed.* I don't want to appear too bookish tonight, but this is an expository preaching conference. So, I want to just magnify the meaning of that word here for you. Paul here coins a Greek term, not used anywhere else in the Bible: *hyperpleonazo.* A compound term he's using here. He put it together. He took the word *pleon,* which means "more," a word of quantity, and added a prefix to it, *hyper,* which means "over, above." *Hyperpleonazo.* He means to express the notion of superabundance. In other words, that was not only enough, but more than enough. Now, if you use this word with reference to pouring liquid into a vessel, it means to overflow. If you use this word with reference to a river that's at spate, it means to be overflowing the banks, floodtide.

Grace doesn't come to us in little bits. Grace comes to us in abundant measure. How much? As much. What do you need? More than you need, you're gonna get it. "*By grace have you been saved through faith and that not of yourselves, it is the gift of God, lest anyone should boast.*" Oh, grace! Grace running over. Not just a little bit, but more than we need.

I don't see how anybody can't live a Christian life. I don't see how we talk about how hard it is. "Oh, I had such a struggle this week." Whenever Paul talked about struggle, he never was talking about living the Christian life. He was talking about trials that came his way because he was engaged in the Lord's business. Whenever he asked for prayer, it was never for his personal wellbeing. It was always that the word would go forth in power. He never asked a personal request for prayer. Read the Gospels. Read his epistles. Whenever he asked for prayer, it was connected with his ministry.

In our testimony services, when we put in our testimony, we always add a request, "Pray for my strength in the Lord." If you know what you've got from above, you've got strength. Use it! Use it! "Greater is He who is in you, than he that is in the world." Stop struggling. Succeed. The song-writer expressed it well: "*Marvelous, infinite, matchless grace freely bestowed on all who believe.*" You don't have to beg for it.

When my wife and I were at Christmastime one year in the shopping mall, she was taking care of her part of the shopping list. I finished my part. I'm not trying to say anything about that except what I said. So, I spent the time waiting on her. I spent it in a little bookshop there in the shopping mall. And a couple, I overheard them talking, a young couple, I heard the lady say to her husband, "John, here's something you can give your dad for Christmas." Now, that didn't sound very Christmas-y, did it? Well, because of that I turned to see what it was she was holding up to John's view. It was a beautifully hand-carved, well-lacquered model ship. Instead of John taking the model ship to look it over for its beauty, he clutchingly grabbed for the price tag, and then I heard him say: "Ugh. Thirty-Five dollars." And then he blurted out, "He's not worth that much." And I wondered what had his father done or left undone to make that son view his father so cheaply. Not that the gift had to cost $35, but the attitude that he was showing by what he said.

And I thought about my own father. Every time my brothers and I would go back home to visit, after we were grown, we could never leave the house before my father would side up to us and say, "Do you need anything?" And if we needed it, we would have it. That's the kind of father he was.

But now, there's another Father. He's rich in houses and lands. He holds the wealth of the world in his hands. Why do we beg God so when he is our Father? "If ye, then, being human, know how to give good gifts to your children, how much more will your heavenly Father give good gifts to you who love him?"

That's why I was talking about grace being in abundance. God doesn't give us pinched-off blessings. They are more than enough. We don't just slide through by cramped conditions. He makes us more than conquerors. Stop struggling! Let grace prevail! I received mercy. Mercy.

"Oh, the deep, deep love of Jesus. Spread His praise from shore to shore. How he loves us, ever loves us. Changes never, never more. How He watches o'er His loved ones, Died to call us all His own, How for us He intercedeth, Watching o'er us from His throne."

I want you to know. I'm always feeling assured. No matter what's happening to me in life. I'm now almost eighty years old, but every day, I'm thanking him for his goodness. Not worried about a thing come hell or high water. When you pass though the waters, they won't overthrow you. When you go through the rivers, you won't drown. When you go through the flames, it won't burn you. That's our God. That's grace. I received mercy.

No wonder as he comes to the end of his passage, he's ready to shout to the "King of the ages, immortal, invisible, the only God, be glory and honor forever and ever." How long is forever? You ought to hear his sermon. How long is it?

You know, sinners order their lives, and they lament their fate singing the blues. The saved offer praise, grateful for grace. If you don't know how to sing and thank God for his goodness without anybody pumping you up—I don't need a choir to get happy!—all I do is think of his goodness to me. I love to hear the instruments. I play one occasionally. But, I don't need a drum to get my rhythm going.

Well, I'm closing. Paul was not the only one who knew something about faith and love that are in Christ Jesus. He was not the only one who knew something about salvation. Fanny Crosby knew something about it. And the many poems she wrote that became gospel songs carry her witness from age to age. When she was eight weeks old, she suffered some eye trouble, and due to maltreatment on the part of the physician, she was blind after that. But she grew up equipped with spiritual insight. No outward sight except shadows, but inwardly, because she prayed, she had insight. She viewed her poetry as her ministry for Christ. The next time you sing "Saved by Grace," think about Fanny Crosby. Next time you rejoicingly sing, "Blessed Assurance," think about Fanny Crosby. Think about Fanny Crosby the next time you prayerfully sing "Savior, More Than Life to Me." Next time you exult in those lines, "To God be the Glory," think about Fanny Crosby, and thank God for her. Next time you plaintively pray, "Jesus, Keep Me Near the Cross," think about Fanny Crosby.

What are you doing that's going to bless somebody else's life? Do you know enough of grace so that when you are gone, long gone, somebody will still be singing or saying something that you left here for them of your testimony? Ah, these are songs of quite simple touch, emotional want, but behind all of them is a sound theology that is mirrored in our text: "Christ Jesus came into the world to save sinners."

Well, I don't have to speak about Fanny Crosby. I can tell my own story. I heard the voice of Jesus saying, "Come unto me and rest. Lay down, thou, weary one, lay down thy head upon my breast." I heard!

You know, hearing implies a voice, someone speaking, and the one that's speaking here is Jesus. There is no voice like his, and if you ever heard him speak, it resounds in the soul so deeply, you ought never to violate what you hear, and you are to always obey what he tells you to do. I heard the voice of Jesus saying, "Come. Lay down, thy weary one." Now, now, lying down the head on his breast. Why on his breast?

Well, let me illustrate it this way. How many of you are mothers? How many of you have ever seen a mother? How many of you have ever seen a mother take a child and cuddle it in order to quiet it? They always hold the child's head to the breast. And what is the child hearing? Oh, maybe a song being sung, but, deeper still, the child is hearing the rhythm of the mother's heartbeat. The child is hearing and feeling that primal tone, that primal sound, that primal note that they heard for nine months. When they're in touch with that primal tone, they are quieted because they are back where they once were in safety. And that is what happens when we pray. We feel and hear the rhythm of God, the tone in eternity. And we feel TLC—tender loving care. Grace.

If you are praying and you've never heard the rhythm of the heavens, then you haven't prayed. When you go into your room, as Jesus told us, and shut the door, the world outside and only you and your God inside, you forget the clock.

I have a study into which I go every day. There's no telephone in there. I don't want a telephone when I'm praying. Nobody can reach me. My wife knows where I am and when she wants me, she comes for me. But, I don't want another voice when I'm hearing the Lord's voice. Prayer is best prayed when we take time with the Lord, when we hear that primal tone again, that rhythm of heaven that puts us back in a state of health. It quiets us in the storms of life. There's nothing that can happen to you that can shake you then.

Oh, yes, I know what it means to be buffeted. In 1993, I was in a hospital. My last two years of my deanship at the university was at stake, and I was ill with a heart condition. I turned my head to the wall, and I whispered to the Lord, "Lord, let me live." I managed to get through the night. The next morning, they had another battery of tests. Sure enough, I had a problem, but I'm here tonight.

What did Hezekiah do? He turned his face to the wall, and he prayed. He got that primal tone again. What do you need from the Lord tonight? What do you need? His grace is as free as the air we breathe. We may each have a full supply if we will obey and his word believe.

I'm here tonight not on any medications for my heart. My brothers and my sisters, I don't know how many of you heard the voice of Jesus say, "Come unto me and rest. Lay down, thy weary one, lay down thy head upon my breast." But, I came to Jesus just like I was. I was weary. I was worn, and I was sad. But, I found in him a resting place, and he made me. I'm not going to say that next word yet because I'm not so much concerned about being glad. What I needed when I came to him was not so much to be glad but to be made.

Are you still in the making? Have you resisted his grace? Paul says, "I do not frustrate the grace of God," that is to say, block it, get in the way of it. What roadblocks have you thrown up that block grace?

I came to Jesus as I was. So did Saul. So did Fanny Crosby. How many others have done the same thing? I came to Jesus as I was: weary, worn, and sad. I found in him a resting place, and he has made me.

We preachers can't take credit for what we are. School didn't make us. He made us, and he's still working on us. And he's not through with us.

I heard the voice of Jesus say, "Behold, I freely give the living water, thirsty one. Stoop down, drink, and live." I came to Jesus, and I drank of that life-giving stream. My thirst was quenched, my soul revived, and now I live in him. I don't know how much longer I have to live, but it doesn't matter to me. I've lived long enough to know the one whom I believe, and I'm persuaded that he's able to keep.

I don't need Paul to tell me he's persuaded. That's his testimony. I am persuaded because I know a great savior. I do. Don't you? I live by his favor. I do. Don't you? For grace I implore him. I worship before him. I love, I adore him. I do. I need him to lead me. I do. Don't you? Heaven's manager feed me. I do. Don't you? Whatever betide me, I want him beside me, in mercy to hide me. I do. Don't you? I want him to use me. I do. Don't you? For service to choose me. I do. Don't you? I want him to bless me, to own and confess me, completely possess me. I do.

Chapter 13

Haddon W. Robinson (1931–2017)

Living Legend 2008

The Preacher

DR. HADDON W. ROBINSON (1931–2017) championed the cause of expository preaching in his teaching, preaching, writing, and leadership. His impact continues to be felt across multiple generations of students who attended the seminaries where he taught, heard the sermons that he preached, or read the books that he wrote.

Born in Harlem, New York, in 1931, Dr. Robinson grew up in a tenement district known as Mousetown where he saw many of his friends turn to crime and violence and, in some instances, suffer an early death. His mother died when he was young, which meant that his father had to work long hours to support the family. Dr. Robinson's conversion to Christ took place sometime in his early teens. Soon after, he heard the Rev. Dr. Harry Ironside preach in one of the churches in the city. When he went home that evening, he wrote in his journal: "He preached for an hour, and it seemed liked 20 minutes; others preach for 20 minutes, and it seems like an hour. I wonder what the difference is."[1] Whenever he would recount that story, he would often say, "I have spent most of my adult life trying to answer that question."

Dr. Robinson left New York at the age of sixteen to pursue his bachelor's degree at Bob Jones University. As he concluded his time at Bob Jones, he also married Bonnie Vick, his college sweetheart, and the woman to whom he was married for sixty-six years. Then, he pursued a master of theology at Dallas Theological Seminary where he graduated in 1955. He and his wife, Bonnie, also added two young children to their family, Vicki and Torrey. After seminary, Robinson accepted a call to become an assistant pastor at the First Baptist Church of Medford, Oregon, where their family remained for a relatively short time until 1958 when Dallas Theological Seminary (DTS) invited him back to teach homiletics, a discipline that was still very much in its infancy in the curricula of most evangelical seminaries in North America. Robinson accepted the offer and remained at Dallas for nineteen years. While at DTS, he earned his master of arts degree in speech from Southern Methodist University and his doctor of philosophy degree in communication from the University of Illinois. Later in life, he received honorary degrees from Gordon College and McMaster Divinity College.

In 1979, Robinson accepted an offer to become the next president of Denver Seminary, where he also taught courses in homiletics from 1979 to 1991. Then, in 1991, he joined the faculty of Gordon Conwell Theological Seminary, where he taught from 1991 to 2007. While at Gordon Conwell, he taught courses, directed the doctor of ministry program, and served for a brief time as interim president from 2007 to 2008. He also maintained an active radio ministry through co-hosting *Discover the Word*, a radio program that was broadcast six hundred times daily and reached an average of two million listeners in North America and around the world. Baylor University named him to its list of the "12 Most Effective Preachers in the English-Speaking World" in 1996 and again in 2018 (posthumously).[2]

Dr. Robinson wrote more than one dozen books, the best-selling of which is *Biblical Preaching*, a book that has sold more than two hundred

---

1. Willhite and Gibson, *Big Idea of Biblical Preaching*, 8.
2. See "Baylor Names"; "Baylor University's Truett Seminary."

thousand copies and is used in more than one hundred and fifty seminaries and Bible colleges around the world.

The Sermon

Our Scripture tonight comes from the Gospel of Luke, chapter 12. It's one of those corking-good stories that Jesus told. In Luke 12:16, Luke says, *"Jesus told him this parable. The ground of a certain man produced a good crop. He thought to himself, 'What will I do? I have no place to store my crops.' And he said, 'This is what I'll do. I'll tear down my barns and build bigger ones, and there I'll store all my grain and my goods. And I will say to myself, "You have plenty of good things laid up for many years. Take life easy, eat drink and be merry."' But God said to him, 'You fool! This very night, your life will be demanded from you. Then, who will get what you have prepared for yourself?'"* Jesus comments: *"This is how it will be with anyone who stores up things for himself and is not rich toward God."*

Some cynic has described preaching as the fine art of talking in someone else's sleep. That is a bit extreme, but certainly one of the occupational hazards of being a preacher. You keep losing people's attention.

When I was a young man first starting in this business of preaching, it disturbed me greatly when folks went off to sleep when I got up to preach. For those of you settling down for a short summer's nap, I must confess it still disturbs me. But, I've taken some consolation from the fact that, even when Jesus was here on earth, there were those who were in his congregation, who heard him preach, who really didn't listen to what he had to say.

One such incident comes from the twelfth chapter of the Gospel according to Luke. We're told in verse 1 that a huge crowd, thousands of people have come to hear Jesus, and he is talking to them about the issues of time and eternity, of hypocrisy and hell. He's telling them that if they fear God, they don't have to fear anything else.

As Jesus is preaching, evidently, a man pushes his way to the edge of the crowd, interrupts Jesus in the middle of his ministry, and he says to him, *"Teacher, bid my brother divide the inheritance with me."* I don't know any more about this man's situation than you do. But, evidently, his father had died, and he and his brother were squabbling over what his father had left. This would not be the first or the last time that families came to great tension over the inheritance. Cold wars in a family, hot court battles have taken place over an inheritance. One thing is certain, that inheritance was this man's entire life. Here he is in the presence of Jesus to hear him preach and all he can think about is what his father has left him.

The sun never shined as brightly, the birds would never sing as sweetly, the flowers would never bloom as beautifully until he got that share that came from his brother. This is probably the younger brother because, in the custom of Israel, it was the older brother that was the executor of the estate. But, whatever it is, this man comes to Jesus, and he wants to get things settled. *"Teacher, bid my brother to divide the inheritance with me."*

Jesus responded in verse 14 in an almost rude fashion. He said to him: *"Man, who appointed me a judge or arbiter between you?"* What Jesus is saying is, "You have no idea who I really am. You want to reduce me to the level of a county judge. You want me to settle a dispute between you and your brother. That's not why I've come."

Now, Jesus isn't saying that that is nobody's business. He knew the human condition well enough to know that you have to have judges and lawyers. But he was saying it was not his business. He did not come to judge or divide between brothers fighting over inheritance.

It is interesting that this is almost an echo of the Old Testament. Back in the book of Exodus, in chapter 2, Moses intervened in a fight between two Hebrew men. And verse 14, one of those men said to him with a snarl, *"Who made you a judge or divider over us?"* Moses wanted to be a judge, and the people wouldn't let him. And here, the people want Jesus to be a judge or a divider, and he allowed none of it.

Sometimes, when we think we're complimenting Jesus, we're really insulting him. It's easy for people to say, "You know that Jesus came to be a great teacher, and if we simply follow his instructions, then warring brothers won't fight anymore. He'll solve all of the tensions that we're in." But, the world didn't need another teacher. People in the first century had better teaching than they could live up to. If he simply came to teach us, he wasted his time.

Other people say, "Well, he came to be an example. He came to show us how to live."

Several years ago, Charles Sheldon wrote a book called *In His Steps*. In this novel, he imagined that a group of people in a community would settle all of their disputes by simply asking, "What Would Jesus Do?" Recently, high school students wore a bracelet with WWJD: "What Would Jesus Do?" I commend them for the effort, but I don't think it's a workable lead. I mean Jesus wasn't married. Jesus didn't have teenagers. I haven't got the slightest notion what he would do with them. I know this, that if I follow his example, I will read into his example what I want to see.

Besides, to follow Jesus' example is to be mocked. It's like you're asking me to go to a concert and stand behind a concert pianist, and she plays one of her more difficult compositions. I watch as her fingers go back and forth across the keyboard. As I watch, I'm amazed at how well she plays and how beautifully she plays. And when she stops, she says to me, "Robinson, now you saw what I did. You do it." My fingers are lead. To set me that example is to mock me.

No, Jesus didn't come simply to teach us. He didn't come to be an example of how we should behave. Jesus came for a deeper purpose. He didn't come to make bad people good or good people better. He came to make men and women who are spiritually dead alive. And to miss that is to miss the reason for his coming.

And then Jesus turned away from this man, and he turned to the crowd. The basis of what he had just seen, he said to the crowd: *"Beware of covetousness. For a man's life does not consist in the abundance of the things he possesses."* Most of the translations say, or some of the translations say, "Beware of greed." You could see how that would happen. Translators are trying to put the Bible into the language of the reader. I can see how they got to that. The word should be "covetousness." They don't know what that is. Let's get something close. Something like that word "greed."

Covetousness is one of those overstuffed words in the religious vocabulary that has lost its cutting edge. We don't take it very seriously. We think that, back in the Old Testament, when God and Moses were working out the Ten Commandments, that they had nine really good ones and threw in the one on covetousness so it would make the list into ten.

In my years as a pastor, I've had people come to confess all kinds of things to me. I don't remember anyone coming and saying, "I'd really like to talk to you. I've got to talk to you about a bad case of covetousness." But, covetousness is simply wanting more and more of what you have enough of already. And Jesus says, "Beware of it. Beware of wanting more and more of what you have enough of already. For a person's life does not consist of the things that they possess."

When Jesus talks about things, what kinds of things does he have in mind? All kinds of things. Big things. Little things. Things to wear. Things to live in. Things to ride in. Things to buy with your credit card. Jesus is saying, "life does not consist of the things that we possess."

But, this word of Jesus gets drowned out in our society. There are thousands of different voices telling you that your life does consist of things. You see it on the billboards as you drive down the highway. It's in four-color adds when you thumb through a magazine. It's the word from the sponsor on television. They sing it to you in jingles on the radio. We're told that life consists of the things we possess and, because we have bought into it, we live in the midst of the greatest junk business the centuries have ever seen.

It is junk, isn't it? I mean, yesterday's mansions become today's boarding houses and tomorrow's slums. Yesterday's car is today's trade in is tomorrow's junkie. Yesterday's beautiful new style becomes something to hang in the closet, and something to give to Goodwill, then something to become rags. We're a lot like the donkey that has a stick over its head with a carrot at the end. The donkey wants the carrot so every time the donkey moves, the carrot moves. It's always there promising to feed but always disappointing.

Jesus comes to tell us: "Beware of covetousness. Beware of wanting more and more of what you have enough of already. For your life doesn't consist of the things that you possess."

Then, in order to nail that truth into our minds, he tells this story. It's a story of a man who is painted in fairly bright colors. There are many things about him that people in our culture and that culture would have admired.

For example, he was wealthy. We don't know his name. We know that he was simply a certain rich man. In every culture, people look up to people who have riches. We always live with the idea that what is important is what you have rather than what you are.

Now, don't misunderstand. Jesus is not saying that riches are wrong. In the Old Testament, Abraham was a man in his culture who was exceedingly rich. David and Solomon were wealthy Near Eastern kings. After Job went through his turmoil, he was rewarded with enormous riches. And those of us who are Christians are indebted to a man by the name of Joseph from Arimathea for providing a tomb for our Lord after the Romans murdered him. And in the early church, those young congregations had to turn to men and women of means to open their means, to open their hearts, to open their homes to those congregations.

No, Jesus is not saying that riches are wrong. But, the Bible does say that riches are dangerous. For every verse in the Bible that tells you the benefit of wealth, there are ten that tell you the dangers of wealth. It's a bit like a fly in fly paper. The fly lands on the fly paper and says, "My fly paper," and the fly paper says, "My fly." That fly is dead. It's one thing to have wealth. The great danger is that wealth can sometimes have you.

This man is rich. What is more, he is industrious. He made his wealth the hard way by working for it. I know that because he is a farmer. I really am out of my league here. I grew up in the ghetto of New York City. The first cow I remember seeing, I saw when I was about seven years of age. I saw it at the Macy's department store. I mean, I have never planted a field. I have never brought in a harvest. But, we live in Lancaster County, Pennsylvania. I've seen those farmers as they have worked. They work hard.

If you had known this man, you would have seen him up early in the morning getting his implements ready for the day's work. You would have seen him at night keeping his records to the light of a flickering candle. He was busy. He was working. And certainly, the Bible never criticizes work. If you're a sluggard, you get no comfort from the word of God. But, there is a danger of working hard, that's working without asking what you're working for. If all we're doing is trying to amass things, and that's that whole sum of what we do, then we often discover when we look back that we have spent our industry on doing nothing but accumulating things.

But, he was not only rich. He was not only industrious. He was also progressive. That is, he came one day to realize that, with all of his wealth, he had gotten more. So, he decided that what he would do is pull down the barns that he had and add new barns to take care of what had come in as crops. Up until now, he had focused on production. Now, he is going to focus on conservation.

Nothing wrong with progress. We all admire it. In fact, there was one American corporation that said that "progress is our most important product." Not light bulbs. Not refrigerators. Progress. But, progress can be an illusion, can't it? Most of the progress about which we brag of is progress in things, not in people. We have made a great deal of progress over the sickle that Ruth used in the Old Testament to work the field. But, we haven't made much progress over Ruth. And the danger of progress is that if it's on the wrong road, you end up nowhere. The faster you go, the harder you go, the further you are away from what really matters.

But, he's rich. He's industrious. He's progressive. He's got it made. He has made his plans for the future. He is gonna take it easy. And it all looks pretty good until something happened that changed him.

Can you imagine the scene?[3] One evening, the rich man sits across the desk from an architect and a builder. Sprawled in front of them is a blueprint. The rich man says, "Look. Once I was the best farm in the area of Jericho. Then, I became the best in the whole Jordan Valley. After I get this done, I'll be the best farmer in all of Israel."

The two men work. Then, as they're working, the rich man's wife comes in and urges him to come to bed. He's been up late all of the last three weeks. He assures her he'll come. Kisses him goodnight and goes to bed. The two men work for another hour. The architect says "Look, I better go home. I'll take this, and I'll get it ready and I'll come back and show you the changes."

So, the rich man takes him to the door. Shuts the door against the night. But, the adrenaline is pumping. He knows he can't sleep so he goes back to the desk and takes out his ledger. So much for the barns. So much

3. In his twenty-first-century retelling of the parable, Robinson borrows from John Ortberg's retelling of the parable in Ortberg's sermon, "It All Goes Back in the Box." He adapts the story and makes it his own.

for the house. So much for the insurance. And as he is working on the ledger, there is a knock on the door. He goes to answer it and suddenly realizes there is a Presence in the room.

The rich man says, "Who are you?"

The Presence says, "I am death."

The rich man says, "What do you want?'"

Death says, "I've come for you."

The rich man says, "There's some mistake. We don't have an appointment. I mean, you never warned me you'd be here."

Death said, "I did warn you. I warned you when I took your partner a couple of years ago. I warned you when I took that young man across the road. I warned you every time you saw a hearse go past you on the highway. I warned you. You just didn't listen. I'm counting you out. Ten, nine, eight . . ."

The rich man says, "Wait a minute. Look, we can bargain. Take half of these things that I've got. You take them and just let me live."

Death said, "I got no use for your toys. Seven, six, five . . ."

The rich man says, "Look, look, look, look, look! I'll give it all! Take everything. Just let me live."

Death with a grin waves its boney hand, and the rich man is dead. He prepared for every contingency and ignored life's inevitability. He prepared for life, and the very thing for which he prepared was taken away.

The next morning, the wife comes down and sees him slumped across the desk. Tries to awaken him. Realizes he's gone. He'd been so busy building barns, he built up stress. He was gone. And so they arranged quickly for the funeral. Everybody comes. The mayor of the town gives the eulogy. He says to the young people, "Here is somebody you can admire. He worked hard. He was the best barn builder in the entire area. You ought to copy him."

The funeral is over. They took the rich man in his coffin out to the cemetery. They buried him and over his grave they put a stone. On the stone, they put the birthdate and the death date. In addition to his name, there was something from the poets. And then the crowd had to get back home. They had some things to do. But, that night the angel of God came through that cemetery. And over that tombstone he wrote a single solitary word—F-O-O-L. Fool.

I don't think this man was an atheist. He was as religious as the next person. But, if you believe that God exists, and you live as though God does not exist, then God says, "You're a fool." There is that question, "For whom will these things be that you have provided?"

Pictures of squabbling brothers fighting over the inheritance. He has learned the hard way that there are no safe deposit boxes in a casket. He's discovered that life does not consist of the things that you possess. What Jesus is saying is, "If you're looking at life, don't decide what life is about when you are in the strength of your youth visioning the future. Nor in the middle of your career. Take some time out. Go to a cemetery, and stand there and ask yourself, 'Does what I am doing stand up to the light of my death?'"

A game of chess is like a parable of life. In the game, there are the pawns. There are some pieces that have the dignity of a bishop. Others have the maneuverability of a knight. Some the power of a queen. Some the value of a king. But, when the game is over, all the pieces are put in the box. It's a parable for life. You play the game against the system. Some are pawns. Easily taken. Some, like the knight, have great maneuverability. Some, like the queen, the king, are protected. But, when the game is over, they are all put in the box.

That's why Jesus says, "Beware of covetousness. Beware of wanting more and more of what you have enough of already because life does not consist of the things that we possess."

If Jesus is on to something, then the question is, "What does life consist of?" So, Jesus turns away from the crowd and, in verse 22, he talks to his disciples. Jesus says: "Therefore, in the light of this story, I tell you: *Don't worry about your life, what you'll eat, or about your body, what you'll wear. Life is more than food, and the body more than clothes.*"

Jesus is saying, "Don't make that the major concern of your life." Don't make the major concern of your life: things. Then, in order to back that up, he gives two examples. One is from the ravens and one is from the flowers. He says in verse 24: *"Consider the ravens. They don't sow or reap. They have no storeroom or barns like the rich man. Yet, God feeds them. And how much more valuable are you than birds? And who of you by worrying can add a single hour to his life?"* I suspect that by worrying you could knock a few hours off your life. But, since you can't do this very little thing, why do you worry about the rest?

The second illustration comes from the flowers. *"Consider the lilies, how they grow. They don't labor or spin. Yet I tell you that not even Solomon in all his splendor was dressed like one of these. And if that's how God clothes the grass of the field, which is here today, and tomorrow is thrown into the fire, how much more will he clothe you? You of little faith. Don't set your heart on what you'll eat or drink. Don't worry about it. For the pagan world runs after all such things. And your Father knows you need them."*

God can be as real to you as paying a dental bill. If you're committed to him, he can meet your expenses. Jesus is saying, "Don't make that the thing that eats you up in life. Don't worry about it. Don't be concerned about it. But, seek his kingdom and all these things will be given to you as well."

When he talks about his kingdom, he is talking about his rule upon the earth. The rule that he has now and that we will have in a glorious way in the future. If you're going to wake up at 2:00 in the morning and worry about something, worry about that kingdom, how you fit into it, where it's going. But, seek his kingdom, and these things will be added to you.

Sometimes, when I think of life, I think of it as a wagon wheel. At the center of the wheel, there is a hub. Out from the hub, there are the spokes. The strength of the wheel is in the hub. I've known men who have put at the center of their lives possessions. They are like this man in Jesus' story. Every one of the spokes contributes to that. They devote their families to it. They arrange their social life. They go to church because it's a good place to make contacts. But their life is centered in getting possessions. Then, one day, there is a downturn in the economy. One day, they lose what they thought they had, and all of life crumbles in.

I've known men who have put at the center of their lives passions—sexual drive. And all the spokes of life are centered in that. They'll sacrifice their marriage. They'll sacrifice their children to it. They arrange their business around it. It's where they get what they would call their "recreation in life." Then, one day, the fire doesn't burn, and they get older, and they lose the attraction, and life crumbles in.

I've known people who have lived for power. I've known people who will sacrifice their families. They will sacrifice their income. They will sacrifice what they do in the community because they want to get a promotion. They want to get elected. They give everything for it. They want to move ahead. They want a promotion. Then, one day, they lose the election. One day, they don't get the promotion. One day, they lose their position, and it can be devastating. Their lives crumble.

What Jesus is saying is, "For your sake, for God's sake, guard your center." There is nothing that is more worthy of the allegiance of an immortal soul than something that is eternal. Guard your center. Give your life to that which will outlast it. Life does not consist of the things that we possess. Don't spend your life trying to get more and more of what you have enough of already.

There's a legend that comes to us from Italy. It's the legend of a wealthy man who owned a villa, and he had a servant that he thought was a very stupid man. One day, in exasperation, the master said to the servant, "Servant, I don't think there is anybody more stupid than you are. I want you to take this staff, and if you ever meet someone more stupid than you are, you give him the staff."

To show you how stupid the servant was, he agreed. Moved out day by day into the marketplace. Met a lot of stupid men. But, he was never quite sure that they were worse than he was. And then, the legend has it that one day he came back to the villa. He was ushered into his master's bedroom. Master said, "Servant, I wanted to talk to you. I'm going on a long journey."

The servant said, "Well, sir, when will you be back?"

The master said, "Well, I won't come back from this journey."

The servant said, "Sir, have you made preparations for this journey?"

Master said, "No, I've been busy about other things. I've not made the preparations."

And, the servant said, "Could you have made preparation?"

The master said, "Yes, but I just neglected it."

The servant said, "Sir, you're going on a journey from which you will never return? You could have made preparations for the journey and you failed to do so?" He took the staff and handed it to him and said, "Here, sir. At last I have met a man more stupid than myself."

Hear again what Jesus is saying. *"Beware of covetousness."* Beware of wanting more and more of what you have enough of already. Life does not consist of the things that we possess. Life consists of giving ourselves to the One who is eternal and spending our strength on that which outlasts it.

Chapter 14

J. (James) Alfred Smith Sr. (1931–)

Living Legend 2009

The Preacher

REV. DR. J. (JAMES) Alfred Smith Sr. (1931–) served with distinction as senior pastor for thirty-eight years (1971–2009) at the historic Allen Temple Baptist Church in Oakland, California, where he is now pastor emeritus. Born in 1931 in Kansas City, Missouri, he experienced a call to ministry and obtained his license to preach at Pilgrim's Rest Missionary Baptist Church in 1948. In 1952, he obtained his bachelor of science degree in elementary education from Western Baptist College, Kansas City. Then, in 1959, he received his bachelor of divinity degree from Missouri School of Religion,

University of Missouri-Columbia, where he later obtained a master's degree in theology, church, and community in 1966. Upon accepting the call to become the next pastor at Allen Temple and relocating to California, he also earned his master's degree in American church history from the American Baptist Seminary of the West, Berkeley, California (1972), and his doctor of ministry degree from Golden Gate Baptist Seminary (1975), Mill Valley, California. During his thirty-eight-year tenure as senior pastor, the church grew from a membership of five hundred to over five thousand with a dedicated staff of both ordained and lay leaders.

He has also performed many other leadership roles in administration and teaching. He joined the faculty at the American Baptist Seminary of the West and the Graduate Theological Union in 1992, and was at one time the acting dean of American Baptist. He became president of the Progressive Baptist Convention of California and Nevada (1979–1981), the Progressive National Baptist Convention, Inc. (1986–1988), and the American Baptist Churches of the West. He has also served as a visiting professor at Fuller Theological Seminary in Pasadena, California, and a scholar in residence at Gardner Webb University in Boiling Springs, North Carolina.

Dr. Smith's writing, leadership, and preaching ministries have impacted tens of thousands of people beyond the walls of the church where he served for nearly four decades. In addition to his contributions through articles, essays, and book chapters, he has published more than seventeen books including his ministry autobiography titled *On the Jericho Road*, and his prophetic reflections titled *Speak Until Justice Wakes*. A vocal opponent of apartheid in South Africa, he spoke out against its evils and injustices before the United Nations in New York City in 1989.

He has received numerous honors and accolades as a result of a ministry that has now spanned more than seven decades. In 1990, the *Oakland Tribune* named him Outstanding Citizen of the Year as a way to recognize his many accomplishments in compassion, justice, and community development.[1] In 2001, he received the Lifetime Achievement Award from the Greenling Institute, a public policy organization in Berkeley. *Ebony* magazine listed him for two consecutive years in its compilation of the Most Influential Black Americans, and it also placed him on its list of the magazine's top 15 greatest Black preachers in 1993.[2]

He and his first wife, Mrs. Joanna Goodwin Smith, were married in 1950 and remained married for fifty-seven years until she passed away in 2007. They reared five children: three sons and two daughters. He is now

1. See "Reverend Dr. J. Alfred Smith Sr."
2. See "15 Greatest Black Preachers."

married to the Rev. Bernestine Smith, who served at one time as the pastor of Allen Temple Arms I and II. Upon Dr. Smith's retirement in 2009, his son Rev. Dr. J. Alfred Smith Jr. succeeded him at Allen Temple, where he served as senior pastor for ten years until his retirement from there in 2019.

The Sermon

When I talked to Pastor Carter, he shared with me that he was concerned about the laity getting off the bench of lazy religion and getting into the work of ministry, that he just didn't want a ministry that was built around himself, that the vision of the late Dr. Bailey was to have staff to equip the laypeople for ministry. He told me he was interested in Ephesians 4 so I decided that I would build my message around Ephesians 4.

Since I'm pastor emeritus, I don't have to try to impress anybody. I've been there and done that, and so I just want to give a teaching message here tonight. Is that alright? Amen! Since I'm going to give a teaching message, I want to take time and read from Ephesians 4. Like Dr. Bailey, I have a high view of Scripture. I believe the Bible does not contain the word of God. I believe it *is* the word of God. So, out of respect, can we stand for the reading of God's word?

> *I, therefore, the prisoner of the Lord, beseech you to walk worthy of the calling with which you were called, with all lowliness and gentleness, with longsuffering, bearing with one another in love, endeavoring to keep the unity of the Spirit in the bond of peace. There is one body and one Spirit, just as you were called in one hope of your calling; one Lord, one faith, one baptism; one God and Father of all, who is above all, and through all, and in you all. But to each one of us grace was given according to the measure of Christ's gift. Therefore, He says: "When He ascended on high, He led captivity captive and gave gifts to men." Now this, "He ascended"—what does it mean but that He also first descended into the lower parts of the earth? He who descended is also the One who ascended far above all the heavens, that He might fill all things. And He Himself gave some to be apostles, some prophets, some evangelists, and some pastors and teachers, for the equipping of the saints for the work of ministry, for the edifying of the body of Christ, until we all come to the unity of the faith and of the knowledge of the Son of God, to a perfect man, to the measure of the stature of the fullness of Christ; that we should no longer be children, tossed to and fro and carried about with every wind of doctrine, by the trickery of men, in the cunning craftiness of*

deceitful plotting, but, speaking the truth in love, may grow up
in all things into Him who is the head—Christ—from whom the
whole body, joined and knit together by what every joint supplies,
according to the effective working by which every part does its
share, causes growth of the body for the edifying of itself in love.

Would you repeat after me? "But to each one of us, grace was given according to the measure of Christ's gift." Would you say to your neighbor, "God's grace for mission impossible"? God's grace for mission impossible. God's grace for mission impossible. Thank you!

Why does the mission given to us appear impossible? If God has the power, and we have the faith, why is the mission impossible? Are we clear about the mission agenda? Is the mission agenda about us or is the mission God's redemptive plan for an unredeemed world? As a pastor, must not I ask myself, "Am I building people or am I building my kingdom and using people?"

Shortly after the Lord led us into successfully building a larger worship center for our congregation, Dr. Robert Hill, now in heaven, the pastor of Taylor United Methodist Church, came for one of our festive services. Before he took his text, he congratulated the Allen Temple people for having the courageous faith to build such a building. But, then, he turned and looked at me and said, "Brother Smith, you all have built the building, but now it's time to build the people."

If Ephesians 1:4 defines the church as being holy and blameless in a world of stain and blame, why is the church's failure the not-equipping of the saints, the perfecting of the saints, and the building up of the body of Christ? Why is it? It's mission impossible because the ain'ts outnumber the saints, the spectators outnumber the participators, and the agitators outnumber those endeavoring to keep the unity of the Spirit and the bond of peace. I want to know if mission impossible becomes mission possible.

Yes, our failure of measuring up to the high standard of God's righteousness makes God's forgiveness necessary. But, our faith-response to God's forgiving love makes God's grace available.

Here we are, captives of our sinful failure but loved by the unearned, unmerited favor of God's love. I believe that there is nothing as marvelous, miraculous, and mysterious as God's matchless love. We call it God's grace. *"Marvelous grace of our loving Lord that exceeds our sin and guilt. Yonder on Calvary's mount, out toward there where the blood of the Lamb was spilled."*

But we live in a strange new theological climate, where the cross is an unwelcome symbol in the halls of postmodern worship. The mention of Jesus' blood is seen as a contributor to divine violence. This cross-less, bloodless

Christology elevates human reason and eliminates the God of Revelation, the Christ of Redemption, and the Holy Spirit of Resurrection. Yes, this new theology, this theology of entertainment, rather than engagement with the Holy God, reduces the death of Jesus Christ to the death of just another martyr like John F. Kennedy or Martin Luther King Jr.

Yes, the God of nature is limited by the laws of cause and effect, but the God that came to see about us in Jesus Christ, the God that came down the escalator of eternity into time has power to calm the raging sea, and when he speaks the winds obey his voice. This God is a God of grace and glory. If we are honest with ourselves, we have to say with the apostle Paul, "By the grace of God, I am what I am."

I believe that every Christian has been graced by God. To be graced by God means to be blessed with God's favor. To be blessed by God and graced by his mercy, fed by his love, uplifted by his power, means God has smiled upon you. He didn't have to do it, but he did! His favor is unmerited; it is unearned; it is undeserved.

"For by grace you have been saved through faith, and this is not of your doing. It is the gift of God, not the result of works, so no one can boast." And no one has to be jealous of anyone else. For what you have, grace gave to you. What the next person has, grace gave to them.

You see, grace in Ephesians 1–3 is saving grace. This grace positions us in the place of acceptance before God; it gives us peace with God. Saving grace helps us face God; saving grace helps us look at God in the face. Saving grace helps us face God in the perfection of Jesus Christ, and our position is in Christ. Before the foundation of the world, we were chosen in Christ to be holy, to be blameless. In Christ, we have been forgiven.

Ephesians 4–6 addresses not our position but our practice. Yes, chapters 1–3 deal with doctrine, but 4–6 deal with ethics. Chapters 1–3 deal with the content of the gospel, but chapters 4–6 announce that our practice is an ongoing process of growth.

Verse 12 of Ephesians 4 speaks of the equipping of the saints. The word is *katartizo*, which means the mending together of that which is broken as if a surgeon would go to work and take bones that needed to be put back together again. That's equipping! A medical metaphor. Before people can do the work of ministry, before they can get up out of their comfortable pew, their own brokenness needs mending. Sometimes, those of us who are pastors spend so much time doing the mending until we hardly have time to do the tending.

Next, Paul uses a metaphor taken from the building and construction industry. He speaks in verse 12 of the edifying of the body of Christ. Edify means to build up, to build up that which is torn down, and also to build up that which is new. Yes, sometimes there are saints that have been torn down by negativity, by the negativity of the ain'ts.

In my own pastoral experience, I've worked hard as an evangelist to bring in new people. Somebody who has been sitting in the rocking chair of religion for a long time will say to him, "How did you get here so quickly?" and will look around and see that those we brought in the front door have gone out the back door.

So, we have to busy about the task of edification, building folk up in the Lord, building folk up to do the work of the Master. New can mean more of the same, but it also can mean to construct that which has never been. It's exciting to lead a cooperative group of people who are willing to trust the Lord into new territory, into new adventures, into new and higher plateaus of kingdom building. When that takes place, edification is exciting.

Yes, when I think about the body of Christ, another metaphor taken from the field of biology, I hear Paul saying that edification should help the whole body to be joined and knit together by every joint, and every part ought to do its share. Yes, I want to say there's room for everybody in the kingdom, there's room for everybody in the local church, that God has a place for everybody. Therefore, sometimes, a pastor becomes a spiritual chiropractor to make sure that those joints are working together. You see our practice is to help everybody to become fully mature in Jesus Christ. And we are in process of looking like Jesus, walking like Jesus, talking like Jesus, serving like Jesus, loving like Jesus, reconciling like Jesus, healing, mending, and tending like Jesus.

We become like Jesus by God's saving grace. Some may call it sanctifying grace, but it's still grace. Saving grace births us into God's church, but saving grace empowers us to serve like Jesus.

Ephesians 2:10 puts it in focus for me. It says, "For we are God's workmanship, created in Christ Jesus to do good works which God prepared in advance for us to do." Who are we? We are the creativity of God's mind. Who are we? We are the design of God's hand. In us, Christ ought to be in the human heart. In us, the love of God, yes, ought to be experienced with a human touch. In us, the word of God ought to be expressed with the human lips. Who are we? Paul said that we are God's workmanship.

In the Greek, that word means *poema*. It's the same word for "poem" in English. A poem is the message of the author. Can God speak through you? I wonder if you can you be God's poem. A poem has a beautiful tone, a beautiful beat, a beautiful rhythm, a beautiful meter all created by the poet to deliver a beautiful message. We are called to be God's masterful work of art. God has graced us with his message for an ugly world.

God is the great poem maker. Are you God's poem? God who created in the first creation earth wind and fire, sand, sea, and stars also created the second creation. He sent the second Adam not only to bring life after death, but to bring life after birth.

You see, I don't worry too much about life after death. Jesus answered Job's question. Job said, "If a man die, shall he live again?" Isaiah couldn't answer it. Jeremiah couldn't answer it. Ezekiel couldn't answer it. Daniel couldn't answer it. Hosea couldn't answer it. Joel couldn't answer it. Malachi couldn't answer it. But, I heard Jesus say, "I am the resurrection and the life. He who believes in me shall never die."

Yes, I'm here to tell you that Jesus has answered Job's question. So, it's not whether there's going to be life after death but life after birth. And Jesus said, "I've come so that you may have life and that you might have it more abundantly." I wonder what kind of life that boy that sits in your Sunday school class will have? On Monday, will he go to a school where he will die intellectually, yes, at an early age? So, we have to be concerned about whether there will be life after birth. And, if so, what about the quality of life? Jesus came to bring life, came to bring qualitative life as well as quantitative life. Old things have passed away. The new things have come. And if anyone is in Christ, he is a new creation.

Yes, the disciples of Jesus are graced by God for mission possible in a mission-impossible world. How is it possible? It is, Ephesians 4:11–12 answers: *"It was He who gave some to be apostles, some to be prophets, some to be evangelists, and some to be pastors and teachers to prepare God's people for the work of service so that the body of Christ may be built up until we all reach unity in the faith and in the knowledge of the son of God and become mature attaining to the whole measure of the fullness of Christ."*

I wonder. Could more church members become Christians, and more Christians become disciples, and more disciples become like Jesus? Could those of us in the pulpit seek our authority not in our titles but in our anointing?

You see, today, some of us name ourselves. But, if I do a close reading of the text, it says: "And *He gave* some as prophets, and *He gave* some as apostles." But today some of us name ourselves. Some of us are now apostles. Yesterday, we were bishops. Still, some of us want to call ourselves prophets, but we don't know what a prophetic word is. But, the book of Ephesians says that apostles and prophets were given to the church to get her established, and these gifts do not extend beyond the apostolic age. The church needs evangelists. They need obstetricians who are gifted in bringing new birth in the church.

Too many congregations are spiritually sterile, and too many churches have too many babies in the nursery. Sometimes, the pastor has to end up changing the disciples. But, then, after the evangelists, there are the pediatricians, those who are giving tender loving care to newborn babes who are growing up spiritually in Jesus Christ. You can't understand your pastor if the only time you hear the word of God is on Sunday morning. You need to be in a home Bible class. You need to be in a Sunday school class where you can start out drinking the milk of the word, and then grow in grace by getting a little bit of meat. So, we not only need the pediatricians, but we need the dieticians to make sure the flock is fed well.

Three times, Jesus challenged Peter: "Peter, do you love? Peter, do you love me? If you love me feed my sheep. If you love me, feed my lambs."

Well, I must not hold you too long. So, I want to close my message the way Paul opens Philippians. He says, "To the saints in Ephesus, the faithful in Christ." You ought to stand somewhere because, if you don't stand—a man that doesn't stand somewhere, can't stand anywhere.

So, you ought to be in somebody's church in Ephesus, in Dallas, in LA, but make sure you are in Christ. "*Grace and peace to you from God our Father and the Lord Jesus Christ.*" Then, in Ephesians 6:24, his parting words were, "*Grace to all who love the Lord.*"

Anybody here that love my Jesus? Anybody here that knows him for yourself? Anybody know that he's a heart fixer and a mind regulator? Anybody here who knows that He will fight your battle? Anybody here who knows that he's the rock of eternal ages? If you know him, you ought to say so. Let the redeemed of the Lord say so. If he's been good to you, say so. If he's blessed you, say so. If you're not ashamed of him, say so.

Well, in my years as pastor emeritus, the words of grace comfort me. If you come to the closing years of your ministry like I have, realizing that your maturity in Christ is just a relative maturity, if you come to the place where I am and realize that you missed preaching some of the deeper doctrines of God's word, if you've come to the place where I am and realize that there's work that you've left undone, that there's things that you wanted to do, but you weren't able to do them, yes, If you understand that your spiritual DNA is not in your works, not in your writings, not in your words, not in your titles, not in your honors, not in your congregation's size, not in your degrees, [then you understand] it's by grace, God's grace. Grace. Incomparable. Grace. Immeasurable. Grace. Indestructible. "*Amazing grace, how sweet the sound, that saved a wretch like me, I once was lost but now I'm found, was blind but now I see.*" Through many dangers. Through many dangers. Forty years, forty Mother's Days, forty Father's Days, forty Easters, forty Christmases. Yes, telling the world about Jesus. I can tell the world about this. Tell the nation, "I'm blessed." Grace! Grace! Grace! Grace brought me!

Chapter 15

Willie Richardson (1939–)

Living Legend 2010

The Preacher

REV. DR. WILLIE RICHARDSON (1939–) is the founder and senior pastor of Christian Stronghold Church, in Philadelphia, Pennsylvania, where he has been a teacher and preacher of God's word for more than fifty-four years. Planted in 1966 with six people, the church now has an active membership of close to 4,400 people. Born in Florence, South Carolina, in 1939, Dr. Richardson moved to Philadelphia with his family at the age of six. After his conversion, he became a committed evangelist, playing an instrumental role in leading his eleven siblings to Christ and his parents rededicating their lives to Christ. He received his bachelor's degree from Philadelphia Biblical University (now Cairn University), he has pursued academic study at Temple University, and he has received the doctor of divinity degree from Geneva College.

In 1975, he and his wife, Mrs. Patricia Richardson, founded Christian Research and Development (CRD), an organization committed to providing resources to support African American families, communities, and churches. The mission of the CRD is to "research needs and methods, and to develop materials on 'Biblical How To's' for the church, specializing in family ministry and church development through seminars, conferences, retreats, and workshops."[1] It also provides in-depth consulting to churches, Christian nonprofits, secular businesses, and educational institutions.

Dr. Richardson maintains an active academic ministry and publishing ministry. He has served as a professor at the Center for Urban Theological Studies (CUTS), Westminster Theological Seminary, an adjunct professor at Messiah College, and has developed curricula for CUTS and CRD. He has published numerous how-to manuals, resource books for families, video materials, and articles for Christian magazines. He is the coauthor of at least three books. His two most recent single-author publications are *Reclaiming the Urban Family* and *Sharing Christ as You Go*. He and his wife, Mrs. Patricia Richardson, have been married for over forty-four years and are the proud parents of four adult children and eight grandchildren.

The Sermon

I love lecturing and teaching, but I didn't come prepared to teach and lecture. I was asked to preach. I like the theme: "Preach Christ." Amen. Amen. So that's what I came to do tonight.

If you will, turn with me to John, chapter 1, verses 16 and 17. John, chapter 1, verses 16 and 17. *"Because he was full of grace,"*—I'm reading from the New Century Version of the Bible—*"Because he was full of grace,"* John 1:16–17, *"and truth, from him we all receive one gift after another, the Law was given through Moses, but grace and truth came through Jesus Christ."* I'd like to also say that I thank Pastor Carter for this opportunity. You may be seated.

Also, I would like to say that we've been under his leadership for the past two years, and I want you to understand: this conference has gotten better over the past two years. I really love the schedule for the old dude. An old dude can work with this schedule. The old schedule was wearing

---

1. See the Christian Research Development website: https://crdonline.org/bio_dr_richardson.php.

me out. The other thing I'd like to say before I get started is that if it was not for Dr. Sheila Bailey, when the Lord took Dr. E. K. Bailey, there would be no more conference, but it was under her dutiful leadership and her commitment to carrying on the legacy. And we thank the Lord for her. I want to just let everyone know.

Let me pray for a moment: Oh, heavenly Father, we thank you so much for this opportunity to gather in your name. We pray, Lord, that you would lead us this evening into your word and speak from heaven to each one of us. That each one of us leave here tonight, we would know that we heard from you, oh Lord, and that you would give us a personal message and encouragement. Lord, we do pray in Jesus name and for his sake. Amen.

If we are anything at all, it is because of God's grace. If we have accomplished anything at all, it is because of God's grace. Grace is more than salvation. That's my main point this evening, that grace is more than salvation. But certainly, it is salvation. In Ephesians chapter 2, verses 8–9, we read—we're very familiar with it, *"For it is by grace you've been saved, through faith. And this is not from yourselves; it is the gift of God, not by works, so that no one can boast."*

In other words, we are saved, we are converted, we've been born again, we've been regenerated, but we're still undeserving sinners. As a matter of fact, what motivates me to get up in the morning and serve the Lord? What keeps me awake at night? I cannot go to bed any night to simply be so tired and go to sleep.

I have to turn the TV on real soft and get something to distract my mind, because, since I've been saved, the only thing I can think about is how to serve the Lord. If I lay down in the bed at night, my mind will race. I'll be thinking of new issues, new situations. How can I do it better? How can I do more? What can God do next? Because he saved me. Because he saved me. The idea that I'm saved by his grace—it is what motivates me.

However, grace is more than that. Most sermons on grace historically have been about salvation. Theological books and commentaries primarily emphasize salvation through Christ to demonstrate grace. Definitions of grace predominantly amplify salvation in Christ. Rightly so. But, grace is more than that.

As a matter of fact, if we just look at the next verse in Ephesians 2, verse 10, we will get an idea that it might be more than grace. First of all, we're told we've been saved by grace, and we didn't do anything to save ourselves. Even the faith that we got that saved us didn't even come from us; it came from the Lord himself. So, in verse 10 it says, *"For we are God's workmanship, created in Christ Jesus to do good works, which God prepared in advance for us to do it."*

Before you were born, God already had his call on your life. Before he ever called you to the ministry, God already knew what he wanted you to accomplish. Before there was a heaven or a hell, before there was even Earth, remember that he put the salvation plan into being even before he created us. So, therefore, that meant that he already had his mind made up on what you were going to be doing, how you were going to be doing it, how you were going to have success, and how you were going to bring glory to our Lord and Savior Jesus Christ. Your mama and daddy hadn't even gotten together yet. So, we get an idea here. He came up with the creation of what he wanted you to do, how he wanted you to do it, even before you came into existence.

So, let us consider some definitions of grace: "God's unmerited favor." Now, I know you've heard that. But that's okay if you're a baby Christian. And you know, that's a nice way to remember it. God's unmerited favor. Yes, I believe that certainly that is what grace is, but grace is more than that.

Now, the next definition is certainly more than that. Grace is God's freely given, unmerited favor towards the sinful and failing, the expression of forgiving, redeeming, restoring love toward the unworthy. That is a little bit more about grace: God's love taking the initiative to meet human needs, whatever those needs may be. Now, that's a lot closer. Whatever the needs are, whatever the situation is, that's what grace is for.

Now, grace is more than salvation because Christ is full of grace. If you will, look at John chapter 1, verse 16 again. In the King James Version, it says, *"And of His fullness have all we received, and grace for grace."* Now, it says in the past tense—and this is very important—that all of us have received grace. Now, of course the initial grace is salvation-grace. But, then, the verse goes on to say that grace for grace, or "grace on top of grace."

Now, you can't just be satisfied with salvation-grace. Now, the Greek word here for "the fullness" means "a vessel filled with liquid to the brim and running over." The metaphor here is trying to help us understand what Christ did for us. He not only saved us by grace, but he has poured his grace on us, in us, all over us. We're wallowing in it, and we don't even know it!

One of the things that Paul told us—we are saved by faith—but we also have to *live* by faith. Now, one thing I've learned is that faith is worth more than money. Faith is worth more than if you have enough people. Faith is worth more than all these things because, if I can get you to believe what I'm trying to get you to see tonight, then you're going to have faith that you are just wallowing in grace, sopping in grace. And whatever comes your way, there's enough grace to handle it!

Now, now, now grace to me, in my forty-eight years of walking with the Lord—see, you've got to be old to be walking with the Lord for forty years—my definition of grace in my experience of working with the Lord— grace is whatever I lack, whatever I come short of, whatever I need, whatever I don't have, whatever would make me fail if I don't have it, that's grace!

Therefore, grace gives me confidence. Hallelujah! Before I met Christ, I was a loser. Before I met Christ, I was such a loser that I would see girls in high school and be scared to talk to them. As a matter of fact, the first time I saw my wife, I didn't even pay her no never mind. The reason I didn't pay her any attention is because she was pretty and beautiful and dignified—a lady. And I felt I wouldn't even talk to nobody like that. I've got to find me a homey-girl to love, find me a girl I could give my nerve up to talk to and, half the time, she still told me "no." So, that just killed all of my confidence.

But, what has grace done for me? A few years later, I saw my wife. Then, her girlfriend called me up, and her girlfriend said, "She's interested in you." And then grace kicked in. Amen! Amen! Amen! She's sitting right out there right now. Amen! Amen!

Now, grace is what gives you confidence. But, grace is humbling. Last night, we were reminded that Jesus made himself nothing. I want to remind you—without Jesus, we're nothing. Not only does grace give you confidence, but it reminds you when you realize all of the grace and what God is do- ing in your life, you realize, if God was to take away his grace, if he was to remove his grace, you are nothing!

I have enjoyed God's grace so much. I believe in God's grace so much. I don't even believe in losing anymore! I'm used to winning! I'm not used to losing! I don't even like to be around people that talk about losing. Don't tell me about how we're not going to do it. We can do it!

As a matter of fact, when E. K. came to me, you heard, he told you this story a number of times. He came to me. He said, "I want to have an exposi- tory preaching conference."

I said, "Well, I don't know. We already have some of those." I said, "They're all about the same, and I don't think we need another one."

But, he said, "No, no, no. Mine's going to be different. We're gonna teach expository preaching. We're gonna do all the things in regular homi- letics that they learned in those schools, then we're going to do some black homiletics. We're gonna to teach them how to do incarnation. We gonna teach 'em how to close. We gonna teach 'em how to celebrate. We're gonna teach 'em how to whoop!"

I said, "Ain't nobody doing that." I said, "Why haven't we been doing that?"

He said, "I'm scared."

I said, "E. K., we can do it. I got enough grace for both us, and I'm sure you got the grace." And tonight, we're here tonight at this conference because of God's grace!

Now, grace is God's favor and lovingkindness given to us who do not deserve it and cannot earn it. Looking at John 1:16 again, *"Because he was full of grace and truth, from him we all receive one gift after another."*

Now, beloved, listen to me real good. Being in ministry can mess up your self-esteem. Being in ministry can make you think you're stupid, and you don't have anything. But, know what the Scripture says here. We *all* have received his grace and, in this version, it says, "We all receive one gift after another."

When I first started out, coming out of school, I jumped out there, and we started doing things. We were winning people to Christ, the church is growing; the church keeps growing. My wife used to tell me, "You're gifted." I said, "I'm not gifted; I'm just a hard worker." I said, "The rest of these preachers around me, they're just lazy." And I kept going. I kept going. And, after a while, preachers started coming to me, asking me, "How do you do this?" and, "How do you do that?"

Then, I discovered that I was gifted. But *you* are gifted too! And *you* are gifted too! And *you* are gifted too! And you need to believe by faith what this verse says about grace! You have gifts you don't know you have! You have gifts you haven't used yet. You have gifts for the glory of the Lord!

Now, I know what it says in verse 17: *"The Law was given through Moses, but grace and truth came through Jesus Christ."* Now, this does not mean that there was no grace under the law of Moses. For there was, there was, because each sacrifice accepted by God was an expression of the grace of God. However, in Jesus Christ, grace and truth have reached their fullness, making them available to us.

We can receive grace and more grace. Even James, the brother of Jesus, said, "He gives more grace." Now, there's enough grace for fallen preachers. There's enough grace for fallen preachers. Now, what I can't figure out is why we've got enough grace for fallen people in the pew. Why is it if we catch a deacon stealing, the whole church don't even know about it? Why is it if we capture a trustee in the bed with Hattie May, nobody don't know about it? How come if, if little Moe up on this third pew near the back, if he's smoking weed, why does nobody know he's high but the preacher?

Preachers have the flesh like everybody else! Now, let me tell you something else. Preachers fall, and they get trashed. Preachers fall, and they get kicked to the curb. Where is God's grace? Where is God's grace? First of all, the grace should not start after the scandal is out. The grace ought to start long before the scandal is out. Grace ought to start with us as preachers extending and dispensing grace to each other!

Now, listen to me. I'm not the only one to notice that when certain preachers preach, their wife doesn't pay them any attention and starts texting all her friends. That's an indication that's something wrong in that house! He's supposed to be your friend; he's supposed to be your buddy. You need to be inquiring, brother, why she's texting while you're preaching? Amen! She's texting because he's not living at home while he's preaching up here. And we need to get involved and extend some grace!

You need grace. You need grace, just to be married! Hallelujah! Wait a minute! God tells us in the Bible that the man is the head of the house, and then scientifically, I just found out recently women use an average of fifty thousand words a day, and a man, God only gave a man fifteen thousand. We need some grace!

In the Old Testament, under the law of Moses, God extended grace to a fallen spiritual leader. His name was David. David not only committed adultery. Now, don't get me wrong here now, the preachers nicknamed me the most conservative preacher in the East. Don't get me wrong. I'm not condoning sin. I'm sure in a few minutes that, if you're my friend, and I get up in your grill, you'd want to get up in mine, right? But, you know we're letting folk fall apart, and then you go get him, you know.

But anyway, here is David. Not only was David peepin' and a voyeur. Let's line up his sins now. Here was the man that wrote the twenty-third psalm on the roof peepin'. Not only, not only did he commit adultery, but then he tried to cover it up and had the woman's husband killed! But, then, God dealt with it.

Now let me tell you about extending grace. If we're supposed to be friends and we're supposed to be pastor-friends, we who are pastors need to pastor each other. We need to help each other. We need to bless each other. You heard that saying, "Friends don't let friends drink and drive"? Well, preacher-friends are not supposed to watch your friends walk away from the Lord, walk in sin. And you're still walking together and you're silent.

There's supposed to be God's grace. Now, understand when God got finished ministering to David—now listen to me real good—he was not taken out of the kingship.

Now, here's something else that we unwittingly do to help the Devil. Listen to me real good. This week, we heard some of the best preaching and teaching you're ever going to hear. We are blessed! We tell all our friends. But let me tell you, everybody that blessed you, the Devil's got a target on his back. The minute you talk about doing God's will and God is using you—listen, I met a lot of great leaders in my time.

I never met Billy Graham, but I prayed for Billy Graham every single week. Covered him in prayer! Because I know the Devil wants to bring him down. Think about it! Think about it! All the great preachers. Think about the preachers in your community that God was using, and now they're gone. They're done. Because the Devil had a target on their back.

Listen to me carefully. Don't believe everything you hear about a preacher! A lot of what's going down to break a person's heart is to hear the horrible things that people are saying about them. We need to extend some grace! Remember now, if we're recipients of grace, we ought to be giving grace!

Now, I hear these stories, too. If a preacher's one of my friends, I'll take him to lunch. I want to hear about it! Is it true or is it not true? I'm not gonna allow my friends to go down the drain, and then watch them and say, "What a shame!" afterward. No. God gave me grace! I want to give them grace! Target's on *my* back! I want to help shield them!

Now, note. Before David's sin, God said, "He's a man after God's own heart." Go ahead and check your Bible out. After David repented, and that's what we're after, we're after repentance, preachers getting other preachers to repent. Amen!

Privately, behind closed doors! You might have to smack them or something, because they've got a lot of pride, but get them to repent! After he repented, the Lord said, "He's a man after God's own heart." *After* he repented! And after he repented, he was still king. They weren't looking for a new pastor.

The restoration of the preacher rests in Romans chapter 5, verse 20. Look what it says. It's a terrible thing when a preacher falls. It's a terrible thing when a preacher sins. It's a terrible thing when a preacher disgraces God. But, look at what the Bible says in Romans 5:20: *"Moreover, the Lord entered that the offense might abound, but where sin abounded, grace did much more abound."*

In other words, there's that grace thing again! And we're not talking about just salvation here. "Where sin abounds"! No matter how bad it is, there's enough grace to overcome! There's enough grace to bounce back! There's enough grace to get up! There's enough grace to start over! There's enough grace to start again! There's enough grace to be used of God again!

There's enough grace for us to be successfully finishing our assignment. There's enough grace—listen, good—for us to finish our assignment. All of us have been given a mission, and God want us to finish it. In John, chapter 1, verse 16 again, we read, *"Because he was full of grace and truth, from Him we all received gift after another."*

I'm just going to say this to each one of you. Use your gifts, talents, and abilities to God's glory. Now, I'm a professional counselor. I teach and train counselors. And, I know as much as I say that, there are hundreds of you out there that don't even believe that about yourself. That's why you need to believe the Bible. Forget about looking at yourself. Just simply believe the book. That's how I got confidence. Just believe in the book! About what God said about me!

Paul is an example of a preacher-friend, what you should do for another preacher-friend. In 1 Timothy chapter 4, verse 14, in his first letter to Timothy, with Timothy pastoring at the church at Ephesus, a difficult, hard task—Paul, when you read the letters, the first one in particular, he [Timothy] had to do some hard things, and Paul tells him what to do. But in 1 Timothy, chapter 4, verse 14, we read Paul saying this to him in the first letter: *"Use the gift you have, which was given to you through the prophecy when the group of elders laid their hands on you."*

Now, I'm gonna show you just how powerful this grace thing is. When you were ordained, when you were installed at the church where you are, when you were born, God gave you natural gifts. That's why a lot of you all don't want to give up your professional job. You're making too much money. You're still hanging on to them natural gifts. When you were born again, God gave you *spiritual* gifts. Romans 12. First Corinthians 12. Spiritual gifts. That's two groups right there.

Now, now, now when you got your assignment, when they laid hands on you, when you were ordained, God gave you enabling gifts. That's not listed anyplace. That's what this means. God didn't give you an assignment for you to fail. God didn't tell you to do anything and didn't give you what you need— your gifts. What Paul is doing here is telling Timothy, "I know your potential, and you know your potential, and I know you can do this. I know you can do it because I know what the Spirit told me when we laid hands on you, when we ordained you, when we installed you in that church. God gave you extra unction. God gave you extra something, and you're not using it!"

He didn't get through to him because he tells him again in the second letter. Look at the second letter, 2 Timothy, chapter 1, verses 6–7. Paul comes back again, and then he tells us and shows us what Timothy was doing just like a lot of us do, why he wasn't using the gifts. *"This is why I remind you . . ."* 2 Timothy 1:6–7, *"This is why I remind you to fan into flames the spiritual gift God gave you when I laid my hands on you."*

Now, he's not talking about using the gifts. He said, "Catch fire!" You remember now. Paul was the man that went down to Lystra and got bricked! Alright? Thought he was dead, throw him on the garbage pile, and by grace, he got up, went back into town, and preached! And they thought a ghost was preaching! It was all by God's grace! Paul knows what he's talking about here! It's God's grace!

So now, Paul's a little irritated here; he's a little impatient with this young man. "Look, you've got the gift. Now, use it! You've got the gift. Catch the fire! Get going! Catch the fire! Get a flame under you!" God is saying the same thing to a bunch of y'all tonight.

Now, let me show you something, verse 7: "For God has not given you, given us the spirit of fear." He has not given us the spirit of fear. Now, I'm not even going to ask preachers to get up and say if you've ever been scared in the ministry, because we're not going tell the truth.

Look. Big Bertha scares you. Big Bertha gets up there and comes up in your office and tells you what you're gonna do, and you just cow down and say, "Okay, Bertha." Fear is what's stopping you from using the gift! Fear is what stops us from preaching on certain subjects. Fear is what stops us from expanding the ministry, fear of not being accepted, fear of having to fight with someone in the church! Fear.

Listen. Maybe it's because I'm from the hood, but I was fighting before I got saved. You ought to be able to fight good after you get saved. You're looking for a fight? You can get one! When you fight with the Lord, it's different. The Lord gives you weapons that are not carnal, but mighty for pulling down strongholds by his grace!

Paul brings this up in 2 Timothy, chapter 2, verse 1, and he says to Tim, "Tim, you then, my son, be strong in the grace that is in Christ Jesus." Get a fire! Just be strong, now!

Now, the truth of the matter. Timothy did submit because later on, Paul talks about it. He was the main one, the only one, the number-one assistant that Paul had. He kicked in and God used him in a mighty way.

Now, some of you do not wanna get to heaven, and God's sayin' to you, "I was gonna do this with you. You were gonna do this! You were gonna conquer this! And you done chumped out because you didn't understand God's grace on your life!"

There's enough grace for our inadequacies. Paul was losing his sight, or he had a crippling disease in his hand, for when he wrote the Letter to the Galatians, he had to use a secretary to help him write the letter. And, he prayed to the Lord three times to heal him. Now, what makes this so significant? Paul had the gift of healing, and he couldn't heal himself. The first two times that he prayed to God, God ignored him. I know you know what that feels like. God will do that to you. You can't demand an audience. The third time, in 2 Corinthians 12:9–10, here was God's answer: *"My grace is sufficient for you, for my power is made perfect in weakness."*

Now, one of the things I do in my church, two things I want to suggest to you tonight. Turn to that place in your Bible, underline what the Lord said to Paul, and I want you to understand that it goes for you, too. Know: "My grace is sufficient." And, know what else he tells you? He says, "For my power is made perfect in *your* weakness," in your lack, in what you don't think you can do, what you don't think you don't have, in what you don't think the church has, what you don't think you can do in the community, what you don't think you can do because you failed the last time you did it. You weren't counting on God's grace! He says here, "My grace is sufficient." Not for anybody. Look at it! For you! For you! "For my grace is made perfect in weakness."

So, Paul took this attitude, and I take the same one. *"Therefore, I will boast all the more gladly about my weaknesses, so that Christ's power my rest on me."* That's that grace! That's that grace! *"That is why for Christ's sake I delight in weaknesses."*

A lot of my church members are here tonight. They sit in meetings with me. A big problem comes up. It's like Job, you know. They come to the meeting with these big problems. "You know, the Chaldeans are upon them, and I'm the only one left to tell you!"

We're having a strategy leadership team, and someone comes in, "Your children were dancing and carrying on, and a west wind came, killed them dead. I'm the only one left came to come to tell you." And then he said to me, after they tell me this bad news, "Why are you so calm?" "God's grace is sufficient!"

"But, but, but you got these problems. How are we going to overcome this?"

"I don't know." I don't mind to see you let people think you know everything. I don't know. I get up and tell the whole congregation, "I don't know. Don't even ask me."

See, the other thing I bring up, too, "Have you all been praying for me? That's one of the reasons I don't know. Y'all ain't praying enough." The other thing I tell them to do, just think about it. I've been on planes, trains, buses, going across town helping preachers, helping to restore preachers and their churches.

As a matter of fact, I had a church call me up. I had never met anybody in the church. Somehow, it got out that I help put fallen preachers back into the pulpit after they repent. You don't repent, you stay where you're staying, alright? Don't be messing up my reputation!

So, I tell my congregation, I'm serious about this! Folks don't pray for you, right? I tell the congregation, "Now, listen to me real good. Whatever your weaknesses are, whatever your vices are, whatever your sins are, pray the same thing for the pastor. Pray the same thing for me." And they look just like some of y'all are lookin'. And I'm gonna tell you the same thing I tell them, "I ain't doing all that nasty stuff that y'all are doin'." But at least you cover me with your prayers!"

I need a witness! James, James, James. Come on up here. Tell us about it, James. James: "See, I'm the brother of Jesus. And God opposes the proud, but he gives to grace to the humble. Now, I want you to know I was proud. Me and my brothers, we were proud. I was proud. I ain't talkin' about them, but I was proud because here was Jesus. He never did nothin' wrong. When the rest of us were getting into stuff, he's sitting back being Mr. Goody-Two-Shoes. Then when we wanted to go some place bad or do something, he wouldn't go with us. Then, when we would cuss each other out, he wouldn't cuss. And, then, all of a sudden, he goes out one day and people start talking about him. Crowds start following him. Then folks start telling you, 'You know what your brother did? He raised the dead the other day. He turned water into wine at the first wedding.' And, I just got mad. I got jealous of him, and I just got further and further away from him. But, what happened that turned me around was, he died! He died! He died! And mama was there when he died! Mama came over and told us he died. Mama was going to the gravesite that Sunday morning and said he died. But, up from the grave he arose! And because he arose, he's more than my brother! He's more than a man! He's Jesus! He's my savior, and by his grace, he saved me!"

"Now wait a minute, wait a minute, there's more grace! Because it's not just for salvation. After he saved me, he called me into the ministry! I'm not worthy, I shouldn't be there. I never walked with him. I never ministered with him while he was living and before he was crucified, and he called me to the ministry! That was enough grace!"

"But then, but then, but then, he made me bishop of Jerusalem! I followed Peter! I was running the whole show! I know I'm not worthy! It was by his grace! But, then he gave me more grace! He said, 'I want you to write about it! I want you to write about what you heard me say at home that you didn't believe,' and I wrote the book of James by his grace, by his grace!"

Wait a minute, John, John, come on up here, John! Come on up here, John! "Y'all know about me and my brother! We was from the hood. We were called 'the Sons of Thunder.' If you wanna fight, we fight. You wanna rumble? We rumble. And I kept hearin' about all the other apostles. They kept dying. They kept being martyred, and I wanted to be martyred. I was ready because I'm tough. I'm bad! And you know what God did to me? Put me on an island! All by myself! Ain't nobody to fight! Nobody to preach to! Nobody to teach! No church to deal with! I'm out there in the cold, in the wet, in the dark, and the Lord said to me, 'Are you bad enough?' And I sat down. I was going crazy. Day after day, no assignments. Nothing to do."

"Then, by his grace, he rolled back the heavens. I witnessed heaven, rolled back the curtains. I saw what he's doing now. I saw what he's gonna do next year. I saw what he's doing next century! I saw what he's gonna do in your century! I saw what he's gonna do at the end! I saw that he was the Lamb of God reigning on the throne! I saw what the end is gonna be! Now Daniel, he told him, 'Seal it up! Don't tell it.' But he said, 'Tell it!' That's why I'm here tonight to tell you, it's by his grace! It's by his grace!"

Peter, Peter, Peter! Come on up here, Peter! "Y'all know me, Mr. Foot-in-the-mouth Peter. Yeah, I was emotional, impulsive. A lot of you preachers and pastors out there are like that; you get impulsive, you get emotional, and you make decisions, and you come out with a demand and an edict, and you say things like, even to your kids, you say, 'You ain't gonna drive this bike all summer!' And it is February!"

"It don't do good to make a statement like that to church folk because they hold you to it! You done made some dumb decisions at church. You done some wrong things! Sometime you wanna hide because it didn't work. Some of those sermons you preach, it didn't come to you. God didn't give it to you. You stole it from the preacher you heard the other night. The Holy Ghost didn't go into the pulpit with you so you fell flat."

"But," take it from Peter, "if you just trust the Lord. Let me tell you, I'm just a fisherman. I don't have any formal education. I did not sit at the feet of Gamaliel like Paul. That's why Paul is eloquent. That's why he's theological. I'm just a preacher! But, I want you to know that on the Day of Pentecost, when I stood up and I broke out, I just preached the best I could, and I just trusted Jesus. I preached before, but nothing like this happened! But, then he poured His grace out on me! He poured it on *me*! And by the time I got to the end of the sermon, three thousand joined the church that day! That ain't because I can preach! It's his grace! It's his grace!"

Now let me just tell you. Willie, Willie, Willie, tell them about your story. Listen, listen, listen. On our twenty-fifth, on our thirtieth church anniversary, at the banquet—my father is one of the other two men who helped me start the church forty-four years ago—my father got up and told them people in the church, "When that boy told me he was gonna preach, he didn't tell me." This is like, thirty years later. He [my father] said, "How in the world is he gonna preach? He don't talk!" I'm an introvert. I don't like being out front. Don't like crowds. But by his grace, I can't be myself. I can't be quiet. It's like, it's like fire shut up in my bones!

By his grace, I gotta preach! By his grace, I gotta teach! By his grace, I gotta carry on! Now, listen to me! You don't want to get in a fight with me. I warn people. Listen, you get in a fight with me, I got so much grace in my life, I don't accept white flags. Don't roll out a white flag! I believe in total victory. Somebody's going down, and somebody's got to be the victory. It's by his grace! When I got grace, when I got the victory, I got it all! It is by his grace!

Chapter 16

H. Beecher Hicks Jr. (1943–)

Living Legend 2011

The Preacher

KNOWN AS A "PREACHERS' Preacher" and designated by *Ebony* Magazine in
1993 as one of America's fifteen greatest African American preachers,[1] the
Rev. Dr. H. Beecher Hicks Jr. (1943–) served as the senior pastor of the six-
thousand-member historic Metropolitan Baptist Church in Washington, DC,
and Largo, Maryland. He pastored there from June 1977 until his retirement
in 2014 when he became senior pastor emeritus. He was only the fifth senior
minister in a congregation founded by ten believers in 1864. During his thir-

2. See "15 Greatest Black Preachers."

ty-seven-year pastorate, the church developed one of the country's foremost Christian congregations, distinguished by its fervent worship and prophetic preaching. The church also launched various social service ventures and innovated technologically, launching closed-circuit video worship services, a radio ministry, and a twenty-four-hour prayer line.

Before coming to Metropolitan Baptist in 1977, Dr. Hicks was licensed and ordained by Mount Olivet Baptist Church of Columbus, Ohio, and served as senior pastor at Second Baptist Church, Mumford, New York, Mt. Ararat Baptist Church, Pittsburgh, Pennsylvania, and the Antioch Missionary Baptist Church of Christ in Houston, Texas. On his arrival at Metropolitan Baptist, he built a stellar reputation for various initiatives that cultivated church life and created partnerships within the community.

Within the theological community, he served as distinguished visiting professor at Wesley Theological Seminary and as an adjunct professor at United Theological Seminary, Chicago Theological Seminary, Colgate Rochester Divinity School, and Howard University School of Divinity.

Dr. Hicks is a 1964 honors graduate of the University of Arkansas at Pine Bluff. A recipient of the Rockefeller Protestant Fellowship, he received his theological training at Colgate Rochester Divinity School, where he graduated in May 1967. Selected as one of the original Martin Luther King Fellows at Colgate Rochester in 1972, he also studied at the University of Nigeria, the University of Ghana, and the University of Science and Technology in Kumasi, Ghana. He earned the doctor of ministry in theology degree in 1975. His dissertation, *Images of the Black Preacher: The Man Nobody Knows*, was published by Judson Press in 1977. In 1994, he received the coveted Merrill Fellowship at Harvard University Divinity School and, in 1999, he earned a masters of business administration from George Washington University. In 2008, Morehouse College honored him with an honorary doctor of humane letters degree.

Dr. Hicks has published widely in religious periodicals and is the author of at least seven books. Three of his more popular books include *On Jordan's Stormy Banks*, *My Soul's Been Anchored*, and *Preaching through a Storm*, the third of which is now in its twelfth printing. He also serves as president of H. Beecher Hicks, Jr. Ministries, Inc., a management consulting firm specializing in church leadership development and team building.

He is a native of Baton Rouge, Louisiana, the son of the late Rev. Dr. H. Beecher Hicks Sr. and the late Mrs. Eleanor Frazier Hicks. He is married to the former Elizabeth Harrison of Selma, Alabama. They are the parents of H. Beecher III, the Rev. Ivan Douglas, and Kristin Elizabeth Hicks. Dr. and Mrs. Hicks are also the proud grandparents of three girls, Austynn, Ashley, and Anya; and grandsons Henry IV and Harrison Hicks.

The Sermon

If you have your Bible with you tonight, let me call your attention to the book of the prophet Ezekiel. The book of the prophet Ezekiel, chapter 1, and we'll simply use the first four verses. Now, if you have it, would you stand that we might reverence the word of God? This is what it says:

> Now it came to pass in the thirtieth year, in the fourth month, in the fifth day of the month, as I was among the captives by the River of Chebar, that the heavens were opened, and I saw visions of God. In the fifth day of the month, which was the fifth year of king Jehoiachin's captivity, the word of the LORD came expressly unto Ezekiel the priest, the son of Buzi, in the land of the Chaldeans by the River Chebar; and the hand of the LORD was there upon him. And I looked, and, behold, a whirlwind came out of the north, a great cloud, and a fire enfolding itself, and a brightness was about it, and out of the midst thereof as the color of amber, out of the midst of the fire.

I want to talk tonight for the next few moments on *the whirlwind and the hand.* You may be seated in the presence of God. If the call to preach was significant in the life of anyone at all, it was most assuredly significant in the life of an obscure priest whose name we know was Ezekiel. If the call to preach was at one and the same time both catastrophic and captivating for anyone born of God to preach, then certainly it was so for the son of Buzi, born some six centuries before the birth of our Christ. If the call to preach was a call in a time of social unrest, national turmoil, and personal grief, such was the time of a preacher named Ezekiel, who gained his fame as you know preaching in a cemetery and witnessing to dry bones. And lo, they were very dry.

In every sense of the word, Ezekiel was really an obscure priest, his identity hardly a household name, no one ever expected him to gain his fifteen minutes of fame. The son of a priest, Ezekiel was called to preach in the thirtieth year of life, a widower by the tragic death of his wife, and counted among the exiles who sat along the flowing banks of the Chebar River during King Jehoiachin's captivity. In fact, when he thought of the pain and when he thought of the angst and the anguish of that captivity and of his place among resistant slaves and depressed exiles, Ezekiel says of himself: *"I sat where they sat, and remained astonished for seven days."*

Of course, Ezekiel was far different from the preacher varieties that are grown in these days. There is no doubt that Ezekiel was called. He did not preach simply because he had an urge to preach nor because he was told by some Sunday school teacher that he had a voice for it. Ministry for Ezekiel was no vocational choice nor was it a professional option. He did not preach because his daddy was a deacon or his mama was a missionary.

Quite to the contrary, Ezekiel was called. God called. One day, in the words of the late Peter Marshall, God gave him a tap on the shoulder. One day, in the words of James Weldon Johnson, God pinned his ear to the wisdom post, pinned his eye to the telescope of eternity, turpentined his imagination, and then set his soul on fire. One day, God stepped into the ebb and flow of his life, stopped him in his tracks, reordered his steps, and called him to preach.

In the old church, when they used to line out meter hymns, someone used to sing, *"'Go, preach my gospel,' saith the Lord. 'Bid the whole world my grace receive, you shall be saved that trust my Word, and He condemned who will not believe.'"*

You need to hear me tonight. Ezekiel was called. Yet there is a danger that this matter of the call, this whole matter of preaching and prophecy may be unhealthily romanticized. There is a danger here, danger for those who either seek to be priests or prophets. The danger for the priest is that he spends so much time at the altar in here that he or she has no notion of what's happening on the sidewalk out there. The danger for the prophet is that he spends so much time in the pulpit where he thinks God is, that he never manages to walk among the people where God really is.

So then, consider Ezekiel. So critical and life changing is his call to the prophetic office that he remembers the day and the hour. In fact, for Ezekiel there were two days. The first came in the thirtieth year in the fourth month, in the fifth day of the month, when the heavens opened and he saw visions of God. The second came in the fifth day of the month, which was the fifth year of King Jehoiachin's captivity. That's when the word of the Lord came expressly unto Ezekiel the priest. So, consider Ezekiel—called—no doubt. Expressly called. No doubt. Yet, the call was not about him.

Do not forget that in the whole of this book, which bears his name, ninety-three times Ezekiel is referred to or addressed as "mortal" or, more literally, "son of man," but never is he addressed by his given name. Perhaps that is to suggest to us that the vocation to which we are called is more important than the person who receives it.

Consider Ezekiel, I say. Preacher, prophet though he may be, he remained the subject of personal and pointed ridicule and misunderstanding. Some even suggest that the circumstances of his exile and slavery occasioned in him a kind of imbalance of a psychological sort. You have only to read his resume. His psychological record is clear. He was known for his erratic speech, given to aphasia, known for violent body movement as well as unusual visionary experiences, and subject to curious attacks of paralysis.

Some say he was clairvoyant. Others suggest he was a medium. Still others suggest an ascetic, an epileptic, a cataleptic, a catatonic, a schizophrenic or, at worse, simply a preaching psychotic. Yet, there is danger here for Ezekiel is called. He knows he has been called. God has called him expressly. There is prophetic urgency that courses through his veins. He remembers the day and the hour. He remembers the minute and the moment. Ezekiel had been called.

Follow his writing. In verse 1, Ezekiel has visions of God but, in verse 2, he is in a whirlwind. Something happened. In verse 1, there is no question of his connection with the Eternal. It is clear that God and Ezekiel have this thing going on, but in verse 4, behold, a whirlwind! In verse 1, God shows up in the life of the prophet, in fact, God shows up and shows out. God unlocks the vault of eternity and the heavens open up. Ezekiel's vision is sharpened to enable him to see the things of God. In verse 1, Ezekiel's ministry is in sync with the destiny God has in store for him. All systems are go. All things are in order.

In verse 1, it looked like deliverance. God himself would intervene and rescue his prophet from the painful circumstances of life along the Chebar River but, then in verse 4, out of nowhere, without any word of warning, without advance notice, without forecast from the weather service, Ezekiel says, *"And, behold I looked and behold a whirlwind came out of the North."*

Perhaps mine is merely a vice grip on the obvious, but I believe that life is like that. You believe in God for verse 1, and then you get caught up in verse 4. One minute your life is on the right path, but the next minute it looks like your world is coming to an end. One day it looks like you've got the Midas touch and everything you touch turns to gold, but the next day, in your personal verse 4, everything you touch crumbles and becomes as dust in your hand. I wish I had some helpers in here tonight.

Maybe you already know this. One day it looks like you got it made and the next day the roof has caved in, the bottom has fallen out, your 401(k) has tanked, your stocks are in the trash, your bonds are toast, hope and help are gone, the burden is more than you can bear. You thought you were living in verse 1, but found out you are now a resident of verse 4.

I need you all to stay with me tonight. I need you to do what they used to say in the Mount Olivet Church. I need you to prop me up on every weak and leaning side. So, listen closely. The tragedy of Ezekiel's whirlwind moment and the tragedy of our whirlwind moment is that he never saw it coming. Listen closely now, the tragedy of Ezekiel's whirlwind moment and ours is that he never saw it coming. He knew where he was. He understood his assignment. He was clear about his call, but when it came to the whirlwind factor in his life, he never saw it coming.

If he had just listened to the weather forecast, no doubt he could have prepared himself for the storm, but he never saw it coming. If someone had taken the time to warn him of the gathering and ominous storm off in the distance, he could have run for safe shelter, but he never saw it coming. And I suspect tonight there are a few people in here right now who have seen their world turned upside down, and you never saw it coming.

You thought it was about ministry, but you found out it was a mess. You thought they called you because they wanted you to lead, but in fact, they intend for you to follow, and there, you are dealing with divided deacons and treacherous trustees and the folk who wouldn't say "Amen" if Jesus himself was preaching, and you never—you never saw it coming.

You don't know what to call it, but you do know it's a hurricane of hurt and a twister of tribulation and a tornado of trouble and a monsoon of misery, or it could be just a common, ordinary, garden-variety whirlwind. But, the truth of the matter is that you're in a mess, you're in it right now: the mess in your church, the messy mess in your marriage, that mess in your life. And the inconvenient truth is this: you never saw it coming. Ah, somebody is not listening to me tonight.

Maybe you'll hear me when I tell you my story. I've been on that street. Ministry in order. The congregation nurturing and growing. Everything moving in the right direction. Plans for new beginnings and casting visions all over the place. Architects designing greater works. In the twilight of my life, feeling the presence and the power of God week by week. Standing on the word, preaching under the cross.

But, in a moment, in the twinkling of an eye, I saw myself standing in the vortex of an overwhelming mess called whirlwind. And I never saw it coming. Now then, lest you think that this preaching of mine is some flight of homiletic fancy, let me assure you parenthetically that the whirlwind is real. We are called, but these whirlwinds we face batter us and blow us off course and leave to us what I call the ministry of the unexpected.

We are called, but this recession we face is no accident. This is what I call a God-cident. Whatever we face, whatever stronghold we run against, whatever enemy comes upon us, it did not take God by surprise. It's a God-cident. If we will not seek his face, if we will not turn from our wicked ways, God sends a wind, a ministry of the unexpected, and we call it a whirlwind.

All about us are the signs of a culture caught in chaos. That's a whirlwind. We live in an age when we have not yet decided who should marry whom. We're playing around with a whirlwind if you don't hear me. We live in an age in which we seek to justify the ambivalence of our time with some spurious notion of "don't ask, don't tell."

I'm going to preach what I want to preach. I ain't scared. You can get quiet on me up in here if you want to, but I'm going say it till I sit down. And even the church, even the church, is struggling with its own identity. No longer able to be the conscience of the culture. Her voice now muted in the cacophony of a nation that worships at the altar of corporate narcissism and personal greed.

Is it any wonder that those who preach do so under pressure? Because we are, we are living in a whirlwind. Stay with me a little longer. Here's the pain that's hard to share, the pain of being called to preach in your own whirlwind. See, you can preach in somebody else's whirlwind. You can give sage advice in the instance of someone else's whirlwind but, when it's in your church and your ministry and there's a whirlwind in your house, that's painful to preach. And it occasions some questions. May I share some questions?

A lot of preachers are in here so let me ask you some questions. How does one preach when the swirling winds of destructive change are all about you? How does one preach when the violent, spiraling notion of incalculable, unpredictable, ministry-destroying, life-threatening storms are swirling in your direction? How does one preach when the currents of doubt come upon you, when the whispers in town are all about you, and when the winds of uncertainty assail you and questioning eyebrows are raised in your direction?

You're talking about preaching under pressure this week. How does one preach and, at the same time, bear to hear the truth you've spoken twisted by knaves to make a trap for fools, or watch the things you've given your life to broken and then stoop to build them up with worn-out tools?

How does one preach when one wonders whether or not, by the tragedy of your own temptations or by the gravity of your own sin, you have somehow sown the wind and therefore you now reap the whirlwind?

How does one preach when you come to the work and creaking stairs of your pulpit with a word of comfort for people when what you really need is a word of comfort for yourself?

How does one preach a word of encouragement to those who suffer with him when the prophet himself is discouraged and dejected and depressed?

How does one preach a word of hope and victory when those you had counted on doubt you and desert you and question your ecclesiastical credentials and walk out on you and leave you alone?

How does one preach when one wrestles not against flesh and blood, but against principalities, against powers, against the rulers of wickedness in high places?

How does one dare, how does one have the audacity to claim to be prophetic when one must preach all the while standing in a whirlwind of your own?

Well, happily, there's an answer to my question. The answer to the question, however, is not in chapter 1. It's in chapter 2. In chapter 1, everything in Ezekiel's life is a blur. His visions are poetic and apocalyptic and at one and the same time difficult to comprehend. The prophet sees creatures with four faces and four wings. It's just a blur. The prophet sees wheels, in fact, the wheel in the middle of the wheel. The prophet sees wheels, wheels that can only be understood at best by learned speculation. The prophet sees wheels.

Slaves saw it. The big wheel run by a thief, the little wheel run by the grace of God. Everything. I got wheels. Everything is moving and in the midst of it all, a throne and angels in worship, everything moving. It's a whirlwind round and round, tossed and driven, caught in the cacophony of human experience.

It's a whirlwind and at the end of chapter 1, Ezekiel is on his face, enabled there to hear the voice of the One who spoke. Sometimes, in the unceasing moments of our life, in those moments when all things seem to be moving in a different direction at the same time, in the whirlwind of our lives, in the unbelievable, unimaginable presence of God, the end of it all, it places us in a prayer posture on our face.

Listen, there are some things, brother pastor, that you are not expected to fix for yourself. All you are expected to do is to get on your face. There are some events of life that you are not designed to understand, and all God wants from you is for you to get on your face. There are some problems you cannot solve. You have no control over the whirlwinds of your life, but you can fall on your face, and it is in that position that you learn how to pray. It's when you fall on your face that you learn what it is to say, "Father, I stretch my hand to thee. No other help I know."

And yet, whatever you do, don't stay in chapter 1. Whatever you do, don't stay in chapter 1. Chapter 1 is designed to describe where you are, but chapter 2 is designed to tell you what to do. Chapter 1 is designed to describe your struggle, but chapter 2 is designed to describe your victory.

I do not know just to whom I'm preaching tonight, but I'm on a little assignment here to tell some pastor-preacher that, if it appears that your roof has caved in or that your bottom has dropped out or hope and help are gone and the burden is more than you can bear, and you are standing in the swirling winds of your own personal, private, individualized, custom-made whirlwind, I came to tell somebody: stand on your feet.

Chapter 2, verse 1, *"Son of man, stand on your feet, and I will speak unto thee."* Somebody, help me preach tonight! Here's what it means. We are living in a time of credibility collapse, in times of those who claim to be preachers and pretend to be prophets. We have preachers. We have prophets. We got bishops and archbishops, apostles, and I believe there's a pope running around here somewhere. We got it all, but they are among the self-proclaimed, the self-ordained, the self-anointed, and the self-appointed.

Ah, shucks. I might as well go ahead and mess this thing up. When it comes to this matter of preaching, when it comes to the matter of ministry, it's not about you. Tell your neighbor, "It's not about you." I know you got degrees on your wall, but authentic preaching is never intelligence-induced.

Prophetic preaching is not about what seminary you attended. It's about the Holy Ghost that attends you. And I might as well say it. We got a whole lot of cute preaching going on. Talk about some cute preaching. I'm talking about some memorized preaching, but what we need is some preaching that is filled with fire and baptized by the Spirit of the Living God.

So, the problem is that the world sees the title, but when we fail to produce as we have promised, the collapse of confidence in the prophet necessarily creates a crisis of faith in the God in whose name the prophet supposedly speaks.

Can we bring this thing down front? When will somebody stand up and preach? Listen. Let me tell you something. We are living in a society that has dismissed Jesus. They have marginalized the church and redefined the self as God. Will somebody please stand up and preach? This is an age that has decided that there are no rules, the Bible is irrelevant, faith is for the feebleminded, there are no commandments, and everybody can do whatever they want to do because there is no such thing as sin.

I just wish somebody would stand up and preach. Even now, there are protesters in the streets who wish to reverse the divine order of human relationships just in order to suit themselves, and who required the courts to condone everything, and who expect the church to accept anything.

I just wish somebody would stand up and preach. Is there anybody in here who will stand on the unadulterated word of God? Is there anybody in here that is willing to preach in season and out of season? Is there anybody here that has any concern about the faith once delivered to the saints?

Wherever you are, whoever you are, now is the time to stand up and preach! Listen, it ain't gonna get no better what I am going to say tonight. Somebody help me! This culture will not afford nor will it tolerate those who are supposed to be prophets, but will prefer instead to be counted among the sniveling, teary-eyed, yellow-spined, half-steppin' preachers who will not and who cannot stand up and fight.

We live in an age that demands of their prophets that they are certain of their call, fixed in their faith, sure of their destiny, and unwilling to back down to the contrary winds of this world.

The church is in need of leaders. The people of God need direction. The faithful need a firm and guiding hand, and the pulpit requires trumpets and not flutes. Wherever you are, even if your residence is in the local cemetery, son of man, stand on your feet!

Here's all I'm trying to tell you. At some point in one's ministry, you must make up in your mind to work with what you've got. I know you're talking this week about preaching under pressure. That's a wonderful theme, but I just came by to tell you that the solution is simple. You've got to work with what you've got. At some point in one's ministry, you have to make it up in your mind that if it doesn't get any better, you've got to work with what you've got. We must deal with what's in our face. Whining will not change the whirlwind. Complaining, pouting, and self-pity will not change your circumstance.

However the wind has restructured the contours of your life, maybe you need to preach like Ezekiel and talk to the wind. So, if you're looking for a sermon to preach in your whirlwind, go home this Sunday and preach this: "The Devil is a liar." You looking for a sermon? Go home and preach this: "No weapon formed against me shall prosper." You looking for a sermon to preach? I'll give you a sermon: "The ungodly are not so, but are like the chaff the wind drives away."

However the whirlwind has restructured your life, you need to get on your feet. The task of prophetic ministry requires, however, more than standing on one's feet. In order to survive a whirlwind situation, more is required than simply remaining vertical.

So, I looked again and the word to Ezekiel was not only to stand. A scroll was given to him and, with it, this word: eat this book. Somebody say, "Eat this book." Ah, Ezekiel was given a scroll, sacred writing, the Torah, the word of God, and with it the instructions, "Eat this book."

What we have here symbolically is the necessity to internalize the divine word. It's one thing to carry the word. It's another thing to internalize the word. It's one thing to preach the word, but another thing to absorb the word. "Son of man, eat this book. Digest this book. Consume this book. Devour this book. Life is in this book. Health is in this book. Healing is in this book. Salvation is in this book. Justification is in this book. Son of man, eat this book!" Ezekiel was given a scroll and told to eat the book.

So, when you cannot find your way, eat the book. His word is a lamp unto my feet and a light unto my path. Eat the book. When trouble is in your way, God is our refuge and strength a very present help in a time of trouble. When you don't have what you need, just eat the book. My God shall supply all of your needs according to his riches in glory. Eat the book. When enemies are around you and death is only a moment away, for I reckon that the sufferings of this present time are not to be compared to the glory that shall be revealed in us, eat the book! In the middle of your whirlwind, eat the book! Yea, though I walk through the valley of the shadow of death I will fear no evil, eat the book! Before you go to worship, eat the book! Before you put choir robes on to sing, eat the book! Before you open your Bible, eat the book! Before you put your preaching vestments on, eat the book! Before you proclaim the word of God, eat the book! Somebody say, "Eat the book!" Eat the book!

Now, listen. I just came here today for the purpose of trying to help somebody through their whirlwind situation. For I discovered that I ain't the only one in a whirlwind situation. There's a whole lot of folk out there, don't hold your hand up, don't hold your hand up, but there's a whole lot of folk, don't hold your hand up, it's a whole lot of folk out there facing the same hell I'm catching.

So, I came here to try to help somebody through a whirlwind situation, and this is what you need to know. Ezekiel says, that when he stood on his feet, chapter 2, verse 2, the Spirit—"*the Spirit entered into me.*"

Wait a minute, you didn't understand the implications of that. Ezekiel had been preaching for a long time. He was already a priest. He came from a family of priests. But, in order for him to get preaching instructions, in order for him to be worth his salt, God had to put him in a whirlwind situation. And maybe that's why you are where you are right now because God knows, in order to get you to the place where he needed you to be, he had to put some Spirit in you. Maybe that's why the whirlwind is here.

The whirlwind is not there to destroy the culture. The whirlwind is not there to upset the church. The whirlwind is not there to bring casualties into the kingdom. So, he sends a whirlwind. It could be that God just wants to plow up the soil of your soul. So, he sends a whirlwind in your life. It could be that God just wants to turn over the sedentary elements of your life. So, he sends a whirlwind.

Ezekiel says: "God finally got my attention." Is God trying to get your attention? "God finally got my attention, and that's when the Spirit entered into me." The underlying implication here is that every child of God, every preacher, every prophet does not have the Spirit. Excuse me tonight, but everybody with a robe on, everybody with a collar turned backward, everybody with six agents and a security detail running behind them, everybody with a whole alphabet behind their name does not have the Spirit of God.

I keep trying to tell you that Ezekiel was a priest. Ezekiel came from a family of priests. He had the priesthood in his blood. God has called him. He now has prophetic credentials and, yet, God has to send a whirlwind to get his attention. It is only after that that Ezekiel says, "The Spirit entered into me."

Now, listen, there's something strange going on when the priest has no Spirit. There's something peculiar going on when the preacher-prophet has no Spirit. There's something strange when there is one who claims to represent God and claims to know God and claims to speak for God yet is unacquainted with the Spirit of God.

There's something wrong with a preacher who won't say "Amen" to anybody's preaching but his own. There's something wrong with a preacher that won't shout every once in a while. There's something wrong with a preacher who won't lift up holy hands every now and again. There's something wrong with a preacher who never gives in to the Spirit. There's something wrong with the preacher who, if he does have the Holy Ghost, he doesn't ever show no sign.

Alright, you all can talk back to me now. Is there anybody here who can remember the day and the hour when the Spirit entered your life? I said, Is there anybody here that knows the Spirit of the Living God in your life? Ah, is there anybody that knows that you've got a little fire burning and a little prayer wheel turning and sometimes—Yes! Yes!—sooner or later you ought to have some Spirit in you?

I don't know about you but, even if it takes a whirlwind, I want the Spirit in my life. If I speak in Hebrew, I want God's *Ruach*. If I speak in Greek, I want God's *Pneuma*, but if I speak as they do down at the Great Holiness Pentecostal AME Baptist Church of God in Christ, even if it takes a whirlwind to get it, I want the Holy Ghost in my life.

Wait a minute! Some of y'all are going to understand what I am going to say now, and the rest of y'all, don't worry about it. You'll catch it after a while. Well, see, the trouble I have with the Metropolitan Church is cause I keep on lookin' for a church that is filled with some folk that have been sweetly saved, sanctified, baptized, and filled, and that with a mighty burning fire, and the evidence of the speaking in tongues. I'm looking for it! I dare you to call for it! I dare you to ask God for it!

Have I got another minute? Here's what I want to say to you. Here's what I want to say. Do not, do not, despair your whirlwind! The whirlwind has a message. The whirlwind says that God's getting ready to do something in your life. Do not fear your whirlwind. The whirlwind says that God is up to something. The whirlwind says that God is about to have some change to take place and the Devil is as mad as hell. The whirlwind says your tribulation works patience.

Don't let the whirlwind discourage you. Don't let the whirlwind get you down. Don't let your enemies turn you around. They'll come at you one way, but I declare, they'll leave seven ways. So, I'll tell you what you do. Thank God for your whirlwind. It'll usher in a new relationship with God. Thank God for your storms. It'll get the church on one accord. Thank God for the rumblings in your atmosphere. It will come as a sound from heaven as of a mighty rushing wind.

Thank God for your whirlwind. It'll appear as cloven tongues like as a fire. Thank God for your whirlwind. It'll make you feel strange. It'll make you act funny. It'll make you run when ain't nobody chasing you. It'll make you cry when ain't nobody hurtin' you. So, I'll tell you that you ought to just thank God. Can anybody say, "Thank God? Thank God for my whirlwind! Thank God for my storm! Thank God for my pain! Thank God for my heartache! Thank God for my enemies!" It'll be alright! It'll be alright! It'll be alright in the morning. Weeping shall endure for a night, but joy, joy, joy!

Last thing. Just keep on standing. It'll be alright. I'm outta here. This is what this word said. The word of the Lord came expressly unto Ezekiel the priest, the son of Buzi, in the land of the Chaldeans, by the River Chebar, and the hand of the Lord was upon him.

There may be a whirlwind in my life. But, I've made up my mind that I'm gonna preach because the hand of the Lord is upon me. I can't give in now because the hand of the Lord is upon me. The Spirit of the Lord is upon me, because he has anointed me to preach the gospel to the poor, and the hand of the Lord is upon me. The coals of the altar are on my mouth, and the hand of the Lord is upon me. Necessity is laid upon me, and woe if I preach not the gospel. His hand is upon me.

Is there anybody here that knows beyond a shadow of a doubt, that the hand of the Lord is upon you? Somebody say, "The hand of the Lord is upon me." I feel his hand, the hand of the Lord. With my messed up self, I feel his hand. With my schizoid self, I feel his hand. With my confused self, I feel his hand. He's got a lovely hand, a holding hand, a healing hand, and I'm so glad. Yes, yes! So glad! I feel, I feel, I feel his hand. Yes, I do! Yes, I do! Somebody say yeah! Say yeah!

Chapter 17

Harry S. Wright Sr. (1931–)

Living Legend 2012

The Preacher

THE REV. DR. HARRY S. Wright Sr. (1931–) is highly respected and widely regarded by preachers and theologians around the country. The former pastor of the Shiloh Baptist Church (1954–1967) in his hometown of Bennettsville, South Carolina, and senior pastor emeritus of the historic Cornerstone Baptist Church (1982–2003) of Brooklyn, New York, he has served both church and academy for close to seventy years. Early on in his ministry, he established a brilliant academic record. As a Morehouse College graduate (1953), he distinguished himself as both a Fellow of the Fund for Theological Education and as a Danforth Fellow. He has also received numerous academic honors, graduate degrees, and awards throughout his life including the doctor of ministry degree from Southern Methodist University, Dallas, Texas, in 1976.

As a young minister in rural Bennettsville, South Carolina, Dr. Wright assumed a key leadership role as a vanguard for civil rights. In the 1950s, he was a pioneer for the integration of schools and public facilities and an advocate for voter registration. As pastor at Shiloh Baptist Church (1954–1967), he acted as a community activist working through the church, the NAACP, the Boy Scouts of America, and other key agencies to advance the cause of service to youth, the poor, the elderly, and the disenfranchised, a work initially begun by his parents.

In August 1967, Dr. Wright moved his young family to Dallas, Texas, where he continued the work of community activism as dean of the chapel and chair of the Religion and Philosophy Department at Bishop College. Under his leadership at Bishop, the L. K. Williams Ministers' Institute experienced rapid growth as a nationally renowned institute for the development of clergy. A gifted preacher and thinker, he mentored an extraordinary group of students including the late Rev. Dr. E. K. Bailey and Rev. Drs. Frederick D. Haynes III, Thomas Spann, Stephen J. Thurston, Ralph Douglas West, Melvin Von Wade, and countless others. He is still considered a "shepherd" to dozens who now pastor large congregations around the nation.

Dr. Wright also assumed the role of interim chief executive officer at Bishop College in 1979. He concluded his fifteen-year tenure as president of the college, leading the school through many challenging years of financial crisis. As president, he was successful in mending ties with the U.S. Department of Education, facilitating the recertification process by the Southern Association of Colleges and Schools, generating new funding support and goodwill within the Texas establishment, and restoring college enrollment. His leadership and devotion were later recognized by the United Negro College Fund which, in 1995, bestowed on him its highest honor, the Frederick D. Patterson Award. In 2011, he was honored by Morehouse, his alma mater, with the Candle Award in Religion, which recognizes alumni who bring light into dark places.

During his twenty-one-year tenure as the beloved senior pastor of the historic Cornerstone Baptist Church of Brooklyn, New York (1982–2003), Dr. Wright led successful capital campaigns to fund and complete a five-million-dollar renovation and expansion plan for the Cornerstone physical plant along with the construction of the Sandy F. Ray Senior Housing facility, a one-hundred-and-fifty–unit facility completed in May of 1984 at a cost of $9.5 million dollars. During his tenure, Cornerstone functioned as a major springboard for ministers' licensing and for developing many young leaders.

Dr. Wright's beloved wife, Mrs. Joan Chequeta Wright, passed away in December 2006. They had been married for fifty years. Now retired in his hometown of Bennettsville, South Carolina, he enjoys being a father and grandfather. His daughter, Deborah C. Wright, lives in New York City, as does another Wright daughter, Schawannah J. Wright. Dr. Wright's third daughter, Harryeta Wright Hill, lives in Dallas, Texas. Her son, John Christopher Hill, is a graduate of Jesuit preparatory school in Dallas and is a 2012 graduate of Harvard University. His son, the Rev. Harry S. Wright Jr., resides in Atlanta, Georgia.

The Sermon

There is a verse that, for a number of years, I have wanted to see if I could find some nutrients in it for me, and then some overflow that I might share with others. There are some passages that a younger preacher, if he or she is wise, may want to wait a while and grow up to. And I have not dared to touch this passage until my last birthday. Now, tonight, in this marvelous setting, I want to drop anchor in a marvelous passage of Scripture. One verse, twenty-fifth verse, thirty-seventh psalm. "I once was young." *"Once I was young and now I am old, and I have never seen the righteous forsaken or their children begging bread."*

When I was a youngster, growing up in my hometown, Bennettsville, South Carolina, I used to watch my daddy shave, and I often admired the thick layers that Daddy used on his face to shave. Standing next to him, many times as a little boy, I would dip my finger in the water in the sink and rub my fingers on my face to see if I could see any hair growing on my face. I wanted to shave. Daddy, in great humor, would say to me, "Harry, hold your horses. Keep your pants on. Enjoy your youth. You'll have the rest of your life to be grown." Words of wisdom from Daddy.

I just finished reading a marvelous book by Susan Jacoby entitled *Never Say Die*. It's a marvelous book which she has written as a kind of critique on our culture, and our efforts in our culture to deny aging and dying, and the extent to which we go to hide the elderly. She uses some terms in that book that have stuck with me. For example, she uses over and over again the word "elderly." Elderly. And another word, "well-derly," the elderly who are well. And then "ill-derly." Three wonderful words that have stayed with me. Elderly, well-derly and ill-derly.

Three other wonderful words jumped out in those pages. The "young-old." She talked about the young-old and put some numbers beside the young-old. Then, what she calls the "old," and the "old-old." The young-old, and the old, and the old-old. Sixty-five to seventy-five: she says, yes, the young-old, sixty-five to seventy-five, the young old. Seventy-five to eighty-five: old. Eighty-five and up: old-old.

Here is, here is a marvelous passage from a sage, an Old Testament sage, looking back over the meandering highway over whence he's come, looking through the rearview mirror and drawing some conclusions based on his age and his tenure in walking with God. He says, "I have been young, I used to be young and now I am old, and I have never seen . . ." This is a conclusion that he draws, a conclusion based not on what he's heard or what he's picked up, but what has been raked off of the hot anvils of his own personal experience. From that conclusion, he makes some suggestions, and tonight I want to borrow from him.

This is autobiographical, and I want to borrow from this Old Testament sage two pleas, two entries, if you please, two invitations, two suggestions, and two promises under the umbrella "A Citation from Experience." My subject is, "A Citation from Experience."

There are two pleas and two promises. *"Don't fret over evildoers. Be not disturbed. Fret not thyself because of evildoers nor be thou envious over the workers of iniquity."* Here is a plea from an Old Testament sage looking back through the rearview mirror of his life and, based on his age and his tenure and his walk with God, he makes an invitation to the young. It's an invitation suggesting a plea and a tip. *"Fret not thyself because of evildoers nor be thy envious against the workers of iniquity."* Why? Because they are not going anywhere. God has got their number. Don't get your blood pressure up. Don't get bent out of shape worrying about the wicked.

What a marvelous and calming relief to know that I don't have to take care of the wicked. Four times in forty verses, forty verses in this marvelous thirty-seventh psalm, four times, zoom the camera in on every verse, four times there is a marvelous phrase: "They shall be cut off." They are going to be cut off. You will look for them, but they will no longer be. Though the wicked may grow tall like the cedars of Lebanon, in a little while, you'll pass by and they will no longer be. Don't fret over those who seem to prosper in their own ways.

One of the marvelous things that I love about my dear wife—she is sleeping beneath the sod in Dallas tonight—we were married for fifty years, and she's upstairs, and she won't mind if I say this. One of the things I loved about her. She never pushed me in fifty years of marriage. She never pushed me to keep up with the Jones's. I loved her for a number of reasons, but she never pushed me to keep up with the Jones's.

We spent fifteen years here in Dallas in a nice household on Wooded Acre Drive and Oak Cliff 522, where they could drive, 75241. Nice old house, three bedrooms, two baths, a nice little swimming pool out in the back. It got crowded from time to time. Four kids, my wife, wonderful mother-in-law. But it was a lot in that house: a lot of prayer, a lot of food, wonderful memories. It got crowded. Three bedrooms, two baths, a swimming pool, two dogs, and it got crowded. Time and time again, fifteen years that we were here, we had opportunities to move up and move out.

Mr. and Mrs. H. C. Foster, that's a name that I will never forget, wonderful people here in Dallas. And a number of times Mr. Foster would come by the house to show us portfolios of houses in other places where we could move up and move out. And my wonderful wife would look at those portfolios, and she never pressed me, she never pushed me to move up and move out. Our house got crowded from time to time—three bedrooms, two baths, two dogs. But we decided that we had some priorities for ourselves and for our children. And we decided to stay in a small house with love and prayer and plenty of food rather than move out and move up with no food.

I was coming out of Myrtle Beach, South Carolina, a few weeks ago on Highway 22 that merges into Highway 501, a brand-new four-lane highway. As 22 merges into 501, there are clear signs on the highway asking people to merge into one lane. Slow down. Prepare to merge into 501. A marvelous highway, but it merges into 501. Clear signs, over and over again. Slowing down. No passing. Merging into 501. I noticed as I approached 501, car after car was zipping by me in and out, passing me, going up ahead.

Then, when I got down to the merge, 22 and 501, I noticed some red lights blinking up ahead. I got a little closer. I noticed South Carolina State Trooper cars, and then some tall, strong State Troopers writing tickets. All of those cars that had zipped by me, in and out passing, they were down at that merge, lights blinking and State Troopers writing tickets.

Now, "fret not thyself because of evildoers. Do not be envious of those who seem prosperous in their own ways." They're not going anywhere. Four times this sage says they are going to be cut off. Though they may grow tall like cedars of Lebanon, you will pass by in a little while.

That's verse 10. I like that. In a little while, they will be no more. So, this wise sage looking back over his life takes off the hot anvil of his crystalizing spirit. Don't fret, and don't envy. But, rather, trust in him and take delight in him. Commit your way unto him and wait patiently. Don't fret. Wait. Don't envy. Commit your way unto him.

That's a marvelous plea, and you can do that if your theology is right. If your concept of God is that nothing moves on the checkerboard of human destiny that catches God by surprise, you can, you can wait for him. So, this wise sage, who has lived a long time, he has tenure. He knows God's identity and his character and his glory. He makes a plea and an invitation, a suggestion.

Tonight, I borrow from him. Fret not thyself because of evil. Don't get bent out of shape. Don't get your blood pressure up. The wicked who seem to prosper—what a marvelous, calming relief tonight to know I don't have to take care of the wicked. Say my prayers, go to sleep, and dream and snore. Let him handle the wicked.

I was eating lunch one day, Bishop College with John Mangram, a great longtime friend, a great scholar. We were sharing lunch in the Student Union building one day, and I remember vividly John was eating a piece of porkchop, and I asked John a question. I said, "John, John Mangram, what do you fear most about God?" John finished chewing that piece of porkchop and said, "Harry, the thing I fear most about God, number one, are his eyes. He sees everything. Then, the second thing I fear about God is God's age. He had no birthday, and he'll have no funeral."

You can relax and rest, not fret yourself and not be envious, but as a promise, you will not be forsaken. Don't fret. Trust. Don't envy. Wait patiently. You will dwell in the land and enjoy the fruits of your labor. And, here is a promise, a divine promise this sage whispered to me on my last birthday. I began to see if I could squeeze some nutrients out of this twenty-fifth verse as a wonderful promise, as a divine promise.

God keeps his promises. God's checks don't bounce. There is no rubber in God's checks. The sage says, "You will not be forsaken. You will not be abandoned. You will not be left. He will not throw you under the back wheels under the bus. You will not be dropped." That's a wonderful promise. He doesn't say it doesn't happen. He says, "I've never seen it." He says, "I once was young. Now, I'm old. And I have never seen it."

He won't forsake you. That's a wonderful promise. He won't forsake you. He won't leave you. He won't abandon you. He won't drop you. Now, your insurance company may drop you, and friends may drop you. Family may drop you. Churches may drop you. This sage says, "He won't drop you."

In addition to that, he says your children won't beg. I like that marvelous, two-prong promise. You won't be forsaken. He won't drop you. In addition to that, your children won't beg for bread.

I have a sister who lives next door to me. She doesn't like for me to say she's my oldest sister. I don't say that. I say she's the firstborn. We live next door to each other. We're very close, and often times, we go out for a snack together. She's retired. I'm retired. We go out together. She's very concerned because I carry a little cash in my pocket. She's 100 percent plastic. She pulls out a credit card and everything, and she gets onto me sometimes. "Harry, why do you carry cash in your pocket. That's risky." She always reminds me. Not a whole lot, but a little cash. So, I say to Olive, and I say tonight, "I carry a little cash in my pocket because I stayed broke so long."

Now, in my retirement, where I've got a few dollars that I don't need right now, I like to feel, credit cards are nice, but I like to feel a little cash in my pocket. I know very well that I am the recipient of dividends of prayers of my mother and my father. I've got a couple of dollars that I don't need right now, but when I touch this cash, I'm aware that I'm a recipient of trickled-down dividends, prayers of my mom and dad.

Often times, heaven may cut checks to answer prayers of the righteous and may not post those checks in their time. It waits oftentimes until they fall asleep and sends those checks down to the children and the children's children of the righteous.

Now, my dad died in 1954, at the age of fifty-four. He's been upstairs a long time. Dad wouldn't mind if I say this. When Daddy died, he died broke. Daddy died broke. Wells Fargo, JP Morgan Chase, by their calculations, Daddy died broke. But, in terms of things money can't buy, he was filthy rich. He and Mama, miraculously, somehow sent five children to college. Five went to college. One went to Fisk. One went to Morehouse. One went to Spellman. Two went to North Carolina Central. We picked them clean.

So, tonight, here I am an honoree in Dallas. I am a legend. Not only that, I am a *living* legend. And tonight, I'm drawing trickled-down dividends from the answered prayers of my mom and dad.

"He won't drop me." I like that. I didn't touch this passage until my last birthday. Psalm 90:10: *"The days of our years are threescore years and ten."* And, if you're strong on extra grace, perhaps eighty years. I'm living on extra. I'm not driving on regular. I'm driving on extra. So, tonight, I quote again this sage. "I have been young, I used to be young, but now I'm old. And, I have some recommendations. Fret not thyself 'cause of evildoers. And don't be envious of workers of iniquity. They are not going anywhere. Like green grass grows up in the mornings and in the evening, it withers and is cut down."

God has got our numbers. But rather, trust and commit and wait. You've got a divine promise, and God pays his bills; there is no rubber in his checks. You won't be abandoned. You won't be forsaken. You won't be left alone. I like that word: he won't drop you.

In addition to that, your children won't have to beg. Now this last word, and I'm through. There was a wonderful woman in Shiloh Church.

I grew up in Shiloh Church. My dad came to Shiloh Church in 1927. Dad pastored that church for twenty-five years. There was a wonderful woman. Her name was Ella Kelly. She's been upstairs a long time. She lived on Sunny Bank, and when Daddy was preaching, her antiphonal refrain was, "He will do it!" Ella Kelly never said, "Amen." She never said, "Preach." She didn't say, "Praise him." She simply said, "He will do it." And she turned the volume up on *will*. "He *will* do it."

Daddy died. I succeeded Daddy. Same church. Ella Kelly was sitting over in the corner. When I was trying to preach, she had that same antiphonal refrain: "He *will* do it." I've tried to zoom the camera in and dissect that antiphonal refrain: "He *will* do it." I picked it apart: He *will* do it.

That's what we would call extrapolation. That's a big word. Ella Kelly was extrapolating. That means to draw a futuristic conclusion based on a past experience. Now, Miss Ella Kelly, every Sunday night, she was extrapolating. He *will* do it.

Who, Miss Ella? The Master. Will do what? Make a way. How? I know what he has already done. He will do it! He will make a way. He will open doors for you. He will put food in the refrigerator. He will put wheels in the garage. He will put clothes in your closet. He will put a smile on your face. He will put a star in your sky. He will do it!

"*Jesus! Savior, pilot me over life's tempestuous sea.*" "*Jesus loves me, this I know, for the Bible tells me so.*" "*Jesus paid it all; all to him I owe. Sin had left a crimson stain, he washed it white as snow.*" "*What can make me whole again? Nothing but the blood of Jesus. What can wash me white as snow? Nothing, nothing but the blood of Jesus.*"

Chapter 18

Jasper W. Williams Jr. (1943–)

Living Legend 2013

The Preacher

REV. DR. JASPER W. Williams Jr. (1943–) was born in Memphis, Tennessee, on July 22, 1943, the first of four children born to the Rev. Jasper W. Williams Sr. and Mrs. Alice Stewart Williams. His father was the founder and pastor of the Lane Avenue Baptist Church in Memphis where, as a child, he began his walk with Christ and was nurtured in the Christian faith. When he was only six years old, he preached his first sermon continuing the family legacy of Williams preachers. His grandfather and his uncle were pastor-preachers as was his father. "My father was ridiculed to the utmost because he allowed me to preach," he says. Nonetheless, for more than seventy years, he remained true to his calling.

Dr. Williams Jr. graduated from Melrose High School in Memphis in 1961 where he excelled in academics. He entered Morehouse College, majoring in Sociology with a minor in Religion, graduating in 1972. On Easter Sunday, 1963, as a nineteen-year-old young man, he was invited to preach at the Salem Baptist Church on Martin Street in Atlanta, Georgia. The congregation was so moved that they extended the call to him to become their next pastor. Disrupting his plan to return to his father's church as an associate minister, he accepted the church's call, officially becoming pastor of Salem in November 1963. Under his leadership, the church grew to more than ten thousand and launched a second campus. In addition to exercising his preaching gifts, he also engaged the Atlanta community in social and political activism, and he led the church to launch a Christian education ministry, a welfare assistance program, counseling services, housing for the elderly, a single-parent support system, and many other ministries. Over the years, he has led various pastors' conferences, establishing the Jasper Williams Preaching Network, and he has served as an advisor for numerous community, ecumenical, and service organizations.

Dr. Williams has received numerous awards including the Rev. C. L. Franklin Masters Award and the Martin Luther King Humanitarian Award. He has been honored as a preacher, theologian, and recording artist by the NAACP and the Gospel Music Workshop of America, and has received honorary doctorates of divinity from Miller University and Temple Bible College and Seminary.

He serves as senior pastor emeritus at Salem Bible Church and preaches as part of the regular rotation. He is a devoted father of two sons, both of whom are pastors, Jasper W. Williams III, senior pastor of The Church, in Duluth, Georgia, and Joseph L. Williams, who now serves as senior pastor at Salem Bible Church.

The Sermon

Tonight, I want to invite your attention to a passage of Scripture found in the twenty-second chapter of the book of Genesis. Verses 1 and 2 will establish the setting. I shall read verses 1–2 and then transition to the verse that I am opting to use as the basis of our subject for tonight, verse 1 and 2.

> And it came to pass that God did tempt Abraham and said unto him, "Abraham" and he said, "Behold, here I am" and he said "Take now thy son, thine only son Isaac, whom thou loveth and

get thee into the land of Moriah and offer him there for a burnt
offering upon one of the mountains which I will tell thee of."

That is the setting.

Verse 14 is the basis of our subject tonight. It reads as follows: "*Abra-ham called that place, 'The Lord Will Provide.' And to this day it is said, 'On the mountain of the Lord it will be provided.*'" My subject for tonight, Jehovah Jireh, the Lord will Provide. Jehovah Jireh, the Lord will provide.

Jehovah Jireh is a compound name for God. Whenever God uses a compound name for himself, something is going on. There is some situation they are in the midst of or there is some circumstance they are under. God wants to use that situation and circumstance to unveil himself. In verses 1 and 2, God says, as I have read, "Abraham, I want you to go upon the mountain and worship me and, as is the custom of the day, I want a sacrifice. And today, I want the sacrifice to be your only begotten son whom you love to death. Abraham, I want you to give me that thing that you love the most, that which you are most excited for. That which is your dream come true, I want it. I want you to give it back to me. Abraham, this is a test."

It was a theological test because God told Abraham that he was going to make a great nation of his son Isaac. Yet, when God decrees that Isaac is to be sacrificed, he's still a lad. He's not married, he has no children, and still God turns around and says, "Kill him." I mean it simply does not make any sense at all.

How do you give up the thing that you love the most, that which you have waited the longest for, that very thing that is the basis of your tomor-row? Abraham was facing a test of epic proprotions that has in it major contradictions. Here was a test that did not make sense. Here was a test that seemingly was very, very, very unfair.

Now, God's name is always revealed to us when we are in the midst of our situation of life. When you are going through something, like being up a creek without a paddle, out on a limb and can't get back to the tree trunk, in a catch-22 with your back up against the wall, at a dead end of the road, in the horns of a dilemma, suffering like buffering, damned if you do, damned if you don't. When you are made to ask questions like, "Why this?" or "Why is that?" It's ridiculous. This is absolutely crazy.

In situations like these, God is getting ready to show you something about himself that he has never ever allowed you to see before. Many times, in these kinds of situations, God is getting ready to call your name. So, the question at the heart of this text tonight and this test that Abraham faces, let me give you the test right here, right now, and see how you would fare in this test. When faced with the choice between the blessing and the Blesser, which will you choose? Because sometimes we can fall so in love with the blessing, that it trumps the Blesser.

But, look at how Abraham responds to the test. Look at Abraham's response that he gave the Blesser about killing his blessing. Verse 3: *"And Abraham rose up early in the morning, and saddled his ass, and took two of his young men with him, and Isaac his son, and clave the wood for the burnt offering, and rose up, and went unto the place of which God had told him. Then on the third day Abraham lifted up his eyes, and saw the place afar off. And Abraham said unto his young men, Abide ye here with the ass; and I and the lad will go yonder and worship, and come again to you."* So, Abraham, facing the trial of his life goes up to the mountain. We pick it up now in verse 6: *"And Abraham took the wood of the burnt offering, and laid it upon Isaac his son; and he took the fire in his hand, and a knife; and they went both of them together."* Here it is in verse 7: *"And Isaac spoke unto Abraham his father, and said, My father: and he said, Here am I, my son. And he said, Behold the fire and the wood: but where is the lamb for a burnt offering?"* There it is in verse 8: *"And Abraham said, My son, God will provide himself a lamb for a burnt offering: so they went both of them together."*

This was a situation of life whereby Abraham himself could do nothing about it. In our lives, and most especially as pastors and preachers, when God puts us in these contradictions of being between a rock and a hard place, up a creek without a paddle, sometimes there is absolutely no way out. God does not want us to have any way out or in the small, minute trivial, what I call "tee-night-ship" problems: how to deal with this musician, where to put that deacon, what to do with that auxiliary, that auxiliary. He will let us figure out what to do in situations like that. Yes, but I am talking about when it comes down to him revealing himself when we are at that thick level. Abraham says, "God has got to fix this himself."

I don't know. I got a feeling that there is somebody in this room tonight that is in the midst of something you cannot handle, and you need God to fix it. So here, in verse 8, Abraham is saying to his son Isaac, "Son, you ask me, 'Where is the lamb?' I don't have the answer or the solution. All I see is the contradiction, all I have before me is the problem. I cannot do anything about this, but one thing I do know is God will provide himself a Lamb."

So, in verse 9, they come to the place and Abraham prepares the altar. I'm picking up now in verse 10, *"And Abraham stretched forth his hand, and took the knife to slay his son."* There it is in verse 11: *"And the angel of the Lord called unto him out of heaven, and said, 'Abraham, Abraham': and he said, 'Here am I.' And he said, 'Lay not thine hand upon the lad, neither do thou any thing unto him: for now I know that thou fearest God, seeing thou hast not withheld thy son, thine only son from me.'"*

Abraham says, "Wait a minute, God, what do you mean now you know?" God is saying, "Now I know that you fear me. Now I know that you have a holy awe of me, a reverence for me. You have a divine respect for me because when you took that knife and were getting ready to come down to your son's chest and slit his throat, with that, you showed me that you loved me the Blesser more than you love the blessing." Bottom line: "Now I know that you honor me."

Verse 13: *"And Abraham lifted up his eyes, and looked, and behold behind him a ram caught in a thicket by his horns: and Abraham went and took the ram and offered him up for a burnt offering in the stead of his son. And Abraham called the name of that place Jehovah Jireh: as it is said to this day, In the mount of the Lord it shall be provided."* Here in verse 14, Abraham says: "I found out Jehovah Jireh. In other words, I found out the Lord will provide."

Now, let me pick this verse: the Lord. It goes back to the beginning when it first came on the horizon it was known as YHWH. Nobody could pronounce that name. Even up to this day, nobody has been able to pronounce this all-consonant name of God. Even the old scribes and priests, when translating the Scriptures, when they would write and come to this Holy of Holies name, they would put down their old pen and pick up a brand-new pen and write YHWH. After years and decades had gone by, they inserted the two vowels ("a" and "e"). They spelled the name Yahweh, the Hebrew vernacular, Yahweh, which translates into English as Jehovah. Which is in our bible identified as THE LORD (in all caps). In all caps: THE LORD is Jehovah. Anytime you find a deviation of that, these other names are other names of God, but all caps THE LORD is Jehovah.

Jehovah Jireh—The Lord will provide. Jireh. The root word for Jireh means infinitive "to see." Abraham names this place "The Lord Will Provide" because the word Jireh is translated "provides." So, the question is, "How does the root word 'to see' translate to 'provide'?" There is one word that brings "to see" and "to provide" together, and that is the one word: "provision." "Vision" means to see, but when I say "provision" that means that something has been brought into fruition. If I make provision for you, that means that I saw to it that you were taken care of. I saw a vision. I took care of a need. I saw provision.

God provides based on his pre-vision. Where did you get that from? "Pre-vision" is synonymous to "previews." When you go to the movie, before you see the movie you went there for, they show you the previews of the coming attractions. That's what God is. God provides. *Provideo.* Providence. God goes before us and sees for us before we get there. God provides based on his pre-vision. So, pre-vision leads to provision. It gives us: God will provide! God will provide!

I can stand here and break it all down, give you the etymology of these words one by one. But, when I finish, you will not have a better understanding of what it means. If I tell you right here, right now, what my old grandmama said about it; my grandmother, we called her what you call yours, "Big Mama," had it more correct than anybody anywhere when Big Mama said, "The Lord will make a way. Yes, he will."

Listen, if you please. The real question here is, "What must God see so that he might provide?" What do you mean, Jasper? I mean that you are caught in that contradiction of your life. There you are going through the stuff and the mess that to you is seemingly unfair. What must God see about you so that you can name that place where you are. That you can name the mess that you are in. Your Jehovah Jireh.

When God looked at Abraham and his situation questioned, what did he see? There were a couple of things that God saw about Abraham. First, we see what he saw in verse 3, *"And Abraham rose up early in the morning, and saddled his ass."* It's right there that God saw his immediate obedience. God tells you to do something, to do this, that, and the other, and you got to pray on it. You never prayed before but, "I got to pray on this. I got to think about it. Let me meditate on it, and let me get it all around me and get into it." And there is really nothing you are allowing God to see because you have not yet acted on what he said.

Even though Abraham did not understand God's command, there was a contradiction, a confusion. There was a conflict. There was on his part no room for regret, no compromise. He did not ask any question; he did not strike any deal. He did not say, "God, let me make a bargain." He didn't call the family in: "What do you think? What do you think? What do you think?" The book here says, "He rose early in the morning." If it had been me, I would've slept a lot longer that day. Probably wouldn't have done it till around noon. He showed God obedience.

The next thing that God saw about Abraham was complete obedience. If Abraham had just gotten up and saddled up the donkey and went halfway to Moriah and turned around, he would have boasted and could have bragged like we do. "Well, Lord, you've got to give me credit. At least I got up, and I got dressed, and I saddled up the ass. And I started towards the mountain." God would respond, "I didn't tell you to get up and get dressed. I told you go to the mountain and make a sacrifice—make a sacrifice."

The question in the church of the day: What is the greatest sin in the church today? We're pastors; we're preachers. What is the greatest sin that goes on in the church? Is it a sin of adultery? No, the adultery goes on in our churches; it's not the greatest sin. Fornication is not the greatest sin. All this that we got now with same-sex marriages, that's not the greatest sin. The greatest sin is not the sin of masturbation. None of that—gossiping, infighting—is the greatest sin. What is the greatest sin? The greatest sin is halfway doing what God said do. Halfway. That's our problem. Just think about it. Half of anything isn't enough. Half of church, half a man ain't worth a dime. Half a woman, half a marriage, half a relationship is not enough. Old folk had it right when they sang, "Ninety-nine-and-a-half just won't do." I wish I had a witness up in here.

God was satisfied when he saw that Abraham responded to his command immediately, completely. When God saw that Abraham did not withhold Isaac, then God was satisfied.

Tell me: are you willing to trust God with your Isaac? You say, "What am I talking about?" The thing you love most, the thing you want to release the least, that which you want to hold the tightest to and not let go—that is your Isaac. Guess what. Everybody in here has an Isaac. Lord, keep my mind clear.

God saw that he mattered more to Abraham than Isaac. When God saw that, then God provided. After he saw, then God provided. The question: what does God see about you? You're talking about, "I can't get this. I can't get that." What do you let him see? Oh, he sees the wining and the dining, and the laying and the playing. He sees the huffing and the puffing. He sees the joking and the jesting and the rumping and the bumping and the jumping. He sees all of that. But, when it comes down to the aggrandizement of his kingdom, what does he see?

Touch the person sitting right next to you. "What does God see?" Don't wait for no answer. Listen, if you please, Abraham had to put Isaac on the altar. God said in verse 12: *"Now I know that you fear me."* It was at that moment, that split fraction of a second, that God gave the solution. Verse 13, *"And Abraham lifted up his eyes, and looked, and behold behind him a ram caught in a thicket by his horns."* The key word in verse 13 to me is "caught." That ram was caught. That was Abraham's ram that was caught, caught, caught.

Jasper Williams. They are honoring you as a Living Legend. I don't know why they are honoring you as a Living Legend. You preached your way in and preached your way out of the times. All you talk about is he died on Friday and got up Sunday morning. Time out for that junk.

We got a new kind of preaching. Well, what kind of preaching is that? Prosperity preaching. Prosperity preaching is about confidence, and Cadillac, and cash. You don't know nothing about it, Jasper Williams, cause it's about what I am going to get.

There you are, twenty-second of this month, you'll be seventy years old. Second Sunday next month, I would have been preaching sixty-three years, on the second Sunday in August of this year, at one church for fifty years. "You are out of time; you're out of step."

So, you want some prosperity preaching? Here it is right here. This ram was caught, caught, caught. How is that for prosperity? I don't have to worry about the church you got for thanking God for the church he caught for me. They don't need to be going around wondering about what kind of car you've got. He's caught the one I'm riding around in.

Isn't it amazing that Abraham did not see and did not hear the ram until just at the right time? Tell me, could it be that you've been waiting five and ten years for something that God would have given you in five or ten minutes? And, the only reason why you are still waiting is because you have not completed your sacrifice.

So, what is your Isaac? Is it your habit? Is it your job, your business, your career, your man, your woman? You've got to say: "I don't understand, Lord, how I'm going to make it and how things will work out. I don't know how I'm going to do it, but I have made up my mind that I am going to do what you told me to do. And you are going to have to intervene."

Hear me now. You cannot hold on to Isaac and expect to get Jehovah Jireh. Until you put Isaac on the altar, you cannot have Jehovah Jireh and all that it brings. It is when he sees that he provides. So, if you give him nothing to see, he holds the provisions because he only responds to faith, faith, faith.

Well, when Jehovah Jireh showed up, Abraham got Isaac back. Verse 13: *"And Abraham lifted up his eyes, and looked, and behold behind him a ram caught in a thicket by his horns: and Abraham went and took the ram, and offered him up for a burnt offering in the stead of his son."* Abraham got Isaac back. God gave him Isaac. Plus, what does he get? Verse 15: *"And the angel of the Lord called unto Abraham out of heaven the second time."* He gets God to call him two times. Verse 16: *"By myself have I sworn, saith the Lord, for because thou hast done this thing, and hast not withheld thy son, thine only son: That in blessing I will bless thee, and in multiplying I will multiply thy seed as the stars of the heaven, and as the sand which is upon the sea shore; and thy seed shall possess the gate of his enemies; And in thy seed shall all the nations of the earth be blessed; because thou hast obeyed my voice."* In other words, "Abraham, you ain't seen nothing yet!" Now, listen, I'm through. If you want to hold on to Isaac, God said: "Go on! Keep him. Do with him what you want. That's all you're going to get."

Well, I don't know whether you'll help me close or not, but let's give a praise pause. How about giving God a praise for his word so far? As I leave you tonight, the Jehovah of the Old Testament is really nothing but the Jesus of the New Testament. Because all the Bible you understand is about

Jesus. Jesus is in the Old Testament concealed, and then Jesus, Dr. Gregory, I learned from you, is in the New Testament revealed. When Abraham said, "Son, God will provide himself a lamb," it was at that moment that Abraham makes one of the most prophetic statements in all the Bible. When I read this, he did not say, "God will provide for himself a lamb." But, rather, he said, "God will provide himself a lamb."

All the Bible in the Old Testament is about the saints and prophets of old who saw the Lord in many different forms and many shapes and fashions. While Moses saw the Lord as a burning bush, and Jacob said, "The scepter shall not depart." Now, the Lord given unto his feet until Shiloh comes. Oh, Lord. Daniel said, "I saw him as a stone hued out of a mountain." Oh, Lord. Joseph said, "I saw him as a horse in a valley." Ezekiel said, "I saw him as a wheel." Solomon said, "I saw him as a Rose of Sharon and as a Lily of the Valley." Oh, yes, I did.

They all saw the Lord: Isaiah, Jeremiah, Ezekiel, Daniel, Amos, Obadiah, Jacob, Nahum, Zephaniah, Haggai, Zechariah, and Malachi, they all saw the Lord. But, nobody saw him any better than Abraham because Abraham said, "Son, God will provide himself a lamb." Do you hear what I'm saying?

That's what he did. He looked down the corridors of time and, two thousand years later, saw that same mountain in that same spot when he was getting ready to kill his only Son. God, two thousand years later, led his son to the top of the same mountain. It changed from Mount Moriah to become Mount Calvary. He said, "God will provide himself a lamb." And God did become incarnated in Jesus, and he provided for the world a way to be saved.

All this stuff we are talking about tonight is not worth a thing because the main thing in the end is going to be whether or not your soul has been saved. Don't you see Jesus going up the road called Calvary? Every now and then he will fall down on his knees saying, "Must Jesus bear this cross alone and all the world go free?" I heard him say, "No, there is a cross for everyone, and there is a cross for me." They raised him high and stretched him wide and then dropped him low. Do you hear what I'm saying?

I heard him saying, "If you're afraid I'll fight, you can nail my hands. If you're afraid I'll run, you can spike my feet. If you're afraid I'll talk too much, pierce my side." They laid him down in a hole three feet deep: one for the Father, one for the Son, and one for the Holy Ghost. He stayed there all night. He stayed there all day on Saturday. He stayed there all night, Saturday night. But, early Sunday morning, he got up out of a dusty grave, stepped up on resurrecting ground. All power! All power! He said, "All Power. I've got all power. All power!"

Chapter 19

Melvin Von Wade Sr. (1944–)

Living Legend 2014

The Preacher

Rev. Dr. Melvin Von Wade Sr. (1944–) has served as a minister of the gospel for close to six decades. Born in Memphis, Tennessee, on September 18, 1944, and reared in Omaha, Nebraska, where his father pastored the Salem Missionary Baptist Church, he answered the call to preach at the age of eighteen. He enrolled at Bishop College in Dallas, Texas, where he received his bachelor's degree. He started his graduate theological training at Perkins Theological Seminary in Dallas, Texas, and completed his education at Faith Theological Seminary in Tacoma, Washington, where he received his master of arts and doctor of ministry degrees. Early in his ministry, he served as senior pastor of the Bethlehem Baptist Church in Dallas, Texas (1965–1972) and the Mount Pilgrim Baptist Church in Houston, Texas (1972–1975).

Then, in 1975, Dr. Wade accepted the call to become the senior pastor of Mount Moriah Missionary Baptist Church of Los Angeles, where he served faithfully for forty-two years (1975–2017). During his tenure, Mount Moriah rose to prominence as one of the leading pillar congregations in Los Angeles. The membership grew to over one thousand people with facilities in excess of $7.5 million dollars. It also built a forty-unit senior citizens apartment complex known as the Mount Moriah Senior Villa. During his pastorate, he also spoke at numerous colleges and universities, served as the citywide revival evangelist for over twelve major cities in the United States and traveled in mission to at least seven foreign countries. In June 2013, he was selected to preach the Senior Statesmen's Hour at the renowned Hampton Ministers' Conference at Hampton University. He is an accomplished singer, songwriter, and author. He has published several books, including a series with his father, Dr. J. C. Wade Sr., and his brother, Dr. J. C. Wade Jr., entitled *These Three* (Nashville: R. H. Boyd, 2005).

Over the years, he has also built a stellar reputation as a gifted mentor and spiritual father to ministers. His wisdom and experience allow him to invest in pastors from across the nation. He has sent out nearly fifty sons of the gospel in a ministry that has spanned close to sixty years.

For a time, he served as president of the National Missionary Baptist Convention of America (NMBCA). The crowning point of his presidency was participating in the historic coming together of the four National Baptist Conventions, a feat which had not been accomplished in one hundred years. He has also served as second vice president of the California Missionary Baptist State Convention, board member of the Council of National Black Churches, board member of the Baptist World Alliance, and board member of the Gospel Music Worship of America, Inc. He is a lifetime member of the National Association for the Advancement of Colored People (NAACP), and a lecturer, teacher, and preacher for the E. K. Bailey Expository Preaching Conference. In May 2012, he received the Ecumenical Award at the Los Angeles NAACP Roy Wilkins Fund Gala and, in October 2012, he was inducted into the Hall of Fame at Central High School, his alma mater, in Omaha, Nebraska.

The Sermon

I call your attention to the 116th Psalm. Psalm 116 from the Apologetic Study Bible, this is how it reads: *"I love the Lord because he hath heard my appeal for mercy. Because he has turned his ear to me I will call out to him as long as I live. The ropes of death were wrapped around me. The torments of Sheol overcame me. I encountered trouble and sorrow then I called on the name of Yahweh. Yahweh saved me. The Lord is gracious and righteous. Our God is compassionate. The Lord guards the inexperienced. I was helpless and he saved me."* Verse 8: *"For you, Lord, rescued me from death, my eyes from tears, my feet from stumbling."* Verse 12: *"How can I repay the Lord for all the good he has done for me?"* Verse 17: *"I will offer you a sacrifice of thanksgiving and call on the name of the Lord. I will fulfill my vows to the Lord in the presence of all his people, in the courts of the Lord's house—within you, Jerusalem. Hallelujah!"* You may be seated.[1]

I want talk tonight from this subject: From Death to Deliverance. And I want to encourage you. I know we have this thing where when the sermon is over we run out. I spoke with Pastor Carter because there is a burden on my heart. I don't know if you heard last night where Dr. Smith talked about pastors who have committed suicide. We're going to have a special time for prayer for that. Maybe you're not in that, where you're thinking about suicide, but you may know somebody. So, we're going to have a moment of prayer at the conclusion of the message, alright? So, don't run out. Don't run out. My brother is going to give the prayer, but I want you to be seated, alright?

From Death to Deliverance. This particular psalm is the fourth of what is commonly called the Egyptian Pashael Hallel. "Hallel" means "song or psalm of praise." The psalms that are called Egyptian Pashael Hallels begin with Psalm 113 and conclude with Psalm 118. They begin with who it is that ought to be praising and conclude with who it is *we* ought to be praising.

This psalm is a personal psalm called a pronoun psalm because it has an abundance of personal pronouns. Well, this psalm is shrouded in mystery. The word "mystery" literally means "to close the eyes or mouth" meaning it is impossible to express a mystery in its ordinary language. Paul Tillich says in his *Systematic Theology*, "A mystery in its truest sense is that which remains a mystery even after revelation." There is a mystery about this text. First of all, there is a mystery about who the author is. There are those who believe that it was David. There are those who believe it was Hezekiah. There are those that

---

1. Note: Rev. Dr. Wade thanks Pastor Carter once again for his hospitality and for bestowing the award, thanks those who came to offer support, thanks the Bailey family, and thanks his family.

say this psalm is about Jonah. Then, others say that this Psalm has nothing to do with an individual but it refers to the nation of Israel.

There is a mystery about the author, but then there is a mystery about what it was that God delivered the psalmist from; we don't know whether it was an illness or some great danger. But, it appears that the psalmist is purposely opaque, nebulous, and vague. We don't know exactly what it was. There is mystery about this but, even though there is mystery, it is balanced by the transparent, the known, and there is some clear revelation.

First of all, we look at his dilemma. The psalmist was in a grave situation, and to let us know how grave the situation really was, notice what this writer does. He personifies death and the grave. The word "hell" that he uses there actually is a poetic name for the grave, and what he does is he depicts death and the grave as being hunters. Like hunters, they have tracked him down. Not only have they tracked him down, but they have encircled him. It was such a crisis situation until death and the grave, like hunters, were encircling him and lying in wait with cords in order to entangle him. That's what he means in verse 3, *"The sorrows of death come past me and the pains of hell get hold upon me."* The words "the pains of hell" literally mean "the distress of the grave." The term "distress" has reference to narrow walls closing in on a man. What this says is that there was something in this man's life that was encircling him and enclosing him like hunters closing in on prey, like narrow walls closing in on a man.

I'm convinced that maybe there's somebody here that can relate to this anguishing experience of the psalmist. The reason you can relate is because of the fact that the lot of the psalmist has either been your lot or is your lot. Somebody right here looking at me tonight, you've had to deal with an abundance of anguish, an avalanche of agony, a conglomeration of calamity, a cornucopia of catastrophe, a litany of losses, a maze of misery, a plethora of problems, a series of suffering. You've been surrounded by sorrow. Like the psalmist, you've been stalked and dogged and traced and tracked by that which resembles death and the grave. It is an awful thing when you become the hunted and the prey. It is even more awesome when the hunters are death-and-grave look-alikes. It is an awful thing to be hunted down by death-and-grave look-alikes. For death says, "You are finished," and the grave says, "Your doom is sealed." It means that the whole motive of the hunters is to seal your fate.

But, then, it's worse when the icons of death and the grave are not only dogging your tracks, but they start encircling, surrounding, and closing in on you. They enclose you to the point that they get dangerously close; in fact, they get close enough to get you in bonds. Verse 16 says: *"Thou has loosed my bonds,"* and bonds are chains which means that these death-and-grave look-alikes have gotten so close until they start restricting your movement. Are you with me? What's bad is you're on the run, trying to escape the icons of death and the grave that have you surrounded, encircled, and have shackled you; and, in your quest to get away, you find trouble and sorrow.

What that means is that you are now in a cul-de-sac. What it means, brothers and sisters, is that when you run, you find yourself in a cul-de-sac of despair. Like the children of Israel—there is an uncrossable Red Sea before you, an unscalable mountain on one side, a wilderness you cannot cross on the other side, and Pharaoh's mad mob behind you. Like the Hebrew boys—a lethal inferno in front of you and an arrogant enraged king behind you. Like Daniel—an envious and jealous crowd behind you, a document of doom that cannot be reversed, and a lion's den in front of you. Like John the Baptist—an enraged Herodias behind you and a chopping block in front of you. Like Jesus—sitting with a demagogic, demonic crowd behind you and a cross in front of you.

I tell you. To be in a cul-de-sac means that you are not only surrounded but you are trapped. And I want to ask anybody in here: Have you ever been trapped? I mean hemmed in on every side—no way out, no place to turn, no means to escape, nowhere to run, nowhere to hide, all doors locked, no ray of hope, no sign of deliverance, no silver lining, darkness all around you. Everybody seems to be against you! You're in a cul-de-sac, and you're trapped and everything's fell through. Have you ever been trapped?

Now, brothers and sisters, whenever you reach a cul-de-sac of despair, whenever you find yourself trapped by the icons of death and grave, whenever you are hemmed in by trouble and sorrow, it looks like doom all around you—you don't have to go to pieces. You don't have to come unglued. You don't have to end it all. You don't have to commit suicide, which is nothing but a permanent solution to a temporary problem. You don't have to go to pieces if you are a child of God.

That's what the psalmist means in verse 16 when he says, *"Oh, Lord, truly I am thy servant. I am thy servant and the servant of thy handmaid."* What he's saying is that he was born in a household of faith. Even though he was born in a household of faith, he did not have parasitic religion. He was not a Cheez-Whiz believer or a synthetic saint. And, you do know that Cheez-Whiz is fake, and synthetic is artificial? He knew God for himself.

And the issue is still the same, brothers and sisters. It does not matter whether or not you're born to godly parents. It does not matter if you've been reared in a sanctified home; it's no matter about your sacred pedigree. You don't get saved by proxy. In fact, based upon the unbelief of the brothers of Jesus as well as Judas Iscariot, you don't get to be saved just by being with Jesus. Are y'all with me here?

The real issue is not propinquity or nearness. It's about . . . mystical, reciprocal indwelling; it's about hypostatic union. Well what is all of that? It's about I'm in him and he's in me. Do I have a witness? You can tell when you are in him and he is in you because what happens is you start speaking about the Lord epistemologically, meaning that you talk about him in the first person singular or plural. Well, what do you mean?

Job said, *"I know that my redeemer liveth, and he shall stand at the latter day upon the earth and, though after my skin ware destroyed in this body, yet, in my flesh I will see God whom I see for myself. My eyes shall behold Him and not another."*

You know the blind man, don't you? *"Whether he be a sinner or not I do not know, but one thing I do know is that where I was blind, now I see."*

You know Martha, don't you? Martha said, *"Lord, if thou hast been here my brother would not have died but I know that even now God can and do whatever you ask him."*

You know Paul, don't you? Paul said, *"I know in whom I have believed. And I am persuaded that he is able to keep that which I have committed unto him until that day."*

You know John, don't you? John said, *"We know that we have passed from death until life because we love our brother."*

You know Paul, don't you? Paul said, *"And we know that all things work together for good to them that love God. To them who are the called according to his purpose."* Paul said, *"For we know that if our earthly house of this tabernacle were dissolved I have a building of God. A house not made by human hands, eternal in the heavens."*

You know John, don't you? John said, *"Beloved, are we not the sons of God? And not yet it does not yet appear what we shall be, but we know when he shall appear we shall be like him for we shall see him as he is."*

You know the old folk, don't you? Or maybe some of you young folk don't know but they said, *"I know I am a child of God although I move so slow."* Are y'all with me here? And I might as well give you my testimony. I'm enjoining with that old preacher. Pastor, do you not know it? I heard an old preacher say that the more I encounter God, the less I believe what I preach. And I'm with him. The more I preach, and the more I encounter God, the less I believe what I preach. Now don't get mad. I'm going to say that one more time. The more I preach, and the more I encounter God, the less I believe what I preach. The reason is because I believe preaching is level-two preaching, and I'm not on level two no more.

I'm at level three. I don't preach about what I heard or what I believe. I preach what I know. I know the Lord will make a way somehow. I know the Lord will provide. I know the Lord will make your enemies your footstool. I know the Lord will pay your bills when you ain't even got a dime. I know the Lord!

I've got to the point where I've learned about the Lord like Olivia Pope. You see, I know what the Lord can do. He is never out of options. Are y'all with me? And let me tell you what else I know. I know the Lord has made me a palindrome promise. Anybody know what the word "palindrome" is about? Have you ever looked at the word "level"? If you spell it forward it spells level, if you spell it backwards, it spells level. God made a promise that it does not matter whether you read it forward or backward, it comes out meaning the same.

Well, I see some of you looking at me strange and funny, so I got to prove my point. Jesus said, "I will never leave thee, nor forsake thee." Now that's forward, isn't it? Let me read it backwards, "Thee forsake nor thee leave never will I." *"I see lightning flashing, and I've heard the thunder roll. I felt sin breakers, dashing, trying to conquer my soul. But, I heard the voice of Jesus."*

Look not only at his dilemma, but look at his dialogue. In verse 1, we find the word "supplication." Supplication means earnest prayer for a grace-favor. Now the psalmist asked for a grace-favor and, based upon verse 4, the grace-favor was for deliverance. And looking at the total picture, things have become so critical in the life of the psalmist that he did not have time to engage in useless rhetoric. He did not have time to engage in what my college dean called it, verbal semanticizing. In other words, just running out of words. But, when we look at it, prayer is really getting to the point.

I'm discovering that many people are engaging in unnecessary rhetoric in their prayer. Now, let me tell you about my friend who's gone to be with the Lord; his name is E. K. Bailey, maybe you've heard of him. He said we have too many folk who are praying "tent prayers"—it covers everything but it don't touch nothing. And we've got too many people that spend their time in salutation, and they're trying to identify who God is. And I can hear God saying, "I know who I am. In fact, I know better than you know who I am. What do you want?"

Now, let me tell you what the old black church used to sing. *"Jesus is on the main line. Call him up, and just tell Him what you want."* Based upon the text, brothers and sisters—I know some of you young folk haven't got there yet—but trouble can so surround you, encircle, seize, and shackle you and shackle you until you don't have time to say much when you pray. Do you not know there are times that trouble can cut and broth and truncate and abridge your prayers?

I'll show you what I'm talking about. If you check this prayer, it is only eight words: "O Lord I beseech thee, deliver my soul." David's prayer in Psalm 30 was thirty words. The prayer of the thief on the cross was nine words. The prayer of the disciples at sea was seven words, and the prayer of the ten lepers was six words. When Peter was sinking in the stormy water, his prayer was three words.

Well, brothers and sisters, one of my young female members was standing—her mama is sitting looking at me right now—she was standing in the midst of a drive-by shooting, and her prayers got cut down to six words. Then, I had another member, a man was trying to rape her, and her prayer got cut down to two words. All she could say was, "Oh God." But, I've been in a place where all I could say was "mercy."

Then, I discovered that, some of us, my little grandbaby is sitting right over there, and one day, Sydney cut herself. Because she was a baby, she was not able to articulate her pain and all she could do was cry. I discovered that, just like her, our pain and our hurt is beyond articulation and sometimes trouble can have you until all you can do is cry.

But, thank God. Y'all ought to thank God tonight. What are you thanking God for? We've got a prayer partner in the Holy Ghost, the divine decoder who decodes our cries, translates our tears, articulates the message of our pain. I've heard and I've carried cries to God, and that's why the old people said, "I love the Lord. He heard my cry and pitied every groan."

Brothers and sisters, I want you to notice something; this is really something here. Notice to whom he addresses his prayer. He addresses his prayer to the Lord who is gracious, righteous, and merciful. That means he is talking to the paradoxical God. I learned watching the O. J. Simpson trial the expression *prima facie*. That word, that expression, it means indisputable evidence so y'all are making me go there.

Now, understand something. Righteousness is straight and, if it bends, it ain't righteousness. Grace bends, and if grace does not bend, it ain't grace. Mercy bends, and if mercy don't bend, it ain't mercy. So, we serve a God who is both straight and bending. Are y'all with me?

Brothers and sisters, look at what this says, for we serve a God who is able. He is able to mysteriously and sovereignly bestow his bending grace and mercy on us and deliver us without compromising his unbending righteousness. He can bend and forgive us of our sins, cancel our guilt, get us out of our sinful dilemmas by grace and mercy without bending his righteousness or condoning our sin. Do I have a witness?

But, then, brothers and sisters, I want you to notice something else. This God who is gracious, righteous and merciful, he inclines. There you go again. I just knew that somebody would have got up and run around the room. Well, ok. Let me tell you what happens. The word "incline" means to lean forward to catch a sound that's otherwise too faint to be heard.

In December of 1986, my father was stricken with a heart attack and had a triple bypass surgery. During the surgery, he had a stroke, and we were told it would leave him a vegetable. That's my mother. You can ask her. While my daddy was in the hospital, my mother-in-law, who was visiting with us, got sick. They placed her in the same hospital as my father, and guess what that did? That took some of my praying strength. Now, my sister Aretha was visiting from St. Louis. She took sick, and we had to place her in that same hospital. That took some more of my strength. Then, my brother James came to help see about Daddy, and I found out he was battling a heart condition called angina. That took some more of my strength.

While dealing with these issues, did you not know there was a demagogic crowd who led a coup in order to put me out? My enemies were so adamantly sure that I was gone, until one deacon went to Dr. E. V. Hill, asking his help in order to get a new pastor. That took some more of my strength. My enemies, seeking to shatter my credibility, placed my name in the news on the front page for racketeering, and then served me with injunction papers while I was preaching at the LA citywide revival. Then, one chairman of the trustees was so brazen, he came to my office and told me, "Why don't you just leave now with a little respect." That took some more of my strength to pray.

As a result of my enemies trying to put me out, I was taken to court twice. Plus, I had taken an all-day deposition. That took some more of my strength. Well, my baby daughter who sits here loves her daddy and couldn't make sense of all this evil attack that was on her father. She got mysteriously sick, and we placed her in the same hospital as my father, my mother-in-law, and my sister. That took some more of my strength. My strength was so sapped until prayer time, I couldn't cry aloud. But, thank God I serve a God that would lean forward and bow down.

He could hear my faintest. I'm sorry, but he will. Do I have a witness? Let me tell you. Dr. Joel Gregory said that everybody ought to have an icon statement that will follow you and live longer than you do. Well, I had an old deacon by the name of Fanez Graham. Fanez Graham, he didn't have good English, but he had great theology. We used to laugh at him thinking he was really ignorant. But, after he died, we discovered that we were the ignorant ones. Every Monday night, guess what he would say? "Show me what prayer can't do. Can't be dead." I've discovered that's bad English, but it's good theology. Look at somebody and say, "What prayer can't do?"

Look at his deliverance. The latter part of verse 6 says I was brought low, and he helped me. The latter part of verse 8 says, "For thou hast delivered my soul from death, my eyes from tears, and my feet from falling." The psalmist says he was brought low so many times; he was weak and feeble and depleted of his strength. But even when he was reduced in person and strength, the Bible says that the Lord helped him. The help he got from the Lord was bountiful help.

Now, to understand how bountiful the help that God gave him is, I learned this word; it's called "juxtaposition." It means to place something side by side for the expressed purpose of comparison. So, I want to compare. Look at what the prayer of the psalmist was. He said, "Lord, deliver my soul." That's all he asked. But, guess what happened? God it says he delivered his soul, he delivered his eyes, and he delivered his feet. Now, he didn't ask for all three of them. He just simply asked for the deliverance of his soul. Now, what that says is that God has a way of giving you more than what you ask for. First of all, God specializes in winning. God specializes in winning.

Well, let me take you to my grandbaby Sydney. Sydney and I were at a basketball game, and the home team won. Now, when the home team won, all this loud music starts. So, I said, "Syd," that's what I call her. "Who is that?"

She said, "That's DJ Khaled."

I said, "OK, well, what is he saying?" You know, because sometimes music can be so loud you can't tell what they're saying.

She said, "All I do is win."

I said, "You know what? That's God's theme song."

Well, there sits Linda. Linda and some young folk of the church decided they were going to bring me, Pastor Claybon, into the twenty-first century, so they decided they were going to get me an iPad. I discovered on the iPad that there is what is called Safari. With Safari, you can search for some stuff, so I decided I was going to search for the lyrics of DJ Khaled's song. So, I did the search and, in my search—Pastor Carter—guess what I found out? Ludacris put some words in it, and guess what his line is? "Because I've never lost."

Now, I've discovered that God says, "I can up you one. Not only do I never lose, I always win. Not only have I never lost, I will never because I always win. Even when it looks like I'm losing, I still win."

Come on with me to Friday. The Bible says that they took Jesus and nailed him on a cross. Now, when they nailed him to the cross, the devil thought that he was losing. When they got him in the grave, they thought he was losing. But, early Sunday morning, they discovered that God's theme song is "All I Do is Win." Not only does he win, but he gives you more than what you ask for. Are y'all with me?

Let me give you this little story. There was a little girl in Sunday school, and the lesson was about love and kindness. So, the teacher asked the students, "Do you know the difference between kindness and lovingkindness?"

This little girl raised her hand, all excited, and the teacher said, "Alright, baby, what is the difference between kindness and lovingkindness?"

The little girl said, "Well, kindness is when you ask your mother for some toast and she gives you toast. Lovingkindness is when you ask your mother for some toast, and she gives you toast with some jelly on it."

Brothers and sisters, I've discovered something. God will give you some blessings. Right now, we're in a building; it's with some jelly on it. Do I have a witness? Brothers and sisters, let me tell you what Deacon Fanez Graham said in his prayer. Listen to what he said. He said, "Lord, I thank you for my needs and for my don't-needs." All of us got some don't-needs.

When you look in the Bible, that's what David meant when he said, "Thou anointest my head with oil, my cup runneth over. Blessed be the Lord who daily loadeth us with benefits."

Malachi says, "He will open the windows of heaven and pour out a blessing that you won't have room enough to receive." Jesus said, "Give and it shall be given unto you." Good measure pressed down, shaken together and running over.

Well, brothers and sisters, the Lord gave this man full deliverance. God specializes in winning. God specializes in giving you more than you can ask for. But, now the final thing is his doxology.

Look at this man, this psalmist, as he begins to interrogate himself. He says, "What shall I render unto the Lord for all his benefits toward me?" He says, "I cannot repay God for delivering my soul, my eyes, and my feet. I cannot repay God for loosing my bonds." He said, "But even though I cannot repay God, there's at least two things I can do. I can render him obedience, and then I can render him praise and thanksgiving."

Brothers and sisters, I've read Psalms 50:15, and God says, "Call upon me in the day of trouble. I will deliver thee and thou shall glorify me." I can relate to what the psalmist is saying because I cannot repay God for saving my soul. I cannot repay God for choosing me. I can't repay God for setting me free. I cannot repay God for writing my name in the Lamb's Book of Life. I cannot repay God for redeeming me and justifying me. I cannot repay God for making me a brand-new creature. I cannot repay God for healing me of leukemia. I cannot repay God for a successful bone marrow transplant. I cannot repay God for winning and delivering and making a way and bringing me through.

But, I tell you what I can do. I can love God with all my heart, my mind, soul, and strength. I can follow Jesus Christ. I can be filled with the Spirit, I can love my neighbor as myself. I can walk like Jesus walked. I can keep his testimony. I can trust in him. I can bring him my first fruits. I can wait on him. I can put my faith in him. I can lean on him. I can deny me in favor of him. I can be a witness for him. I can lift up the name of Jesus. I can be one with my brother. I can love my neighbor. I can turn the other cheek. I can walk the second mile. I can feed the hungry. I can clothe the naked. I can give drink to the thirsty. I can praise him in spirit and in truth. I can bless him in the beauty of holiness. I can praise him with my whole heart. I can bless him while I live. I can praise him in the sanctuary. I can bless him in the convocation. I can put on the garment of praise. I can bless with a great shout. I can fill my mouth with praise. I can bless, saying "Amen." I can praise him by saying "Hallelujah." I can bless him by making a joyful noise. I can bless his holy name. I can praise him with all of my heart.

I—I. I—I will bless the Lord at all times. His praise shall continually be in my mouth. My soul shall make a boast in the Lord. The humble shall hear, bear up and be glad!

Oh, magnify! Magnify! Magnify! Is there anybody here that don't mind magnifying, who'll lift up the name of Jesus? Is there anybody here who can say that he's worthy! Because he's worthy! I said, "He's worthy!" Is there anybody here that can say he's worthy? Hey. He's worthy! Every time I get a chance, I try to praise him. Bless the Lord, O my soul, and all that's within me bless, bless, bless!

Go bless him because, one Friday he died, they put him in the grave. I don't mean no harm, but the old preacher used to say you haven't really preached until you say, "Early, early, early." Hey, hey, hey. Yeah. I don't mean no harm but, if my brother was up here, he'd say, "I know he's alright. I know he's alright." The old preacher said, "Ain't he alright? Ain't he alright?" How do you know he's alright? I tried him! Hey, can you say yes? Yes, yes, yeah, yes!! When I think of the goodness of Jesus and all that he has done for me, I get a classic case of I can't help myself. Hey! Hallelujah! Hallelujah!

You wonder why I carry on like I do? You don't know like I know what the Lord has done for me. You don't know like I know how many times he made a way. You don't know like I know how many times he paid my bills, and I didn't have a dime. Hey! You can't stop me. You can't even block me. I know. Hey!

Chapter 20

Clay Evans (1925–2019)

Living Legend 2015

The Preacher

REV. DR. CLAY EVANS (1925–2019) was the founder of Fellowship Missionary Baptist Church, where he served as pastor for fifty years. Over the course of a ministry that spanned close to seven decades, he became a pastor to pastors around Chicago and across the nation, thus earning him the affectionate nickname, "the Godfather." Even after his retirement as pastor at Fellowship in 2000, he continued to preach at funerals in and around Chicago and in churches throughout the United States. A mentor and spiritual father to so many, he helped launch the ministries of close to one hundred people. A friend and ally to Dr. Martin Luther King Jr., he served as an influential leader in the Civil Rights movement in the 1960s. In addition to his exemplary civil rights advocacy work, especially as it pertained to exposing unjust living conditions that poor Blacks faced in Chicago, he also built a national reputation as a renowned choirmaster and gospel singer.

Born a sickly child in 1925 to sharecropping parents in Brownsville, Tennessee, Dr. Evans came into the world the fourth of nine children. He did not speak until he was two and a half years old—his parents feared that he could *not* talk—and the nine siblings shared one bed with some sleeping on the floor when the children got older. The whole family engaged in the exhaustive work of sharecropping. The kids could only attend school, a one-room schoolhouse, three months a year, December to February, during the off-season from farming.[1]

At the age of twenty, Dr. Evans moved to Chicago with dreams of becoming a mortician. "I wanted to be successful," he said, "and the only black person who was successful in town [Brownsville] was an undertaker."[2] Unable to find work in Chicago, he got a job working a conveyer belt at a pickle factory. He also attended and eventually became a member of the Tabernacle Missionary Baptist Church, the same church where his powerful and unique singing voice was discovered. In 1946, he married a fellow choir member, Mrs. Lutha Mae Hollingshed, the woman to whom he remained married for seventy-four years. Together, they helped to found and organize the Fellowship Missionary Baptist Church (originally called the Hickory Grove Baptist Church) on September 17, 1950, in a rented chapel at a funeral home with less than ten people. The Evanses would also become the proud parents to six children and the proud grandparents and great-grandparents to many more.

Unfortunately, Dr. Evans was not able to travel to Dallas to receive his Living Legend award in 2015, the year that he was honored, on account of his ongoing health challenges. However, even in the years leading up to his death, he would preach from time to time around Chicago. He preached the sermon that is preserved in this chapter to the people at Fellowship Baptist, his home congregation, just a few months before his ninetieth birthday. As a token of

1. In his description of Evans's childhood years growing up on the farm, Zach Mills writes, "The sharecropper's life was painfully monotonous. The Evans family arose each day before sunrise, usually shortly after 4:00 am. They ate breakfast. Then they walked to the fields to work. The backbreaking labor was unceasing. The sun was unrelenting. The Evans family labored non-stop except for brief rests during dinner and supper. The women got even less rest than the men. The Evans women left the fields early to prepare the family meals." See Mills, *The Last Blues Preacher*, 12.

2. Mills, *The Last Blues Preacher*, 49.

kindness, the leaders at Fellowship sent the audio version of this message so that it could be included as a chapter in this volume. Dr. Evans preached this sermon, titled "Jesus Is Passing By," on February 1, 2015.

The Sermon

Take your Bibles—I know everybody has Bibles—and wave your Bibles at me. Not your apparatus. I know it has the word of God in it but I like Bibles. Repeat: *Bible-carrying, Bible-reading, Bible-believing, Bible-practicing makes a strong Christian, and strong Christians make a strong church.*

I have to say this to you. In order to make a strong church, not only do you need strong preachers in the pulpit, and Fellowship sure enough has one [Dr. Jenkins], the pulpit is well taken care of; he needs some strong members in the pews. So, the pulpit and the pews go together. If you keep that, God will be with you.

Strong preacher, teacher, leader in the pulpit. Strong members in the church, in the pew. Don't talk your preacher down. Talk him up. Support him. If you can't say something good, keep your mouth closed. You may be seated.[3]

I talked a little bit on this the other day, and I want to preach it to you today. Matthew 20:29–34, starting with the twenty-ninth verse.

> And as they departed from Jericho, a great multitude followed him. And, behold, two blind men sitting by the way side, when they heard that Jesus passed by, cried out, saying, "Have mercy on us, O Lord, thou son of David." And the multitude rebuked them, because they should hold their peace: but they cried the more, saying, "Have mercy on us, O Lord, thou son of David." And Jesus stood still, and called them, and said, "What will ye that I shall do unto you?" They say unto him, "Lord, that our eyes may be opened." So Jesus had compassion on them, and touched their eyes: and immediately their eyes received sight, and they followed him.

"Lord, that I might receive my sight." I wish that would be our prayer, every one of us. "Reverend, I've got sight." You're still blind! Even if your sight is 20/20 physically, you're still blind.

---

3. Dr. Evans sang "Amazing Grace" just before the introduction to this sermon in which he invites everyone to take their Bibles out and wave them at him. Everyone had been standing during the song and during his opening remarks so he invited them to sit at this point in the sermon.

How many of you wear glasses here today? The majority of us are wearing glasses or contact lenses or something. For sight is very, very important. It's such a problem when you can't see.

Helen Keller was born blind and unable to talk. What a handicap! You don't know what you're missing when you can't see. Fellowship, you don't really know it, I don't think, but it fits into my sermon.

I'm blind in one eye. It's been like that for twenty-five or thirty years. I'm not going to tell you which one because, if you knew which one, you'd sneak up on me on the blind side. I ain't going to give you that advantage. One of my eyes has been replaced as a cosmetic. You can't tell which one it is. People who have known me for a long time will ask me, "Which eye are you blind in?" I ain't going to tell you. But when you're born blind . . .

Now, in this passage of Scripture, there are a few things I want you to know. Number one. It took place on the Jericho Road. The Jericho Road was a bad road. Nothing wrong with the road. Some of the people were bad on it. Just like on your street where you live, some people are bad on the Jericho Road.

Now, the man, they robbed him, beat him up, stripped him, left him half dead. You've heard that story. The priest passed him. The Levite passed him up, but the Samaritan picked him up. Your street can be called a Jericho Road. My street. You don't have to be bad. You can do some good.

Here in Matthew, it says there were two blind men. Mark talks about one blind man . . . . Jesus and his disciples were on the Jericho Road on the way from Jericho to Jerusalem. That's the road you took from Jerusalem to Jericho. Here are two men, blind. It's like the song. If you are blind, you don't have to be deaf if you can hear. So, he heard a crowd coming down the road, and he asked somebody, "What's all that about? Who are they?" They said to him, "Jesus! Wherever you live, Jesus makes the difference."

I don't care where you live or what you're doing. If Jesus is there, everything's going to be alright. They said, "Jesus is passing." I want to say to somebody who is here. You've got a need, but Jesus is passing. You don't have to leave like you came, Jesus is passing down your road. That's number one. He passed by a while ago and some of you don't even recognize, when others were singing, that was your message for the day. Jesus is passing. That was the one thing on my mind.

Whatever your situation is, cry out whatever your needs are. These blind men had a need. You may be sitting there looking and smelling good but you have a need. Recognize his passing. Jesus of Nazareth, Jesus, Son of David, he's already been by before I got up. Some of you recognized him. Some of you didn't.

This man said, "Have mercy on me!" I don't care how good you've been. You need mercy. There are two columns. There's the mercy column, and there's the mid column. The mid column thinks you're alright where you are. "I deserve this. God ought to be good to me." Get out of that column! You ain't all that good!

But, the more you begin to cry out, prayer changes things. There were those in the crowd, you've always got some of them, who said, "Be quiet. You're too loud. You're too emotional." But, the more people tell you to be quiet, the louder you ought to cry.

If you have faith in God, I don't care what your situation is, Jesus can change it. These blind men felt, "If I can get to Jesus . . ." Jesus says to cast your cares upon him because he can . . . whatever it is. You can be poor, blind beggar, all of that. Some people won't help you, but he will. The Bible says that the blind men cried out even though the crowd tried to discourage them. Ever had anyone try to discourage you? You're trying to get ahead and they are so negative? That's why we sing, *"Pass me not, O gentle Savior, hear my humble cry. While on others thou art calling, do not pass me by."* Encourage somebody again and tell them, "Ask Jesus. Don't pass you by."

Look at that thirty-second verse. Jesus did what? He stood still! He was passing by. Not only is he passing by this morning, he passes by all the time. If you have a need, the Bible says in the thirty-second verse, "He stood still." You might not believe it, but he's standing right in front of you now. Tell him what you want. Now, don't be so general and say, "Lord, bless me." You have a specific need, and they had a specific need. "I want to receive my sight. I need sight!"

I want to share with you for the next four or five minutes that we are blind, physically blind. I told you about that I only have one eye. They have what they call seeing eye dogs that navigate you. Well, when you have a dog, spell it backwards. God will see you through. He stood still, and you get the resources later.

But, they cried out, "I want to see." I used to get up and say, "Just bless me!" Tell the Lord specifically what you want, if you've got a need, whatever the need might be. I said to them the other day that you've got to have sight.

My brother Joe and I were going back down to Tennessee. On a day like today, I was driving where you could hardly see. And, he said to me—now this is the secret some of you know. Some of you know my nickname, that they call me Pete. Don't *you* call me Pete?—so, he said to me, "Pete, why you driving so slow?" I said, "Man, I can't see." He said, "Man, if you can't see, you're driving too fast." But this reminds me that even though you may have physical sight, there are some of us who are mentally blind. Blind!

Some of you talk to your children until you turn blue, or whatever color you turn. You'll talk to a friend, and they'll tell you, "I can't see, mentally, I can't comprehend. Mentally, I can't see you." Your mother-in-law taught me a lesson. Many times, when people don't agree with you, they're not being mean. They're green. They just can't see it! I've had to say that about some things, some things you just don't wanna see. Remember that it's sight, insight, hindsight, no sight.

There was an insect that we call the lightning bug. What is strange to me about a lightning bug is that they always light up behind after they pass something. I said, "What good is a lightning bug? It's lighting up after it passes the object," and some of us don't see a thing, like a lighting bug, until it's too late.

If you had seen what you were getting into when you got married . . . too late! Too late! Too late! Have you ever did that? You make your choice, but you make it too late to do you any good.

Lord, give me sight! Some foresight. Insight. Let me see! Thank you for physical sight, but you can have all of that that you want. If you ain't got no insight, you're in terrible condition. So, you're got to be just like it talks about in one of the Gospels. Bartimaeus. Lord, give me some physical sight. Give me some mental sight.

Now, sometimes our sight is distorted. We don't have good sight. Right sight. There's a story I once read, or somebody told me, that there were three blind men. They touched an elephant and they said, "What is an elephant like?" One of them said it was like a wall. They touched his side. The other one touched his leg. "Like a tree," he said. Another touched his tail, "Like a rope." Many of us have a distorted vision of God. Let me go!

But, I want to relate to you. Being physically blind is bad, mentally blind is bad, but spiritual blindness is the worst kind of blindness. To be spiritually blind, so blind that you can't accept Jesus, blind, you come to church, but you're still blind. I ain't gonna give my money. I'm not gonna tithe. We can't trust God with all of our heart and lean not on our own understanding. But, in all of our ways acknowledge him. Will he guide you? Will he direct you? He shall. He will. He will. He will. I wanna leave that with somebody.

You've got some problem right now, but you are spiritually blind. It's no secret what God can do. What he's done for others, trust him and never doubt, he will bring you out. "Lord, I'm blind!" Here's what the Lord can really do.

Some of you don't know how to really trust God with your money, with your tithe. If you can give your tithe from your heart, he will bless you and keep you. Can I have a witness?

Is there anybody here that knows the Lord will fight your battle? He will bring you through? That even in the storm of life, he can speak to your storm. Tell somebody, "He will speak through your storm!"

Some of you got a distorted view. You don't believe God is saying today what he started yesterday. How many of you believe he can? How many of you believe that he can open doors? How many of you believe he can put food on your table? How many of you really believe that he can take that enemy and make him a friend?

Can he do it? Thank you, Lord! The Bible said that when they pleaded with him and begged with him, that he said, "Have mercy." Then, the blind men said, "Open my eyes, that I can see." Then, he touched the eye and it came open. Now, when the Lord opens you up, you understand him. Hallelujah!

When the Lord opens up whatever you're doing and makes a way for you, you ought to follow him. Can I get a witness? Follow him! Say, "Where the Lord leads me, I will follow." God bless you!

Let me just tell you this. Someone really needs to know that the Lord is passing you by. Passing your way. He's passing right down your pew. And if you call him, he will stop right in front of you. He'll say, "What do you want? What do you need?" And if you tell him, he will answer you. He will!

Chapter 21

Lacy Kirk (L. K.) Curry (1926–)

Living Legend 2016

The Preacher

Rev. Dr. Lacy Kirk (L. K.) Curry (1926–) was born on October 1, 1926, the seventh of eight children born to Dr. Milton King (M. K.) Curry Sr. and Mrs. Lena Clabon Curry in Wichita, Texas. In 1934, when he was eight years old, the family moved from their home in Amarillo, Texas, to Omaha, Nebraska. After graduating from high school, Dr. Curry attended Denver University (Denver, Colorado) where he received his bachelor of arts degree, Berkeley Baptist Divinity School (Berkeley, California) where he received his master of divinity degree, and Northern Baptist Seminary

(Lombard, Illinois) where he received his doctor of divinity degree. He has also received numerous honorary degrees such as the doctor of humane letters from the Tennessee School of Religion (Memphis, Tennessee), the doctor of divinity from Arkansas Baptist College (Little Rock, Arkansas), and the doctor of humane letters from Georgetown College (Georgetown, Kentucky). As a young adult, he pastored several churches including St. John Baptist Church, Tulare, California (four years), New Zion Baptist Church, Ogden, Utah (four years), and Mt. Calvary Baptist Church, Chicago, Illinois (five years).

In January of 1973, he organized the Emmanuel Baptist Church, where he pastored for thirty years (1973–2003). With ten charter members, the congregation grew in its first year to over seven hundred members. Initially, the church met at Morgan Park High School in Chicago but, after its rapid growth, Pastor Curry led the church to build a sanctuary at its present location at 8301 South Damen Avenue, Chicago, Illinois. The church also launched Emmanuel Christian Academy as a leadership training center for children in the Chicago area. Upon his retirement after thirty years of service, he remained in Chicago and received the designation of senior pastor emeritus.

In addition to his preaching and pastoral leadership, Dr. Curry has held numerous leadership roles at the local, regional, and national levels, including his roles as a board member of the Northern Baptist Seminary, a board member of the National Baptist Convention, Inc., Church Extension chairman, treasurer of the Salem District Association (Chicago, Illinois), president of the Interdenominational Ministerial Alliance (Chicago, Illinois), chaplain of the Cook County Department of Correction (Chicago, Illinois), and treasurer of the Baptist General State Convention of Illinois.

Dr. Curry married his first wife, Mrs. Dorothy R. Davis, of Jackson, Georgia, in 1955, and they remained married for fifty years until her passing in 2005. They reared four children. Later, he married his second wife, Dr. Verdie L. Robinson of Detroit, Michigan.

The Sermon

The Gospel of St. John, chapter 9, verses 1 through 7, and then verses 8 through 41. But, I want to read these first seven verses here from the King James Version. You may remain seated, if that's alright with the pastor. *"And as Jesus passed by, he saw a man which was blind from his birth. And his disciples asked him, saying, 'Master, who did sin, this man or his parents, that he was born blind?' Jesus answered, 'Neither hath this man sinned, nor his* parents, but that the works of God should be made manifest in him.'" Verse 4: "'I must work the works of Him that sent me while it is day. The night cometh when no man can work. As long as I am in the world, I am the light of the world.' When he had thus spoken, he spat on the ground and made clay of the spittle, and he anointed the eyes of the blind man with the clay." Verse 7: "And said unto him, 'Go, wash in the Pool of Siloam,' which is, by interpretation, 'sent.' He went his way, therefore, and washed and came seeing."

In the preceding chapters of this Scripture, we find the Lord Jesus being engaged by the Jews and the Pharisees and the scribes in conversations regarding the prevailing doctrines and laws of Moses and the chief priest and rulers. All through the rest of this chapter—it's interesting that this whole chapter seems to swing on doctrines and rules and regulations and what ought to be and what causes a thing to be and so forth.

In chapter 8, the scribes and Pharisees brought unto him a woman taken in adultery. They said to him that Moses said that she should be stoned. The Bible says Jesus wrote on the ground and said to them, "He that is without sin, let him cast the first stone." When no man did it, he told her to go and sin no more. This suggested that he had power to forgive sins. He told her, "Go, and sin no more." You wouldn't hardly say that unless you have some power and some authority to forgive sins. So, that caused another flair-up in their relations.

The Bible says that they later took up stones to kill *him*. But, he passed through the midst of them and went further, farther. In chapter 9 here, the Bible says that he passed by and saw a man that was blind from his birth. He saw a man which was blind from his birth. He saw a man—the man was blind—and it doesn't say whether he knew he was blind from his birth, but it says he was. Now, whether he knew that or not, I don't know at that point.

His disciples asked him, "Master, who did sin, this man or his parents that he was born blind?" His disciples, fellows who'd been with him, been following him, been seeing him do miracles, they asked him, of all the questions they could've asked him, they asked him, "Master, who did sin?" They could've asked him, "Does he have any children? Has he eaten? How old is he?" But, they asked him, "Master, who did sin? His parents? Did he, this man, or his parents, that he was born blind?"

Now, as a little something irregular, how could a man have sinned to cause his own blindness, if the blindness came from sin? They ask the question, "Who did sin, this man?" Now, the question, it seems like to me—it's not regular. I don't know that much about English and all that kind of stuff, but how could they ask a question, "Did this man sin?" How could he sin, and it caused him to be *born* blind? I could see, maybe he sinned after he was born and caused his blindness, but to be *born* blind? But, that's the question that they ask.

Jesus answered, "Neither this man nor his parents, but that the works of God should be made manifest in him." Now, the scholars probably know better than I that the prevailing thinking was, in that period, that *all* what we call "abnormal" or "irregular" stuff was caused by sin at some point. *All* irregular stuff caused by sin. Somebody sinned. Somebody sinned.

If God is all-perfect, all-kind, all-loving, how can he make something that is not normal? How can he be a loving God and fair with everybody and all, and then make a man, allow a man to be born blind? Seems to me, that would be contradictory to your idea, your concept, or your belief. If he's loving and kind and merciful and all of this kind of stuff, then you know, at least he could have given the man a chance to *go* blind. But if God caused a man to be *born* blind, it seems to me you've got make some kind of adjustment or something in your thinking and your theological base concept or whatever they would call that in school.

Jesus said, "Neither this man nor his parents." But, then he counters that and says, "That the works of God should be made manifest in him." The preacher last night spoke about God causing some things to do, some pitfalls, some valleys in your life. I guess maybe that's why Job, the book of Job, doesn't seem to have any, here's a man who doesn't have any ancestry. So, we can't talk about him, his parents having done something to cause him to wind up in the jam he was in.

And my family, all of us, all eight of us children, have glaucoma. Papa had a bunion on his right foot, and all of us have that. Some things seem to go in the stream. And those folks who know about genetics and hormones and all that kind of stuff, they can tell you about that. But, some things follow up, seem to follow up, run in the family. But, then, how's this man *born* blind when his parents are not blind? Then, you got to say, "Well, something must've happened." So, I guess the general thinking was sin.

Now, if it's sin and it's in the world and the universe, you've got to have a start. Well, if God made the world, what kind of God is he, going to make sin? So, you've got conjecture of thought here that might give you a problem.

Jesus, the Bible says, looked at the man. And, the disciples asked a question, "Master, who did sin?" Jesus proceeded to spit on the ground, make spittle, anoint the man's eyes and told him to go wash. And the man did it and came seeing.

I am drawn to this text because I think, in my traveling now, that there's a group of ministers out here, perhaps, and mission workers and so forth, who are perplexed about the successes of life when you work so hard in your church and in your community to do this and that and the other; and, it appears that you're not getting the success result that you've planned. You've wondered to yourself, "What have I done?" Your wife may be wondering, "What are you doing that I don't know about? Why is this church not growing?"

Isn't it normal to think that, if a thing is going along and something's wrong with it, then something is wrong somewhere for it getting to be in that shape? Is that normal thinking? I think so. I think so. I think so.

So, this text comes to me tonight and raises a question in my mind. This man born blind, he didn't have anything to do with it apparently. His mother and father didn't have anything to do with it apparently. Nobody on the street had anything to do with it. So, it seems to be somewhere in God's lap that this happened. And, the question may be, What kind of a God is this? Can we trust a God, can we trust a God who would allow you to be born blind and then expect the man born blind to say, "God is fair"?

Can you trust a God who will allow you to marry a fellow who's nice and kind and all like that, shoes shined, and hair combed if he has hair? Can you trust a God like that? And if so, why am I not pastoring a church house like this, choir like this, men like this, operation like this? How can he be fair and allow me to do all that I do normally and yet have what we call a handicap? That's my introduction. [Laughter]

The Bible says that Jesus passed by, saw a man, and then the disciples said, "Master, who did sin, this man or his parents, that he was born blind?" I want to raise three areas quickly as to my disposition to this as a way to think about it. Maybe not right and true, but *a* way. Sometimes *a* way is better than *no* way, even if it's not the *best* way.

First thing, I think. The Bible says Jesus saw the man as Jesus was passing by, and the man was blind from his birth. To be consistent in our theology and systematic in our faith, if God is the Father of Jesus and Jesus is his Son, then Jesus automatically had an obligation to assist and help his Father's children. The man's his brother if God is his Father and he created all human beings. So, Jesus passing by, saw the man and began to help him. Why did he do that? Basically, if God created all of us, whatever the man's condition was, he was still his brother.

So, if a policeman will arrest a woman and think, "This is my sister," I think your problem is solved. That's all he has to do. Just consider every woman his sister, consider every man his brother, and go ahead and arrest him, however you want to do it. But, you have an obligation. If you believe that God is your Father, and the Father of all creation, you have an obligation to help him. The disciples didn't feel that they had that obligation. They wanted to know what caused him to be blind.

When you feel that God is your Father, and every man is your brother, you have an obligation. The blind man never asked him for sight! He felt a personal obligation. The Bible says, "He saw him as he passed by."

I think one thing he saw was the man's blindness did not change the elevation of his status as far as humanity is concerned. If God made us, and He's fair and honest, even if you're *blind*, you are no less a human being than a person who has eyes. And, if that's true, then blindness is no more a hindrance than anything else in your life, just a matter of how you're going to treat it.

Jesus felt an obligation. "This is my brother, and I think I need to see after him." I think if you take that position to start with, it will give you light on some other things. Jesus saw the blind man as he passed by.

Secondly, when Jesus saw the man's need, he proceeded to prepare the means by which the man could be healed. He did not ask the man any questions about his ID. They're not asking about his voting card, his registration card. He did not ask the disciples for any advice or any help. He knew they didn't have the right spirit because they were worried about his blindness instead of his sight. They said, "Was he born blind?" They never asked him, "Does he have any sisters? Do his parents need help?" They weren't worried about his plight!

"Who did sin?" When you approach life always making your first jump to the negativity in life, you're always going to have perplexity. You're always going to be in a quandary about what to do when you think about sin first.

As part of my sixty years of preaching, I preach about sin every once in a while. I discovered it's very hard to drive a person to what's good and right. You have to be drawn by what is good and right. There's nothing in us personally to make us want to go. But, we can be drawn. So, they said, "Jesus said, 'If I be lifted up, I'll draw . . .'" You can't make a woman love you, but you can do some stuff to draw her. Better to be drawn than driven!

He didn't ask the disciples for any help. He spat on the ground, made some clay spittle out of it. Used what he had! I wish I had time right in there.

The man was lying at the pool thirty-eight years or somewhere around there. I don't know if he spent all that time at the pool, but wherever he was. When the Lord got ready to heal him, the Lord told him, "Take up your bed!" He didn't tell him, "Go get some new hands! Go get some new legs!" He didn't tell him, "Go get anything new!" He took what the man had! Told him, "Use what you got! Use what *you* got!" Don't go looking for the deacons and the trustees and crying to them. What do *you* have? "Take up your own bed!"

The man took up his bed and went to walking down. He looked back and said, "Jesus, why do you want me to carry my bed?" He said, "Because when I heal a Negro, I heal him so good no one can ever tell there was ever anything wrong with him! But if you got that bed, somebody will ask you, 'Man, why you carrying the bed?' Then, you got a chance to witness, because you got the bed on your back! Before you were carrying the bed, the bed was carrying you! But, when I fix you, you can carry your bed!"

Finally, finally, there's an element in our Christianity and in life—I'm coming to my subject now—there's an element in life called an "upgrade." I received a call not long ago from a telephone company, and they said I had a problem with my phone. They said, "Mister, you need to upgrade it."

I said, "Upgrade it?"

"Yes, you need to come in and get us upgraded so you can do this and do that and it won't be so long bringing up the stuff that you pull up on here. You need to upgrade it."

When I got to the telephone company, the fellow said, "You need a new one."

I said, "No, I have not learned all that I need to know about this one I have. And I don't need *more* stuff since I haven't conquered this stuff. Plus, I don't have the money."

They said, "You don't need it this month."

I said, "That's why I don't have it." I said, "Can you upgrade it?"

They said, "Yes, we can do this and do that and the other."

I'm probably feeling that many of our problems in life come because, in this Christian work, we sort of feel like, "I'm not winning. I'm not hitting the home run. I don't—I can't build a church like this. I don't have a large membership like this."

I'm the last of ten children, eight that lived, and all of my family pretty much under God have been what you call successful. My oldest brother was president of Bishop College for twenty-seven years. My next oldest brother was very successful at the post office. My next brother was a dentist. My next brother was an optometrist. My sister was an accomplished musician. My next brother was a bank vice president. My next brother was a physician. And, I was just a baseball player.

I started preaching and pastoring a church: twenty-seven members, twenty-seven names, twenty on a Sunday, maybe, ten if I talked about sin that Sunday. I was getting $20 a week, and I lived fifty miles up the road. I was pastoring in Tulare, California, living fifty miles up the road in Fresno, California. Some of the ministers said, "He's going to school, he's so smart, and all that. But he doesn't have any members. His church is not growing." It kind of got to me.

Some of them came in my pulpit and said, "You know, if the Lord called him to preach, he'd know how to preach. He wouldn't be trying to go to school to learn how to preach." In my pulpit, they did all this kind of stuff. And another fellow in town who hadn't been past the fifth grade, he had a house full, and I had twenty-seven names and so forth.

So, I did. I did get a little discouraged. Then, we had a church meeting, had fifteen at the church meeting in the offices wanting to raise me from $20 a week to $50 a week. I said, "No, we can't do that. We need a parsonage. I need to move here on the ground where I can work with the community and so forth." A woman in the church said, "Pastor, let's be real. Let's be reasonable. They want to raise you to $50?"

I said, "Yes."

She said, "Let's be real, let's be real. You can't preach, and I haven't felt nothing since you've been here."

And I said, "Well, you know, I'm sorry about that. I have been trying, though." Anyway, I said, "Well, what do you think we should do?" I'm thinking to myself, "Maybe not 50. Maybe 40?" But, I said, "Well, sister, what do you think we should do?"

She said, "Well, we can't do no 50. We can't do no 50."

I said, "Well, officers think they can do it."

She said, "No, we can't do that."

I said, "Well, what do you think we should do?"

She said, "We should cut it."

And I said, "Well, cut it how much?"

And she said, "Hell, cut it out." [Laughter]

Well, I'm driving a car, driving a '35 Studebaker. This is in 1962. I'm driving a '35 Studebaker, and my son the comedian says, "It was smoking, so people thought we were delivering barbecue on the run." Anyway, well I said—and I polled, I knew I had the vote—I said, "Well, whatever the people say." So, they voted to raise me to $45.

Anyway, on the way home, my wife says, "Honey, you know I love you," and this and that and the other, and "I'll do whatever you say. But, I think these people don't appreciate you. You really need to go on. You get a church in a big city, and you get a church in San Francisco. You got these children, you know. We got to get these children through school." It kind of got to me. It kind of got to me.

I went home, and my brother called, president of Bishop College, and he said, "How'd it go, tonight?" I said, "Well, it went alright." I told him what happened. I said, "Well, you're all successful. You're president of a college, and your brother this and my brother's that, and I'm just playing ball getting $300 every year, getting AAA, still don't get called, a wife and three children."

And my brother said, "Maybe you ought to go to teaching school." My brother said to her, "Listen, honey. He's saving souls. He's saving souls."

She said, "Yeah, you're president of a college, and your brother's this."

And he said, "Yeah, all of that, but Lacy's saving souls. Lacy is saving souls."

I'm through now, but here's my point. Here's my point. I had to readjust my thinking to the idea of assisting. In baseball, you call it moving or running, so you bunt the ball. You don't drive the runner in, but you get him in scoring position. So, I played baseball all those years, never sat on the bench. And the manager says that I knew how to move the runner. I knew how to get the runner in scoring position.

I think Jesus is calling us, whatever our situation is—don't be concerned. Not everybody you pray about is going to be what you call "healed," but I think we have an obligation to "upgrade" the situation. President Wade, I think we've got an obligation. Whatever it is that we're talking about—be satisfied! Upgrade the situation!

However, you find him, lift him some. There's something you can say to help him. Whatever—he's blind. He's sick. He's lame. Jesus saw the man with the withered hand. He didn't give him a new hand. When he got through with him, he was able to use the hand that he had.

I'm through now. My soul is happy. So, I may never pastor a crowd like this. This is a larger crowd than I think I've ever spoken to in my life. I've played baseball before a whole lot more than this, but when you're talking about Jesus, well, I'm satisfied! I can't pastor a crowd like this, but I can help the man that is pastoring. I can pray for him! I can move the runner! I can get him in scoring position! I can go down on my knees, and I can move the runner! I can get him in scoring position!

Jesus says we've got an obligation. Don't worry about how he got blind! Don't worry about how he got sick! Move the runner! Get him in scoring position!

Jesus went to the cross—I can't save all of you, but I'm going to get you in scoring position—went in the grave, stayed all night Friday night, Saturday night, Sunday. Early, early, he rose up! And, I found out I was in scoring position!

Yay! Thank you, Jesus! Praise his holy name! He's real. He's real. Real in my soul! He has washed and made me whole! His love for me is like pure gold! Yay! Thank you, Jesus! Excuse me now, but my soul is happy! Yay! Thank you, Jesus! I can move him in scoring position! I may not heal him, but I can move him in scoring position! I can upgrade him! Whatever he has, I can upgrade it! He doesn't have to have something new. We can fix what he has and make him usable in God's service.

Chapter 22

Robert Smith Jr. (1949–)

Living Legend 2017

The Preacher

Rev. Dr. Robert Smith Jr. (1949–) holds the Charles T. Carter Baptist Chair of Divinity at Samford University's Beeson Divinity School, where he teaches Christian preaching.[1] Previously, he served as the Carl E. Bates Associate Professor of Christian Preaching at the Southern Baptist Theological Seminary in Louisville, Kentucky. A gifted and popular teacher of preachers, he received Southern Seminary's Findley B. Edge Award for Teaching

---

1. This short biographical profile has been adapted from the faculty profile page on the Beeson Divinity School website. See https://www.beesondivinity.com/directory/Smith-Robert.

Excellence in 1996. An ordained Baptist minister, he served as pastor of the New Mission Missionary Baptist Church in Cincinnati, Ohio, for twenty years, the same church where he received his call to preach at the age of seventeen. While pastoring at New Mission, he also embarked on his educational journey earning his bachelor of science degree in 1984, his master of divinity degree in 1988, and his doctor of philosophy degree in 1993. He joined the faculty at Southern in 1995 and the faculty at Beeson in 1997.

Dr. Smith has served as a cowriter in a study of Christian ministry in the African American church in the book *Preparing for Christian Ministry* and as coeditor for the book *A Mighty Long Journey: Reflections on Racial Reconciliation.* He has also served as a coeditor for *Our Sufficiency Is of God: Essays on Preaching in Honor of Gardner C. Taylor.* His 2008 book *Doctrine That Dances: Bringing Doctrinal Preaching and Teaching to Life* was selected as the winner of the 2008 Preaching Book of the Year Award by *Preaching* magazine and the 2009 Preaching Book of the Year Award by *Christianity Today.* In 2010, *Preaching* magazine named *Doctrine That Dances* one of the twenty-five most influential books in preaching for the last twenty-five years.[2] In 2014, he published *The Oasis of God: From Mourning to Morning—Biblical Insights from Psalms 42 and 43.*

Dr. Smith has spoken at more than one hundred universities, colleges, and seminaries in the United States, Great Britain, the Middle East, Africa, Australia, New Zealand, and the Caribbean. His research interests include the place of passion in preaching, the literary history of African American preaching, Christological preaching, and theologies of preaching. At Beeson Divinity School where he received the school's Teacher of the Year Award in 2005, he teaches Christian preaching and other electives in homiletics. He and his wife, Dr. Wanda Taylor-Smith, are the parents of four adult children (one of whom is in heaven).

The Sermon

Romans chapter 3. I want to read verse 21–25. The passage is probably dealt with in verses 21–31 but it is so pregnant that I won't be able to deliver it full-time. I want to talk about the grace effect. The grace effect. Hear these words from the word, Romans 3:

> But now a righteousness from God, apart from law, has been
> made known to which the Law and the Prophets testify. This righ-
> teousness from God comes through faith in Jesus Christ to all who

1. Duduit, "25 Most Influential Books."

believe. There is no difference, for all have sinned and fall short of the glory of God and are justified freely by his grace, through the redemption that came by Christ Jesus. God presented him as a sacrifice of atonement through faith in his blood.

I want to contend that God has delivered us by the "but how" of sin, through the "but now" of justification of faith in Christ Jesus, for the "but then" of praise in the power of the Spirit. God has delivered us from the "but how" of sin through the "but now" of justification of faith in Jesus for the "but then" of praise and the power of the Spirit.

The "but how" of sin. How did God deliver us, and how did we fall into sin? Horace, the Roman poet from the first century, said, "Never bring a problem to the stage unless it deserves to be solved by God." "Never bring a problem to the stage unless it deserves to be solved by God."

A problem has been brought to the stage by Paul. It is a problem that not only deserves to be solved by God, but it is required to be solved by God. Paul tells us that this problem is sin and only God can solve *that* problem.

It's S-I-N with "I" in the middle. *It's me, It's me. It's me. Oh, Lord, standing in need of prayer! Not my mother, or father, sisters or brothers, but it's me, standing in the need of prayer.*

Sin is not simply an action. Sin is an attitude. Sin is not simply the denotation of an action; sin is the description of who we are as sinners. In fact, we live in the now-ness of sin, before we participate in the verb-ness of sin. It's what David is saying in Psalm 51:5: *"I was born in sin, and shapen in iniquity,"* that is, I was guilty before I was born, and I was sinful before I was conceived." David goes on to say in Psalm 139:23–24, *"Search me, O God, and know my heart. Try me and know my thoughts and see if there's any evil in me and lead me in the way everlasting."*

We live in the now-ness of sin—person, place, thing, state of being—before we participate in the verb-ness and the activity of sin, for the verb-ness carries the action of the noun.

It's really what Jeremiah is trying to get across when he talks about sin, not so much as the definition, but as a description. He says in Jeremiah 17:9, "The heart is deceitful and desperately wicked, who can know it?" Then, he admits in verse 10 and says, "But the Lord knows the heart."

It's what Robert Robinson, the great poet and songwriter, meant when he wrote the song, "Come, Thou Fount." *"Oh, to grace, how great a debtor daily I'm constrained to be. Let thy grace Lord, like a fetter bind my wandering heart to thee. Prone to wander, Lord, I feel it, prone to leave the God I love. Here's my heart, Lord, take and seal it. Seal it for thy courts above."*

Hear him saying. He says, "Let this grace, Lord, like a fetter, bind my wandering, wandering heart to thee. I'm prone to wander, Lord, I feel it."

Do you ever feel that? It's your Achilles's heel. It's the place where you're most vulnerable. It's the place where you need a quadruple security guard around a certain area in your life to keep you from wandering. *"Prone to leave the God I love."*

If not for the grace of God, every one of us has the propensity, proclivity, and the possibility of spitting in the face of the sovereign God. I know you think you're incapable of doing that, but "let a person take heed while he or she is standing lest they fall."

I see Peter, who really did love Jesus. The Lord has already warned him, "Peter, before the rooster crows you're going to deny me not once, not twice, but three times." Peter says, "No, Lord, I'd die with you before I'd deny you." And sure enough, it would happen.

Jesus has informed him that he's praying for him. Hear these words in Luke 22:31–34, *"Simon, Simon, Satan hath desire to sift you as wheat. But I prayed for you, that your faith."* Not that you would not fall, you're going to fall, but "that your faith would not fail, after you have turned back, after you have been converted within the brothers."

So it is that Peter did deny the Lord because we are prone to wander, Lord, we feel it. Do you feel that proneness? Do you feel that desire to say to the Lord every now and then when someone has gotten on your nerve, "Lord, if you just give me thirty good seconds to really say what I really feel, to lay my religion down, I'd feel so much better." Prone to wander. To return back to the little black book, to try what you tried years ago, because the pressure is on. Your nerves would be much more relaxed if you could just turn back for just a moment. Prone to wander, Lord, I feel it. Prone to leave the God I love.

But, grace is designed to deliver us from the "but how" of sin. Timothy George, our dean [at Beeson], has written a book, *Amazing Grace*, in which he talks about sin and uses the traditional theological terminology. Sin equals lawlessness. He retains the theological traditional dictionary, but he provides us with a contemporary relevant vocabulary. He says that sin is like an addiction.

If a woman who is a crack woman gets pregnant and smokes crack for the nine months of her pregnancy, chances are that the baby will be a crack baby. What did the baby do to be a crack baby? Nothing except to be a born of a crack mother.

You and I become sinners because we were born to sinful parents. Now, what grace does is deliver us from the "but how" of sin. Never bring a problem to the stage unless it deserves a God to solve it.

Paul brings and stacks up the problem of sin in a prodigious way. Chapter 1 of Romans, verses 29–31, he says of the Gentiles, "You're arrogant. You're boastful. You're deceitful. You're evil. You're murderers. You're disobedient to parents. You're slanderous. You're heartless. You're ruthless. You are sinful." Then, he says in verses 24, 26–28, of that chapter, "God gave them up to their sinful passions."

Never bring a problem to the stage unless it deserves a God to solve it, and no one else can. The Jews like that kind of preaching. "Preach, Paul! Tell those Gentiles how no good they really are."

Then, Paul comes to chapter 2 and says, "I'm going to talk about you, also. You call yourself a Jew, in verse 17 of chapter 2, and yet you have all the advantages. You've got the Law and the Prophets and the cultic system, that is, the priestly system. You've got circumcision," which is a symbol of being in a covenant relationship with the community of God and the God of the community. "You've got all of these things, and yet you have also committed sin."

Jews are sinful. Gentiles are sinful. Then, he says in chapter 3, verse 10, *"There is none righteous, no not one."* And, then, in verse 23, *"All fall short of the glory of God."*

"Never bring a problem to the stage unless it deserves a God who can solve it." There is no one that can solve this problem of sin except for God himself.

Now, we see God moving to solve this problem of sin. In fact, he does it by offering himself on the cross as the only one who can solve the problem of sin. As a result today, I stand here to tell you that I'm saved. I've been saved three times. Yeah, I've been saved three times. I don't call this heresy. At least hear me out. I've been saved three times.

The first time I got saved was in preexistent eternity. Before I even experienced life, God elected me. Had nothing to do with my works. Had nothing to do with my merit. God elected me. I know that word "election" bothers somebody, but it's right there in the Scripture. God elected me. The first time I got saved is in preexistent eternity, and God wrote my name in the Lamb's Book of Life.

Then, he left the weights. For God never reacts to anything. He preacts to everything. In other words, God acts before there's anything to act on. That's why Zedekiah could say in Isaiah 46, *"He knows the end even before the beginning begins."* I got saved in preexistent eternity.

I got saved in past history even though God had already elected me, even though Calvary was plan A and not plan B, even though Jesus died in the mind of God in preexistent eternity. John says in Revelation in chapter

16, verse 8, *"I looked behind the altar, and I saw a lamb that looked like it had been slain from before the foundation of the world."*

God elected me then. But, just because he had been slain from the foundation of the world, he still had to be slain in past history. In AD 30, Jesus, who had died in the mind of God in preexistent eternity, had to die on the cross for our sins. I got saved in AD 30.

But, then, I got saved not only in preexistent eternity, not only in past history, I got saved in my history. In May 1956, I heard the gospel. I was seven years old, and I responded to the gospel. God saved me on the basis of what he had done in preexistent eternity and past history, and I took and acted upon it in my present history.

Therefore, brothers and sisters, what this really means is salvation is a complete fact. I've been saved from the penalty of sin, from the power of sin, and one of these days, I'm going to be saved from the very presence of sin.

God has come to deliver us from the "but how" of sin. Not only that, God has come to deliver us from the "but how" of sin through the "but now" of justification by faith in Jesus Christ, the "but now" of justification by faith in Jesus Christ.

Here is Paul speaking to us about how God has actually done this. The curtains have been drawn up until verse 21 of chapter 3. The windows have been closed, the doors have been bolted, and there is no hope until these words "but now" come from the lips of Paul. It's the hinges that turn the door.

"But now." It was Deacon Lloyd Jones who pastored the Westminster Church in England, a Welshman, who said, "There are no more two wonderful words in all of Scripture than these two words, 'but now.'" But, these two words have to be placed in the right order. It's not "now but," "but now." It's not even "now" because now indicates something has happened, but "but now" indicates something has changed. "But now."

If you take and put a positive statement before the redemptive conjunction "but," the theological conjunction "but," then that which follows the theological conjunction "but" is inevitably negative. For instance, in Judges 2:18, God raised up a judge, and as long as that judge lived, God gave that judge victory over the enemies of Israel. Verse 19. "But!" When that judge dies, Israel returns and reverts back to their old corrupt ways. The positive preceded the "but," which means that the negative succeeded the "but."

You've got to be able to put the positive in the place behind God; it's "but God's." But, if you take and put the negative before "God's," that means that the positive will inevitably follow.

For instance, the very first time we see this phrase in Genesis 8:1, the last part of Genesis 7 says that the watery flood was on earth for one hundred and fifty days. Chapter 8:1: *"But God remembered Noah and the waters receded."*

Joseph says to his brothers in Genesis 50:20, *"You meant unto me for evil, but God meant unto me for good to save many people alive."*

Psalm 30:5: *"Weeping may endure for a night, but joy comes in the morning."*

Psalm 34:19: *"Many are the afflictions of the righteous, but the Lord delivers him from them all."*

Psalm 73:26: *"My heart failed, but you are the strength of my heart."*

Matthew 19:26: *"With man it is impossible, but with God all things are possible."*

I find it very interesting in that fifteenth chapter of Luke, the prodigal son in verse 21, the prodigal son has given his speech of apology to his father. He says, "Father, I have sinned against you and against heaven and I am no longer worthy to be called your son." The father never lets him get to "Make me one of the hired servants" because once a son always a son. Verse 22 says, "But the father said," in spite of what the son said, "'Put a robe on him. Put a ring on him. Put shoes on his feet. For my son was once lost, *but* he is now found. He was once dead, *but* he is now alive.'"

That great word that we find in Romans 5:7–8, *"It's rare that a man would die for a righteous man. Perhaps a man would die for a good man, but God commended, God demonstrated His love toward us, in that while we were yet sinners, Christ died for the ungodly."*

Paul says in Romans 6:23, *"The wages of sin is death, but the gift of God is eternal life through Jesus Christ our Lord."*

I know you're tired of these theological "but's," but I've got to just say a couple more. For when I think about the magnitude of what it took for God to save me, I've got to get the "but" in the right place.

Ephesians chapter 2:1: *"There was a time when you were dead in trespasses and sins, but because of God's rich mercy, and great love, He has made you alive in Christ Jesus."*

Then, he moves to verses 12 and 13, where he says this, *"You were one-time strangers to the commonwealth of Israel. You were foreigners to the covenantal promise, without God and without hope in the world. But those of you who are far away are now made to be drawn nigh by the blood of Jesus Christ."* You've got to get the "but" in the right place.

That's why the songwriter would say, *"I was sinking deep in sin far from the peaceful shore, very deeply stained within, seeking to rise no more. But, the master of the Sea heard my despairing cry, from the waters lifted me, now safe am I. Love lifted me. When nothing else could help, love lifted me. There is a name I love to hear. I love to sing it's worth, it sounds like music to my ear, the sweetest name on earth, Oh, how I love Jesus. Because he first loved me."*

These words, "but now," are like echoes of mercy and the whispers of love. For God has delivered us from the "but how" of sin through the "but now" of justification by faith in Christ.

The words. Oh, it's such a small word. I like the big words of the Bible. I like justification. I like sanctification. I like propitiation. I love adoption. I love ecclesiology. I love those words.

But, according to Matthew 5:18, before one "yod," which is the smallest letter in the Hebrew alphabet, or one tittle, the extension of it, before it passes, heaven and earth will pass away. Zechariah 4:10: *"Don't despise the day of small things,"* and even small words.

"But now" is two monosyllabic words. There are some words in the Bible that are very small and don't cover very much space, but they are profound in their depths.

I love the King James Version of the Bible. Now, I know that if it was good enough for Paul and Silas, good enough for the Hebrew children, good enough for Ozela and Robert Smith, then it's good enough for me.

But, when I read Isaiah 55:1, "Ho, come to the waters. Buy milk and buy wine without money and without price." Just a word: "Ho."

Matthew chapter 28, verse 19–20. *"Lo."* I mean, why not just say I'm with you to the end of the world? But *"Lo, I'm with you always until the end of the world."*

John 3:16: *"For God so loved the world."* I mean, why not just say he loved the world a lot? But no, He *so* loved the world. How much is so? What is it like to be so tired and so sick and so hungry that it's inexpressible, inexplicable?

How do you deal with the word "O"? *"O, the depths of both the wisdom and knowledge of God. How unsearchable are his judgements and his ways are past finding out."* O, the depths. *"O, how I love Jesus! O, how I love Jesus! O, how I love Jesus because He first loved me." "O, for a thousand tongues to sing my great redeemer's praise, the glories of my God and king, the triumphs of his grace."*

What is it like to tell God how much you love him? What are you going to do to serve, and all you can find is a monosyllabic word that consists of one letter, "O"?

Now, here are two words that don't occupy much space. "But now" plunges us into an unfathomable depth, and brings up to us jewels that we'll never be able to truly mine or understand in this life. I really believe that, even in eternity, we'll still be growing in our knowledge of just how much God loves us and how faithful God really has been.

Paul says in verse 21, he says that there is a rightness of God that has been revealed to us apart from law to which both the Law and the Prophets testify. This is the righteousness that comes with faith to all who believe. For there is no difference. "For all have sinned and come short of the glory of God."

The Law and the Prophets testify. The law was never designed to save us. The law was designed to reveal, not to restrain our sin, but to reveal our sin. To reveal our sin. Not to redeem our sin, but to reveal our sin. It was a mirror that showed us our sin, our mess. It showed us, but it couldn't do anything for us.

The prophets would come later on, and they would prophesy about the redeemer who would redeem us from sin. So, you will hear Isaiah say in Isaiah 9:6, *"Unto us a child is born, unto us a child is given, and the government shall be on his shoulders and his name shall be called Wonderful Counselor, Mighty God, Everlasting Father, and the Prince of Peace."*

Now, the Law and the Prophets are testifying about the authenticity of this Jesus who has come in order that we might experience the "but now" of justification by faith in Jesus Christ himself.

Here they are. This all is being spoken about when Jesus walks with these two on the road going from Jerusalem to Emmaus, a seven-mile trek. The Bible says in Luke 24:27 that Jesus, *"beginning at Moses, the Law and the Prophets, showed them how the Old Testament was written concerning himself."* They were witnesses. But, now we see them epitomized and personalized by Moses and Elijah on the Mount of Transfiguration. There, in Luke 9, there they stand. They are three earthly witnesses—Peter, James and John—but they are not celestially conditioned. They cannot handle all that glory.

But, Elijah and Moses have been in heaven. Elijah's been there for eight hundred years, having caught a chariot of fire pulled by horses. The fire had rings of fire and he out-threw death.

Moses had been in heaven for fifteen hundred years, having died. God had rocked his body between two mountains until his soul crept out from his body, and embalmed him with heavenly fluid, and buried him in an unmarked tomb.

Now, they show up on the Mount of Transfiguration testifying about Jesus. Now, they speak. It's as if they're saying to Jesus, "Look, you go on and take our documents. Since you are the end of the law," Moses is saying to Jesus, "Go on and take the law. You've fulfilled it."

Elijah is saying, "Since you are the end of the prophets, take the prophetical scroll. For you have fulfilled that as well."

The only conversation is about Calvary. In Luke 9:31, the Bible says that they talked about the exodus, the *exodon* that would take place in

Jerusalem. It was an accomplishment, not a tragedy. They were in essence saying to Jesus, "Go on and die because we are here, and we have been in heaven on credit. We have been in heaven all of these years based upon what the prophet said that you're going to do. Go on, Jesus, and die because, if you don't die, we're going to receive an immediate eviction. We're not going to be able to stay in heaven so go on and die."

There on that cross, Jesus will die because, for generations, justice had been demanding full payment. All that God offered was an installment payment.

Once a year, Yom Kippur, the great Day of Atonement, there was an offering that was made. Justice got tired and said, "I want to be paid in full." And mercy said, "You will one of these days." The psalmist said in Psalm 80:5–10, *"Mercy and truth met together. Righteousness and peace kissed each other."* There on the cross, justice and mercy got together, and Jesus took and paid it all for us. In fact, when he died in Mark 15:38, the Bible says that, when he died, that the veil in the temple was ripped from top to bottom. Now, what really was taking place was God was tearing up the mortgage note. Then, Paul picked up a pen of inspiration and dipped it in the ink of illumination and said, *"Jesus paid it all, all to him I owe. Sin had left a crimson stain, but he washed it white as snow."* Oh, brothers and sisters, I'm glad that when I get to heaven, I will not be there on credit. I will be there because Jesus has paid it all for me.

Well, not only that, but it is also a matter of seeing how we are being escorted to look at this great justification. God has taken and delivered us from the "But how" of sin through the "But now" of the justification by faith in Christ in order that we might reach the "But then" of praise to the power of the Holy Spirit.

In verse 24, we're escorted into the courtroom. It's the courtroom of justification. Notice. We're justified freely, verse 24, by his grace.

The Romans were familiar with judicial cases. They had a strong judicial system. Forums and sit-ins and so forth and so on. But, the Jews couldn't understand it particularly when the connection was made from the Levitical system of bringing a sacrifice. From Christ not bringing a sacrifice, but Christ being the sacrifice himself. *"Behold, the Lamb of God who comes to take away the sin of the world."*

This is what happens in the court scene. We are standing there in the courtroom of God. There's God sitting on the judgment seat, and there are the witnesses for the prosecution. The Law and the Prophets testify against us because we're guilty.

Then, there is the prosecuting attorney. According to Revelation 12:10, Satan is the accuser of the brothers and sisters who accuses them day and night. It looks bad for us. The verdict inevitably and unmistakably will be guilty.

But, then, someone comes from the side. He really is our advocate. He really is our defense attorney. John says in 1 John 2:2, *"Brothers, I write unto you that you should not sin, but if you sin, you have an advocate, Christ Jesus, the righteous, who is the propitiation, the satisfaction and the covering and cleansing of our sin. But not only our sin, but the sin of the entire world."*

I can see Jesus saying to the Father, "Father, you cannot condemn this person because new evidence has been entered into the records. This individual cannot be sentenced and cannot even be judged because it goes against the law of double jeopardy." Which means you cannot try a person twice for the same crime. "I've already been tried for his crime and, therefore, since I've been tried for his crime, he must go free."

"Therefore, there's now no condemnation for those who are in Christ Jesus," who walk not after the flesh but the Spirit. I realize that, for some, this may be intellectual but it just gets in my soul. Had it not been for what he has done, then I could not do what I'm doing now.

I'm on shouting ground now. This makes me happy! This makes me rejoice because this is what heaven is going to be about. We go to the courtroom of justification, and God looks at us and says, "You are an individual who appears to be one who looks as if he or she has not even sinned." One of these days, when sanctification has fallen down at the feet of eternity and glorification will take over, *"it does not yet appear what we shall be, but we know that when He appears, we shall be like Him for we shall see him as he has come."*

Go with me to the auction block of redemption. Verse 24 says that we have been redeemed. *"He has redeemed us by His blood."* Now, the Jews understood what redemption was. Even the Romans understood when it came to slavery. Now, they had the agora, the marketplace. It was a place where they sold goods, but they also sold human beings. They stood in line to be purchased.

All of us must come to understand that God has bought us back twice. He owned us in creation but we failed. Therefore, he came back to buy us through redemption so that he owns us. We are now his. We are like Hosea who was told in Hosea 3:1–3, *"Go back and buy your wife Gomer back. Bring her into your home, love her, and tell her not to leave again."* That's what God has done for us. He has bought us back.

Oh, I know we are not what we ought to be, but he bought us back. I realize we are stained and tainted, but he bought us back. I realize that we don't seem to have much worth, but he bought us back. I'm a wretch but I'm his. He bought me back.

So, I've been to the courtroom, the courtroom where I have been justified. God has taken and put the charges on Christ, so much so that as Paul said to Philemon in Philemon 18, *"Whatever charges Onesimus has incurred, then charge it to my account."*

We've been to the auction block of redemption, but finally, we go to the altar of propitiation. Verse 25. The Bible says that we have been the recipients of propitiation by his blood.

The Romans would try to appease the anger of their gods by offering sacrifices to their gods. Sometimes, in other cultures, they would offer their own children in order to satisfy and to expiate their god, to propitiate their god, so their god would turn from his wrath.

Brothers and sisters, we have experienced real propitiation. We cannot appease God. I don't care what you bring. *"Nothing in my hand I bring. Simply to the cross I cling."*

God is not interested in your degree. That will not appease God. God does not care about what kind of house you live in—it's his anyway. That won't please God. But, God takes and brings Godself. The only way God is appeased and satisfied is when God offers himself.

You hear Isaiah saying in Isaiah 53:10, *"It pleased God to bruise Him,"* because we're not only saved by grace, but we're saved by wrath. In other words, we're saved by the wrath that we deserved by the wrath that Christ took for us.

Therefore, we come, if you will, to the altar where the high priest once a year would take two goats. One goat he would kill. He would take the blood and come to the Holy of Holies, and he'd spread it over the lid of the ark of the covenant, which represented the presence of God in the midst of His people. It was overlaid with gold and gold inside it. *There* was Aaron's rod that budded. A dead tree brought to life which prefigured the cross of Calvary where life would come from a dead tree. *There* was the manna that represented the provision of God, that Christ came to provide salvation for us. And *there* was the decalogue which represented the word of God. Christ did not come to bring a word from God. He is the Word of God! And *there* the blood was sprinkled over the *hilasterion*, the mercy seat, and that represented that God not only satisfied himself, but he covered our sins.

If there was anyone who really needed covering out of everyone in the Bible, David needed it. So, David can say using that same word in Psalm 32:1–2, *"Blessed is the man whose transgressions are forgiven and whose sins are covered."* We have been covered by the blood of Jesus Christ.

Well, brothers and sisters, God has come to deliver us from the "how" of sin, through the "but now" of the justification by faith in Christ, to and for the purpose of the "but then" of praise in the power of the Spirit.

This passage has an intra-trinitarian soaking. God's there; the Father; the Son's there. You say, "The Spirit's not there," no, not explicitly, but there's always a trichotomous activity whenever God moves. You cannot talk about God as Father and Son and leave out Spirit. It's Jonathan Edwards who says that God has forever known himself in a sweet and forever society as Father and as Son and as Holy Spirit always and forever. It is John Newton who says, "Since there is no jealousy in the triune God, it is impossible to over-praise the Father and the Spirit in the adoration of Christ."

The Spirit is moving in this passage. How do I know? Because the Spirit reveals sin to myself. The Bible says in John 16:7–9, "*When the Spirit of truth has come, he will convict the world of sin, and of righteousness, and of judgment.*"

You can't even see the magnitude of your sin until the Spirit shows it to you. The Spirit reveals Christ to us because he does not come to talk about himself. He comes to talk about Jesus. So, the Spirit is moving throughout the passage like God the Father and God the Son and God the Spirit are verily involved in this Trinitarian transaction.

I became acquainted with grace many years ago in a very profound way. It was not even in church. It didn't have anything to do with a sermon or a song the choir had sung. I remember that day, December 25, 1960. I lived at the address of 452 Milton Street of Mount Auburn in Cincinnati, Ohio. It was Christmas Day. I was eleven years of age. My brother Willy was seven, and both of us wanted bicycles. Now, it was hard for us to sleep that night because we'd keep getting up and looking under the tree, and nothing was there.

Finally, we went into the room and underneath the tree there were two bicycles. One was an English racer that had power steering and power brakes. That was my bike. But, my brother Willy, he got a Huffy, which meant that it was manually-steered and manually-pedaled. He made the mistake of getting on my bike before I could get on it. And we had a "Come to Jesus" meeting. Out in the side yard of the house, my mother stepped out, and I'm glad she stepped out because he was seven. But, he was getting the best of this eleven-year-old boy and we knew we were in trouble. Mama said something that just astounded us. She said, "Hit him, little Robert. Hit him, Jimbo," which is my youngest brother's nickname.

We couldn't believe it. We stood there inactive. Mama said, "If you don't hit each other, I'm going to tear both of you up." We began to fight, and when we stopped, she said, "Keep on hitting each other." I know it seems cruel, but we kept on hitting each other. When we stopped, she said, "Hit each other again," until blood began protruding from our nostrils.

Then, she stopped. She said, "You've broken my heart today." She said, "On this day, when we should be having a celebration, you're fighting each other. Don't you know that there were times when I didn't have any money in my purse? I saved the money that I needed that you might have money to buy your lunch at school. When I didn't have some clothes, they were tattered and torn, I wore them so that you didn't have to wear holey clothes, that your friends wouldn't make fun of you."

She kept pulling back the curtain of memory showing us where she brought us from, the sacrifices that she made. We said, "Mama, whip us," but Mama was already "whipping" us. We were crying not because of what she did, but because of what she refused to do. Mama was showing us grace. Don't you know? We never fought again because we never wanted to break the heart of our mother.

Oh, brothers and sisters, that really is grace. It's God rolling back the curtain, a memory now and then, showing you where God brought you from and where you could have been. It's God reminding you of the pitfalls that he's brought you out of, and he did it for his name's sake. I'm glad tonight. Brother, let me make my own music tonight. I'm glad that God has come to a place where he gives us grace in order that we might see how wonderful God has been.

Therefore, I've made up in my mind that I will forever lift my eyes to Calvary, to view the cross where Jesus died for me.

"How marvelous was the grace that caught my falling soul. He looked beyond my faults and saw my needs."

He looked beyond my vile and gave me victory. He looked beyond my brokenness and gave me wholeness. He looked beyond my debts and gave me dignity. He looked beyond my faults and gave me faith. He looked beyond my misery and gave me mercy.

One of these days, since he looked beyond, I'm going to look to him and bow my head, and thank him because he brought me, thank him because he kept me, thank him because he never left me, praise him because he saved me. Praise him! Praise him for the grace effect that continues to have effect in my life!

Chapter 23

Joel C. Gregory (1948–)

Living Legend 2018

The Preacher

Rev. Dr. Joel C. Gregory (1948–) holds the George W. Truett Endowed Chair of Preaching and Evangelism and directs the Kyle Lake Center for Effective Preaching at Baylor's George W. Truett Theological Seminary. He is also the president of Joel Gregory Ministries. For decades, he has averaged preaching and teaching more than one hundred and fifty times per year in twenty states and internationally. In 2018, in a national poll conducted among more than five hundred professors of preaching, Gregory was named as one of the twelve most effective preachers in the English-speaking world. Then, in 2019, his colleagues at Baylor University recognized him as an Outstanding Professor.

He holds the bachelor of arts degree summa cum laude from Baylor University, the master of divinity degree from Southwestern Baptist Theological Seminary, and the doctorate of philosophy degree from Baylor University. He taught preaching at Southwestern from 1982 to 1985.

Among other engagements, Dr. Gregory brought a plenary message at the Baptist World Congress in Seoul, South Korea, and preached the closing message at the 2015 Baptist World Congress in Durban, South Africa. He has preached in venues as varied as Westminster Chapel, Spurgeon's College, and Kensington Temple, London, as well as Regent's Park College, Oxford. His ministry has taken him to the International Seminary at Buenos Aires, Princeton Theological Seminary Chapel, and Princeton University Chapel, as well as scores of seminaries and universities across America. He is the founder of the four-day Proclaimers Place® with sessions in eighteen states, England, France, Italy, Greece, Israel, Germany, and Switzerland, as well as each summer at Regent's Park College, Oxford, since 2005. More than fourteen hundred ministers have attended these seminars.

Among his pastorates, Gregory served as senior pastor of Travis Avenue Baptist in Fort Worth and First Baptist in Dallas. He was twice elected without opposition and unanimously as president of the 5400-church Baptist General Convention of Texas (BGCT). He brought the Southern Baptist Convention annual sermon in 1988, "The Castle and the Wall," widely recognized as a landmark message. He was for years the preacher on five hundred radio stations for the *Baptist Hour*. He is married to Joanne Michele Tomlin Gregory, and they are the parents of four adult children.

The Sermon[1]

Ephesians 1:

> *I pray that the eyes of your heart may be enlightened in order that*
> *you may know the hope to which he has called you, the riches of*
> *his glorious inheritance in his holy people. (NIV)*

A horse cannot see straight ahead. The eyes of the horse are on both sides of its head. It must move its head back and forth to see. A dragonfly has

---

1. Dr. Gregory received the Living Legend award in 2018, but did not preach a sermon that year. He lectured on the history of the E. K. Bailey Preaching Conference. He preached the sermon preserved in this chapter at the Conference circa 2005. The title of the sermon is "The Eyes of the Heart," and it is an exposition of Ephesians 1:18.

compound eyes. These enable the bug to see in slow motion. That is why the bug can zap another bug. The common billboard pigeon can see a range of colors that humans cannot see. The world of ultraviolet and infrared is visible to the pigeon. The house cat cannot see colors, but only sees shades of gray. But the cat has great depth perception and can land and leap on a mouse. The snake "sees" in a different way. The snake has heat perception sensors in its head. That enables it to strike perfectly. The kingfisher bird has two kinds of vision, one for soaring over the water to spot a fish and another for diving beneath the water to catch the fish. It has double vision. As a believer you also have a double vision: *physical vision and the eyes of the heart.*

Her entire life of thirty-nine years was spent in a tiny, remote corner of England called West Yorkshire. She lost a sister to tuberculosis. She grew up in an Anglican parsonage that was so poor that she scarcely had anything to eat. She went to a boarding school that was so bad it became memorialized in her book. When she was a little schoolgirl, the other girls would hurry after school to visit the shops, but she would just sit at her desk and look and look at the woodcuttings printed in her simple textbooks. She would look at them and say marvelous things about them that stunned her teachers. That little girl, Charlotte Brontë, became a famous writer whose novel *Jane Eyre* can be found on the bookshelf next to Shakespeare, Milton, and Chaucer. Why? She looked at that little world with the eyes of the heart and saw more than anybody had ever seen there. Because of that, she had to express those things in her books. Why was this obscure young woman so gifted as a writer? She looked at life *with the eyes of the heart.*

One of my friends, John I. Durham, is a retired professor who taught Hebrew and the Old Testament. Yet, for decades he has made his avocation the study of the biblical paintings by the Dutch painter Rembrandt and has since become a world expert on the artist's works. He does not have an art history degree or formal training, other than his background of teaching the Old Testament. While visiting museums from Amsterdam to St. Petersburg, he just looks and looks at Rembrandt's paintings so long that he makes the guards nervous. But, he has seen things that no one else has ever seen in the one-third of Rembrandt's paintings that are biblical. He has even written a book called *The Biblical Characters of Rembrandt.* John has done that because he looks at those paintings *with the eyes of the heart.*

Someone writes about an experience of novelist Douglas Coupland. While walking along the Mall in Washington, DC, he noticed a large number of tourists with white canes. As he got closer to them, he realized it was a group of blind people. When they heard him walking toward them, they handed him a camera and asked him to take their picture. Coupland said that, at first, he was astonished. He remarked, "Later on, I was thinking that wasn't so bad. Even though they cannot see, they believe in sight." Indeed, without physical eyes, *they could see with the eyes of the heart.*

In our circumstances of life, that describes us as believers. We're a group of people who can't see right now, but we believe in sight. We look at things with the eyes of the heart because we believe important things are there, even if we do not see them at first. In fact, we are people who bet our lives on things we cannot see, yet we believe in seeing them someday.

In 1671, Blaise Pascal offered a famous quote that can even be found on T-shirts today: "The heart has reason that reason knows not of." Tweaking that saying a little, I would rather say, "The eyes of the heart have a vision that vision knows not of."

Within that long, 169-word prayer in Ephesians 1:15–21 is an expression that Paul uses: ". . . the eyes of your heart, having been enlightened . . ." That's the only place in the Bible where that expression—"the eyes of the heart"—is used. The Essenes used a similar phrase, as did St. Clement of Rome much later. It's an interesting phrase. For those of you studying Greek grammar, it's a very rare accusative absolute. It just leaps off of the page and stands there, as if Paul was praying this: ". . . that the eyes of your heart, having been flooded with light." It means that something had happened in the past, and he could still see it.

Have you ever been out picking peaches in an orchard on a bright, sun-drenched day? If you close your eyes, you can still see an image of the peaches and the leaves against the closed curtain of your eyelids. Paul had something similar happen to him on a spiritual level. Likewise, as believers, you've had something happen to you that lit up the eyes of your heart. That lighting up of the eyes of your heart should not just be a momentary flash or a brief strobe but an experience that lasts, just like viewing that image of the tree after closing your eyes. God can flood the eyes of your heart to see things you can see no other way. In fact, only the eyes of the heart can see the things that really matter.

In Ephesians, the apostle hands to you a prayer about just that reality—the eyes of the heart. Paul prays that the eyes of your heart might be enlightened, flooded with light, or illumined. Here at the seminary, we may need that reality more than others. We think about those who are so distant from the things of God that the eyes of their hearts need to be enlightened to see them. But, that may even still be truer of those of us who are so close to them every day. We can take the knowledge of God and systemize it by parsing verbs, declining nouns, labeling the eras of church history (patristic, medieval, and the Reformation). We can even take a course in homiletics and learn to craft sermons. Yet, having done all of that, so close to holy things, we must see *with the eyes of the heart.*

This text very simply puts forth some things that you can only see with the eyes of the heart. *The apostle says it is only with the eyes of the heart that you can see the hope of his calling.* You have a sense that the voice never died in the ears of Paul that he heard on that road to Damascus: "Saul, Saul!" It all began with a call in the past. Yet, to the Thessalonians, Paul said that, not only is that call *behind* him, but it's also *alongside* of him. He said, *"He is calling me to walk worthy"* (2 Thess 1:11). Later down that journey, he said, *"This one thing I do. I press forward, toward the prize"* (Phil 3:14). It was an upward future calling that was also behind, before, and alongside him. Every step of the way, that calling created for him a sense of hope.

Paul says that we can know the hope of his calling only when God illumines the eyes of our hearts. In Ephesians, the calling of God refers to his call that creates new spiritual life. It is an effective call that is more than just information; it changes everything. It is a call that creates within us the certainty of hope. It is not a call with information but a call with transformation. We use the word "call" in common ways: margin call, will-call, outcall, recall, phone call, and others. These calls do not transform the situation. The call of God is like a jury summons. It creates a different situation. The call of God is like being drafted into the military. It creates a different situation. The call of God is like a 911 call. It creates an urgent new situation.

The apostle isn't referring to hope in the subjective sense. We use the word "hope" in two ways. One is *emotional*, which deals with that personal, sentimental aspect of hope. We use the word "hope" in an emotional sense when we say, "I feel hopeful," or, "I am losing hope." Paul's Greek readers knew about that. They considered hope to be temporary consolation in the midst of life's uncertainties that never went away.

Paul uses the word "hope" in an objective or *concrete* sense—that out there beyond him with a capital "H," there is hope. We use the word in that way when we say, "Our new quarterback is our only hope for the team," "Our new CEO is the only hope for our company," "The attorney is the only hope we have to win the case," or, "The only hope I have is my doctor." In this sense, hope means there's somebody out there beyond us who is the object of our hope, the direction of our hope, and the content of our hope.

Unlike vaporous emotions that are like thin clouds which burn away under the heat of the noonday sun, the object of our hope is represented by a Person who is out there, beyond us and separate from us. That is what Paul prays for in this passage: "that the eyes of your heart may be opened wide," in order that you see your concrete, substantial, transcendent Hope out there, beyond you, outside of you and existing before you.

In view of current events happening throughout the world, there appears to be no hope. Realistic physical eyes see no hope in the human

JOEL C. GREGORY (1948–)   235

situation alone. The "atomic clock" has moved closer to the midnight hour of atomic annihilation. At this time, North Korea and Iran threaten nuclear war. The nation is more divided politically at this moment than at any time in living memory. The distance between the affluent and the poor is greater in the U.S.A. than any time in memory. All of these macro issues do not even begin to address our individual personal hopeless problems that defy any finite solution.

When you look with your physical eyes, there seems to be no hope. In our modern culture, those lacking spiritual vision will see no hope. Consider the words of actor Charlie Sheen: "There was so much more despair and hopelessness for me at the end than there had been the other times I supposedly got clean. This last go-around was overwhelming." You can only view hope, however, with the eyes of your heart.

On March 1, 1954, the young, brash American evangelist Billy Graham held his first crusade in London. Everybody thought it would fail. The Anglican Church said it would set Christianity back, and he would not be able to fill any arena. One member of the Labor Party even tried to introduce a bill that would prohibit him from being allowed into the country. He couldn't find anywhere to preach. Finally, he booked Harringay Arena, and somebody said that he wouldn't have more than a couple of thousand people there. He didn't think he would get that many people to attend either. But, to everyone's astonishment, the crusade lasted three months, and the Harringay Arena was filled with over twelve thousand people night after night.

In the midst of all that, Billy Graham received a call from Jock Colville, the private secretary to Winston Churchill, the most famous man in the world at the time. Colville said that the prime minister wanted to see him at noon, before his lunch scheduled at 12:30 with the Duke of Windsor. Remembering it later, Graham said he walked past the Duke into the office of 10 Downing Street, and there he sat: Mr. History. He waved his cigar toward a chair, and the young evangelist sat down. Churchill tried to make a lame joke. He said: "Marilyn Monroe and I together couldn't fill Harringay Arena." (Colville's writings mention that Churchill had been nervous about the meeting. Apparently, the prime minister had paced the room, asking himself, "What do you talk about to an evangelist?") But then Churchill looked at him and somberly said, "Young man, do you have any hope? I have no hope." Graham said that the most famous man in the world who had been the embodiment of hope made that statement to him over and over.

Only the eyes of the heart can know the hope created by his calling. But that's not all. Looking back to that call, the apostle looks forward to something else. For he writes, *"Only the eyes of the heart can know the riches of His inheritance in the saints."* Now, "inheritance" is a loaded word. An inheritance can either raise emotions of gratitude and hope or bitterness and disappointment. I've noticed that even when you say the word, the ones who have gotten one, smile; and those who didn't don't smile.

Let me be disclosing. I have a petroleum inheritance. I receive checks regularly. My maiden great-aunt Beulah Hornback died at 103 years of age in Jack County, Texas, without a will. When you die without a will in Texas, it creates a complicated mess. Aunt Beulah was one of twelve siblings, and she had no children. Thus, the courts had to track down the nephews and nieces of eleven siblings all over the United States. There were grand- and great-grand and great-great-grand nephews, and we all got an equal part. Early in the twentieth century, she had inherited some mineral rights from someone who defaulted on a loan. That's the source of the Gregory oil fortune. Every month, I get a check for less than the amount of a stamp. Needless to say, I don't think much of my inheritance.

What is an inheritance? It is the legacy, or heritage, that somebody leaves. It's the bequest. In a sense, it's the residue that is left over at the end of life. An inheritance consists of the tangible results of a life of labor. When you leave an inheritance, you leave the distilled residue of everything you have done for a lifetime.

It's astonishing in a way that Paul would attribute that very same subject to God. The very thought sounds strange and foreign. God, as he really is, will have an inheritance. What would God want to inherit? Wouldn't you think that God would want to inherit something that he made? He is the infinite Creator, but it does not strain his power. He merely projects a thought, and there shines ten thousand luminous suns beneath his throne. On a Saturday afternoon, he could make a galaxy if he wanted to, fling planets off his fingertips—or, rather, speak the word and they would come into existence.

Only the eyes of the heart see that. Otherwise, you look at the universe with the same eyes as Richard Dawkins, a British ethologist, evolutionary biologist, and popular science writer who holds the Charles Simonyi Chair for the Public Understanding of Science at Oxford University. Not only does he not see God, he cannot see why scientists he respects see God. Of "good scientists who are sincerely religious," Dawkins names Arthur Peacocke, Russell Stannard, John Polkinghorne, and Francis Collins, but then says, "I remain baffled . . . by their belief in the details of the Christian religion." To use the old analogy, Dawkins is like the proverbial ox chewing his naturalistic cud in the field that spies Wordsworth writing poetry about the field or Constable painting the field and then wonders why those things over there do not have their noses in the same grass.

A few months ago, while I was speaking in Raleigh-Durham, a Duke University astronomer invited me to dinner. I had no idea how to make small talk with an astronomer, so I finally asked, "How big is the universe?" He shot back, "Fourteen billion light-years to its outer edge." I asked for an explanation. He told me what that meant. If I could harness a beam of light and ride it at 180,000 miles per second, it would take fourteen billion years to get to the edge of the known universe.

The naturalist William Beebe (1877–1962), an ornithologist with the New York Zoological Society and inventor of the bathysphere, would often visit President Theodore Roosevelt on his estate at Oyster Bay, Long Island, in New York. In his book *The Book of Naturalists: An Anthology of the Best Natural History* Beebe said that, after an evening of discussion about things on the fringe of human knowledge, he and the president would often go out on the spacious lawn under the gables of the famous presidential home. They would look, with or without glasses, up at the night sky and focus their attention on the faint glow in the corner of the constellation of Pegasus. Then, Roosevelt recited the following to Beebe:

> That is the spiral galaxy of Andromeda.
> It is as large as the Milky Way.
> It is one of a hundred-million galaxies.
> It is 750,000 light years away.
> It consists of 100 billion suns.
> Each larger than our sun.

Then, Roosevelt would grin at Beebe and reflect, "Now, do you think we are small enough? Let's go to bed."

Yet, I wonder if that is the right deduction. God cannot have a conversation with a nebula. No binary star system ever woke up in the morning and called his name. We may be way too impressed with God's interest in cosmic space. God can do "big" any time he wishes to do so.

When the last sun sets, when the last wave ebbs, when the stars fall out of the sky, and the sky rolls up like a scroll, what will be God's inheritance? When this time and space and universe are gone, what will be the residue for God? What will God have as the legacy, the heritage or the inheritance for what he has done in time and eternity?

God's inheritance will not be this planet. At 25,000 miles around its equator, this earth will one day die out like a burned-out piece of charcoal. God's inheritance will not be the Milky Way with its 100,000 light-years of stars spread over space. Moreover, God's inheritance will not be any of the twenty galaxies in this neighborhood.

There is another use of the word "inheritance" that stretches our minds. Earlier, in verse 14, Paul talks about our inheritance with God, but in verse 18, the idea is different. It is the staggering thought that God wants to inherit us. *We are God's inheritance.* The inheritance of God will be those of us who have been redeemed by his Son, transformed by his cross and the Holy Spirit, and renewed by his saving power. The God who could have *anything* as his inheritance has designated *us* as his inheritance.

Only the eyes of the heart can see that redeemed humanity is of supreme value to God. At first, any morally sensitive person who has read Ephesians would recoil and say, "Who am I, this tiny speck of protoplasm in a universe of a billion luminous atomic furnaces, who am I to think that a Creator wants to inherit me more than all of that?"

Well, Paul says he does—that the ultimate thing he wants to inherit is redeemed humanity. You can cut that down to Texas size. The biggest ranch under one fence in Texas is the W. T. Waggoner Ranch, eight hundred square miles of land covering over six counties around Vernon and Wichita Falls. If the parents had to choose between keeping their eight-hundred-square-mile ranch or the life of their beloved daughter or son, there would not be a moment of hesitation. They'd say, "Take the ranch; I want my child."

Seeing with the eyes of the heart that God wants to inherit you by no means implies some delusional self-regard or some egomaniacal self-obsession. It is best not to think too much about it in personal terms, but it *is* necessary to think about this in terms of the person on the other end of the pew from you. No matter how worn, haggard, or ill that individual may be, he or she will be the inheritance of God. When the race is run and the life is done and the crown is won, that person will be what God inherits. The God who can have anything wants that person at the other end of the pew to be his inheritance. That is the ultimate basis of human worth, dignity, value, and respect, and, conversely, the death of all disregard, prejudice, and dehumanization. But, you can only see that with the eyes of your heart.

God looks at this from one other perspective, and that's the rugged now. Only the eyes of the heart can see the power of God. Behind me is the call of God, creating hope. In front of me, I'm God's inheritance, but I know something about myself. Unless I experience the power of God, that call of hope behind me is just a charade, and the inheritance in front of me is just an illusion. I need his power in the rugged now.

That's why Paul writes, *"Only the eyes of the heart can know the exceeding greatness of his power toward us who believe."*

Last May, I was reading an article in *The New Yorker* magazine about the greatest physics experiment that will ever be done. Outside of Geneva, on the border of France, twenty nations have banded together to design the biggest particle accelerator ever built. At a hundred meters underground and seventeen miles across, it's enormous. The purpose of it is to accelerate subatomic particles until they hit one another to see if something is there that the scientists believe is there but have never seen.

A 1964 physicist named Higgs worked out mathematically that, along with electromagnetism and the strong and weak forces, there is another thing out there. They named it after him: the Higgs Boson. No one has ever seen this special particle which gives everything its mass, but the scientists know it's there. They have built this enormous machine to smash electrons so they can see it. They intend to see what they know is there but what they have never seen.

We're in a similar situation as believers. We have bet our very lives on a power that we can't see. There's nothing empirical to verify it. It doesn't yield itself to vision, and that's why Paul says, *"I hope that the eyes of your heart, having been enlightened, can see the power of God."* You've studied this passage. He turns the dictionary upside down with synonyms for "power." Nowhere else in his writings does Paul use more than two of them. Here, he uses four of them together. They refer to God's power that is in reserve, which becomes active and overcomes all resistance because of its inherent strength. You can almost feel him straining against language. He says, "No, that's not enough." So, he puts in front of the word "mega"—God's mega-power in reserve. Paul still is not satisfied, so he takes another word—a word that only he uses—that gives us our word "hyperbole." It means, "I am throwing this into an entirely different sphere." The word refers to his hyperbolic mega-power. You can tell that Paul is frustrated because he can't express what he says; you see only *with the eyes of the heart.*

For those of us in faith-related work, there's a great deal of distortion we encounter concerning the power of God. Some recently called a misunderstanding of God's power "radio-orthodoxy"—that kind of pandering to the dramatic or the spectacular. You've seen it if you watch late-night televangelists: They wave their arms and people fall down. Is that the power of God? I think not. God's power is a quiet power.

Here is a man who all of his life has been manacled with a demonic habit that he can't break; it fetters him. And then, slowly, a new reality comes into his life. Not just in one big crisis, but little by little those chains are broken. There's a woman who all of her life has been haunted by some phobia. Every morning it sneers at her, and every night it haunts her as she goes to sleep. Then, suddenly over the years and the miles, she hears the word of the Galilean, "Fear not." Gradually, under that sound, it fades away. There's nothing spectacular or dramatic about that. It's just like Jesus said it was: *"The kingdom of God comes without observation."* That is the little leaven that leavens the whole lump. That tiny seed becomes a mighty shrub. His quiet power is always there; you just have to have eyes to see it.

Somewhere this morning, rays of sunlight muted by the clouds came into a baby's nursery, and it didn't even wake up the baby. At the same time, that solar power was lifting millions of tons of water out of the Gulf, creating the winds that blow it over the land and dumping it out as rain. But, it didn't even wake up a baby.

God's power is quiet power, and you only see it *with the eyes of the heart*. I was pondering this passage a while ago sitting in the dirt on the floor of the only surviving transept of the basilica at Cluny, France, which in medieval times was second in size only to St. Peter's, the biggest church in Christendom. All that is left is a transept, more than a thousand years old. I sat down at the base of a pillar and looked up at the arches and those canopies. They were so numinous that even today, you're not quite sure if you're looking at the canopy or at heaven.

I wondered what it might have been like for a medieval serf or peasant to come into that vaulted space, look up and up, and not be sure where the basilica stopped and heaven started. I sat there, and I thought about that arch being there half of the two millenniums back to Jesus in Galilee. I thought about empires coming and going, medieval fortresses falling, the Sun King reigning, and Napoleon marching over that very ground. That very day in that little town, they celebrated the liberation from Hitler when the Allies came through Cluny. I sat there in that silence, and I saw it—a power that was there before us and without us. It can be there after us and without us, but you only see it *with the eyes of the heart*. May God flood the understanding of our hearts with light so that we see.

Chapter 24

Lloyd C. Blue (1933–)

Living Legend 2019

The Preacher

Rev. Dr. Lloyd C. Blue (1933–) has a long and abiding legacy in discipling and training men to be effective Christian leaders, husbands, and fathers. Born in the small town of Laurel Hill, North Carolina, in 1933, Dr. Blue spent his young adulthood in Los Angeles, California, following his family's cross-country move in 1951. His conversion came in 1954 while he was serving in the Navy. When he returned to Los Angeles, he entered pastoral ministry. He began preaching in 1962 while a member of the Solid Rock Baptist Church in LA. Years later, he would move his membership to Mt. Zion Baptist Church, where he worked with and was discipled by Rev. Dr. E. V. Hill. It was Dr. Hill who recommended him highly to Bill Bright, the founder and president of Campus Crusade for Christ (now known as CRU), an organization he served for fifteen years. He also served for a time as the pastor of Israel Baptist Church in Hamilton, Ohio. His pathway of ministry eventually led him to Texas, where he currently serves as the senior associate minister at the Cornerstone Baptist Church in Arlington. An ordained Baptist minister, he pastored for thirty-one years and established himself as a national and international preacher and lecturer.

Dr. Blue graduated from the Institutional Baptist Theological Center in 5th Ward, Houston, Texas, with a bachelor of theology, along with his master of arts degree from Union University of Los Angeles, California, and his doctor of ministry degree from the University of Central America in Kansas City, Missouri.

He has also served in many leadership roles as a director for several ministries including director of Pastors Development Ministries at Seminary without Walls in Mendenhall, Mississippi, and director of evangelism and men's ministries at Concord Church in Dallas, Texas. In 1993, he felt led by the Holy Spirit to develop a full-time ministry related to church growth. Currently, he serves as president of that ministry, Church Growth Unlimited, Inc., which provides consultation to church leaders on church growth and development.

An accomplished author, Dr. Blue has published widely, including the book *Developing Oneness in Marriage: A How-to for Husbands,* and popular pamphlets such as *Mechanics of Expository Preaching, Church Growth Unlimited,* and *How to Live the Abundant Life.*

He and his wife, Mrs. Tressie V. (Johnson) Blue, have been married for sixty-five years, and they have one son, Lloyd Blue II.

The Sermon

Colossians 1:24–29:

> *Now I rejoice in my sufferings for your sake, and in my flesh I do my share on behalf of His body, which is the church, in filling up what is lacking in Christ's afflictions. Of this church I was made a minister according to the stewardship from God bestowed on me for your benefit, so that I might fully carry out the preaching of the word of God, that is, the mystery which has been hidden from the past ages and generations, but has now been manifested to His saints, to whom God willed to make known what is the riches of*

the glory of this mystery among the Gentiles, which is Christ in you, the hope of glory. We proclaim Him, admonishing every man and teaching every man with all wisdom, so that we may present every man complete in Christ. For this purpose also I labor, striving according to His power, which mightily works within me.

Now, the text has already been read, and I need to tell you up front that I'm not going to exegete those six verses. As a matter of fact, I'm going to violate a whole lot of exegetical principles and expositional laws. I'm going to do some stuff that I would teach my students never to do.

But, I wanted those six verses read because they say that to be legitimately expositional, you've got to have at least four verses. So, you've heard. So, now I want you to focus on the last two verses. I've been battling around with the Lord for the past few days about this. And I don't know why I do; he always wins. But, in these last two verses, he gave me the burden to share with you here tonight.

And those last two verses simply say, *"We proclaim him, admonishing every man, teaching every man with all wisdom, so that we present every man perfect, complete, mature in Christ. For this purpose also I labor, striving according to his power which mightily works in me."*

For us tonight, I want to talk about God's expectations. God's expectations. What does God expect of us as preacher-teachers, of anyone who handles the word of God? What does God expect?

Some people get the idea that only preachers are supposed to do this, but you won't find that anywhere in Scripture. Every born-again believer is a proclaimer. Now, there is the called out from the call, but all are called. We all have the responsibility of proclaiming Christ. That's our job. That's our job. So, tonight I just want to pull out these two verses and talk to you about what I see here as God has directed me. He's my boss so he calls the shots.

The first thing I see here is God expects us to proclaim Christ. God expects us to proclaim Christ. Now, some translations say "him," but the "him" is Christ. We proclaim Christ. That's our job. And for us as preachers and pastor-teachers, that's our full-time job. You may do some other stuff, but your real job is proclaiming Christ. Second Corinthians 4:5: *"For we do not preach ourselves, but Christ Jesus as Lord."* We do not preach ourselves, but Christ Jesus as Lord.

Why was Paul so fired up about preaching Christ? What made that such a priority for him? Now, he's writing this letter from prison. He's in jail for obeying the Lord and proclaiming Christ to the Gentiles. Now, if he'd been willing to backslide, he might not have gone to jail. But, Paul was against backsliding. We preach him! We preach him. Why?

Well, if you look back at Genesis, we can find out why Paul was so fired up about this. God made Adam; he gave him a body to communicate. Then, he gave him a soul, mind, emotion, and will, a mind to think, emotions to react, and a will to make choices. Then, he gave him a spirit. God himself opted into Adam's spirit, switched him on, and called him to function properly in his office as a man. Then, God through Adam's spirit taught his mind, controlled his emotions, directed his will, and governed his behavior so that, when God stood Adam before creation, all creation could look at Adam and see what God was like.

God was in Adam expressing himself through Adam to all creation around Adam. Whatever God said, Adam said. Whatever God did, Adam did. And God said, "Good. Very good! As long as you're dependent on me, you're going to live! But, the day you decide to go independent, son, you're going to die." And sure enough, the day came when Adam believed the Devil's lie that he could be a moral and spiritual adult without God! The same God that opted in and switched him on, opted out, and Adam died!

He survived, body and soul. He still had a body to communicate. He still had a soul, mind, emotion, and will, but spiritually, he died. He died. He died. Now you know why Jesus said, *"I am come that they might have life!"* John 10:10, *"And have it more abundantly."* Why? Because everyone born since Adam was born dead. Adam was created in the image and likeness of God, but we were born in the image and likeness of our father Adam. We came into this world saying "no" to everything God said "yes" to and "yes" to everything God said "no" to. That's why you must be born again. I need to hurry up and tell you that if you were born before Adam, this has nothing to do with you at all.

Paul was excited about preaching Christ because he knew that all we lost in Adam, we could get back in Jesus. For Jesus Christ is the life of God restored to all humanity! That's why it is so vital and so necessary that we preach Christ. Preach Christ! Preach Christ! Preach Christ! Well, we preach Christ to proclaim Christ.

But, the second thing that I see here is that God expects us to perfect the saints, to perfect the saints. That word "complete" in the text carries with it the idea of "perfecting" or "completing" or "maturing." It's all the same thing. It simply means to grow up in Christ. He makes it plain that we are to proclaim Christ, admonishing every man and teaching every man and with all wisdom, so that we may present every man perfect, complete, mature in Christ.

Now, what does it mean to admonish? The word "admonish" simply means "to warn," or "to help set someone's mind in proper order." Now, I need to hurry up and tell you that the only way to do that is with the word of

God. What you think will not set anybody's mind right. You're gonna have to use the Bible. If you're gonna help anybody, you're gonna have to use the word of God.

Now, in the day in which we live, there's a couple things that I think, pastors, we need to be excited about when it comes to warning people. We need to challenge and warn people. One is forsaking the assembling of ourselves together. That ain't no biggie. We've been hearing people say ever since we've been here, "You ought to go to church. You ought to go to church. You ought to go to church." But the writer of the Hebrews 10:25 says, "*Forsake not the assembling of yourselves together.*"

Why is that so important? You see, here is what makes it so important: because there is the danger of drifting away. You see, every time you miss a service or Bible study, every time you miss one, it becomes easier the next time. That voice that gnaws at you, it gets quieter and quieter. And pretty soon, you've drifted away. That's the Devil's plan. You see, he wants to isolate you from other believers. If he can isolate you from other believers, then he can do the job on you that he's been wanting to do all this time.

He already knows he's lost you. He knows that. But what he doesn't want, he doesn't want to lose anyone else *because* of you. So, if he can just get you to just drift away, he will isolate you. The way he does it, he gets you out to the tree, and then he gets you up the tree, and then he gets you out on the limb. Then, he runs back to the tree and saws off the limb. And while you're falling, you can hear him say, "Stupid!"

I mean, it's so simple. It's so simple. I'm almost embarrassed to tell you. It's a program to isolate you from other believers. That's his thing. Who gets all excited about everybody missing church? The Devil does. He rejoices every time you decide, "Well, I think I won't go today." He says, "Praise the Lord!"

So, preacher-pastors, I think that we need to do more to warn people about drifting away. Now, if the researchers are right, we are losing thousands of churches every year. Thousands! Not one or two. Thousands! Every year! Why? Drifting away. Just drifting away.

Well, there's another thing that I want to call our attention to, and that's forsaking the business of sharing the gospel with unbelievers. You see, as believers, your responsibility as believers is to share Christ with other nonbelievers that they too might know the joy that you have. But now, the Billy Graham Association, the Southern Baptist Convention, Campus Crusade for Christ International [Cru], all these organizations who do all this research and stuff, they say that about 90–95 percent of the people that go to church on Sunday have never shared Christ with another person. That's mighty near everybody, y'all. But, what they said also about that same figure is that this is the number of people who are not sure about their salvation. Just maybe the problem is, I'm not sure of what I have, so I'm not fired up about sharing it with somebody else. It's hard to share with somebody else what you aren't sure you have. But you know something? When you know, you know you know. Keeping it to yourself is just not something you're able to do.

The night that I got saved [while in the Navy], I got in my car afterward, and I said, "I ain't telling nobody what just happened to me!" And I wasn't sure what just happened to me. I knew I was under new management, but I didn't know how to figure it out. I didn't have no hands to put on it. And I said, "There won't be no point in telling anybody, because won't nobody believe it anyway!" because I was one of the Devil's right arms. I was 145 pounds of solid sin from stem to stern. I was either doing it or watching somebody else do it. And I said, "If I tell anybody, they're gonna laugh me to scorn! Nobody's gonna believe it!"

I woke up the next morning, my friend was laying in the next bunk. And it just popped out, I said, "Ben, I got saved last night." I didn't mean to tell him. I was gonna keep it to myself. I'm waiting for Ben to laugh, and he looked at me and he said, "I wish it had happened to me." I took my shaving kit down, and I noticed that my hand didn't shake. I took the bottle down, and I recognized that I didn't need it no more. I took it down to the latrine and broke it in the trash can, and there's about ninety guys standing around. They said, "Blue, have you lost your mind?! What are you doing?!" I said, "I got saved last night!!" Before nine o'clock that morning, my commanding officer had sent for me to tell me how glad he was that I had gotten saved. About then, I had told everybody I saw! Yeah!

But, it reminded me of a young lady in our church. She got married to this guy secretly because he stood to inherit a whole lot of money if he had finished certain grades in school so they got secretly married because they were in love. So, she came to see me and she said, "I just can't hardly stand it." And, I said, "What seems to be the problem?" She explained the story and I said, "I don't see nothing wrong with it. You're legally married, so what's the problem?" She said, "Well, you know, we walk in church and I sit on one side and he sits over there somewhere, and I see all the girls looking at him, and I just want to get up on the back of the pews and say, 'He's mine! He's mine!'" When you know, you know. You just want to jump on something and say, "He's mine! He's mine!" Yeah, we need to warn people about that. Well, I need to hurry on because the train's coming. Warning, warning, warning.

But then, he says, "Teaching every man" or "instructing," which refers to clearly communicating the word of God. That's one of the things that makes this conference so important. It helps you to clearly communicate the word of God.

But, listen. There is an issue that bugs me because I believe it was one of the things that I neglected as a pastor. Now, let me just read the verse to you. First John 4:10, it says, *"In this is the love, not that we love God, but that he loved us and sent his Son to be the atoning sacrifice (propitiation), the atoning sacrifice for our sins."*

The love of God. The love of God. Brother pastors, I want you to take it from an old fellow that's been there, done that. Think in terms of spending more energy teaching and preaching on of the love of God—the love of God. You see, it's hard to respond to somebody if you don't know how much they love you. It's a little difficult to do that. I believe that was one of my biggest mistakes.

Listen, how can a believer trust God not knowing that God loves them? How does he do that? If I don't really know how much God loves me, how do I trust him? And if I don't trust him, how can I obey him? It's my dependence upon him that enables me to obey him! And it all begins with me understanding he loves me! He loves me! He loves me!

Paul helps me out with this in 2 Corinthians 5:14. He says, "I'm constrained by the love of Christ. The love of Christ constrains me. It's the love of Christ that controls me! It's the love of Christ that compels me! I'm captivated, activated, motivated by the love of God!" That's what kept him going! That's why he couldn't quit! When he wanted to quit, he looked with eyes of faith up on a hill called Calvary. When you look up there, you see the ultimate expression of the love of God! That's *God* hanging up there! You do know Jesus is God, don't you?

The love of God, that love of God, the love of God, somehow or another—we have to get excited about the love of God! He loves you! He always has, and he always will! But it's hard to trust God if you don't know that he loves you. You tends to want to think of him as a big, bad judge waiting to slap you around for messing up, when he's really standing there with arms stretched, saying, "Come on, son. You did the same thing last week, but I still love you. Come on. Come on!" He loves you. God loves you! God loves you! God loves you!

He said, "with all wisdom." We're to preach and teach the word of God with all wisdom, with all wisdom. Now, that's preaching and teaching with the proper use of knowledge. You come to this conference, and you gain knowledge, and you go back home to preach and teach. But, you've got to exercise some wisdom!

There's a transformer out there hanging somewhere on a pole with all the megatons of electricity flowing into Dallas. It comes up there to that transformer. That transformer receives what it flows, and it feeds it into this building at just the right amount, the 210, or the 110, or the 220, just whatever is the voltage. But, if you move that transformer, then all those megatons of electricity will blow the building off the foundation. Just blow it off!

My brother preacher, you're the transformer! It's good to come to this conference. It's good to get all you can get. Get all you can get. Store all you can store. But, then break it down. Break it down and feed it into your people at the level they can receive it. *"With all wisdom, presenting everyone complete, perfect in Christ."*

Perfecting is helping people to grow up in Christ! It means to present them mature in the faith. It means helping them to become more like Jesus. When was the last time you sat down to prepare your sermon, and the first thing you did was say to yourself, "How is this going to make my folk more like Jesus? How is this going to help them to be more like Jesus?" If that's not your goal, to help them become more like Jesus, then what are you preaching for? What are you seeking to achieve? That was Paul's goal! Paul says, "My purpose is that they may know the mystery of God, namely, Christ!" He said, "That's my purpose."

Now, I got to quit. There's one more thought that I want to close with here. Verse 29 gives some people problems. God expects us here to perform with power. He expects us to perform with power. Some commentators say that verse 29 is a picture of Paul's prayer life. I have no argument with the fact that Paul had a tremendous prayer life. No way he could accomplish what he did had he not had a great prayer life.

But that's not the context. What he said—watch what he said. Watch what he said. He talks about proclaiming Christ to the lost and presenting mature believers to Christ. His labor and his striving was to proclaim Christ to the lost and present mature saints to Christ. That was his ambition. That was what he worked for. This labor and striving was like that of a marathon runner. And that marathon runner is going for all that he or she can, and they just can't make it by themselves. Somebody comes out on the track and comes alongside and gives them a shoulder to hang on and help them across the finish line!

Is what Paul is saying here, "I'm working at it like it like it all depends on me"? Knowing that it all depends on him, "without the power of the Lord Christ, I can't do it!" And brother pastor, brother preacher, you have to have the power of Jesus Christ operating in you. If you're going to proclaim Christ to the lost and present mature saints to Christ, that is not a job you can do on your own. No. You can't do it by yourself.

So, Paul says, "What I'm doing is I'm working at it *like* it all depends on me." You see, you can't live on the couch and have God do it, and you can't go out without God and do it. It's a partnership. You've got to be available to God, and God available to you. The two are working together to make it happen because you can't do it by yourself. Some folk have said, "I'm gonna get it done if it kills me." And it did. It did. It did.

Paul says, "Now, I'm going on with the Lord. I'm gonna trust God." And we see some verses where Paul says, "*I can do all things . . . not of myself, but through Christ who strengthens me.*" And then in Philippians 2:13, he says, "*For it is God who works in me both to will and to do of His good pleasure.*" I can't do it by myself, but I know that God can. Faithful is he that calls you who also will do it. The God who called you will do in you and through you what he has called you to do.

Aren't you glad about it? Yeah! God who called you to proclaim Christ, you need to let him do it. You can't do it so let God do it. The God who called you to perfect the saints, let God do it. You can't, but God can. So, let the Lord, in you and through you, do all that he demands of you.

God will perform with power, and he'll do it through you. I know he will! I know he will! Let God do it! Let God do it! Let God do it! Yeah! yeah! Let the Lord do it! Put your trust in God! Stop trying to do it on your own. Trust God, and let God do it!

I learned a long time ago. "*I trust in God wherever I may be, out on the land, or on the rolling sea. For billows roll, he keeps me soul. My heavenly Father.*" Yeah. My heavenly Father, my heavenly Father, watches over me! Yes, he does! Yes, he does!

Do you know he will? Do you know he will? If you know he will, say yes! Say yes! Say yes! Yes, he will. Yes, he will.

Let God do it! Let God do it! The old folks used to sing a little song. They sang, "*Let Jesus fix it for you. Yeah. He knows just what to do. And whenever you pray, just let Him have his way! O, Jesus! Yeah!*"

Oh, he knows. He knows just what to do! Yes, he does. And whenever, whenever you pray, just let him, let him have his way! Ah, Jesus! Jesus! Jesus will fix it! Let him fix it for you. Oh, for you. He knows. I'm glad he knows just what to do! Whenever you pray, just let him have his way! Jesus! Oh, Jesus! He'll fix it for you!"

Recommended Reading

Alcántara, Jared E. *Learning from a Legend: What Gardner C. Taylor Can Teach Us about Preaching*. Eugene, OR: Cascade, 2016.

———. "Past Masters: Caesar A.W. Clark—Small Stature, Giant Message." *Preaching* 31.4 (2016) 46–47.

———. "Past Masters: A Poet in the Pulpit: Manuel L. Scott Sr." *Preaching* 30.4 (2015) 54–55.

Bailey, E. K. *Farther In and Deeper Down*. Chicago: Moody, 2005.

Bailey, E. K., and Warren W. Wiersbe. *Preaching in Black and White: What We Can Learn from Each Other*. Grand Rapids: Zondervan, 2003.

Blue, Lloyd C. *Developing Oneness in Marriage: A How-to for Husbands*. Dallas: Searchlight, 2011.

Crawford, Evans E., and Thomas H. Troeger. *The Hum: Call and Response in African American Preaching*. Nashville: Abingdon, 1995.

George, Timothy, et al., eds. *Our Sufficiency Is of God: Essays on Preaching in Honor of Gardner C. Taylor*. Macon, GA: Mercer University Press, 2010.

Gilbert, Kenyatta R. *The Journey and Promise of African American Preaching*. Minneapolis: Fortress, 2011.

Hicks, H. Beecher, Jr. *Images of the Black Preacher: The Man Nobody Knows*. Valley Forge, PA: Judson, 1977.

———. *My Soul's Been Anchored*. Grand Rapids: Zondervan, 1998.

———. *On Jordan's Stormy Banks*. Grand Rapids: Zondervan, 2004.

———. *Preaching through a Storm*. Grand Rapids: Zondervan, 1987.

Hill, Edward Victor, Sr. *A Savior Worth Having*. Chicago: Moody, 2002.

———. *Victory in Jesus: Running the Race You Are Meant to Win*. Chicago: Moody, 2003.

Jackson, Walter Kingsley. *I Let the Lord Do It*. N.p.: Campbell Road, 2003.

LaRue, Cleophus J. *The Heart of Black Preaching*. Louisville: Westminster John Knox Press, 2000.

———. *I Believe I'll Testify: The Art of African American Preaching*. Louisville: Westminster John Knox, 2011.

Mitchell, Henry H. *Black Church Beginnings*. Grand Rapids: Eerdmans, 2004.

———. *Black Preaching: The Recovery of a Powerful Art*. Nashville: Abingdon, 1990.

———. *Celebration and Experience in Preaching*. Nashville: Abingdon, 1990.

———. *The Recovery of Preaching*. New York: Harper, 1977.

————. *A Word for All Seasons*. Valley Forge, PA: Judson, 2012.

Mitchell, Henry H., and Ella Pearson Mitchell. *Fire in the Well*. Valley Forge, PA: Judson, 2004.

————. *Together for Good*. Valley Forge, PA: Judson, 2007.

Mitchell, Henry H., and Emil M. Thomas. *Preaching for Black Self-Esteem*. Nashville: Abingdon, 1994.

Mitchell, Henry H., and Nicholas C. Cooper-Lewter. *Soul Theology*. San Francisco: Harper & Row, 1986; Nashville: Abingdon, 1991.

Patterson, A. Louis, Jr. *Joy for the Journey*. Lithonia, GA: Orman, 2003.

————. *Prerequisites for a Good Journey*. St. Louis: Hodale, 1994.

Redmond, Eric C., ed. *Say It!: Celebrating Expository Preaching in the African American Tradition*. Chicago: Moody, 2020.

Richardson, Willie. *Reclaiming the Urban Family*. Grand Rapids: Zondervan, 1996.

————. *Sharing Christ as You Go*. Christian Research Development, n.d.

Robinson, Haddon W. *Biblical Preaching*. Grand Rapids: Baker Academic, 2014.

Scott, Manuel L., Jr. *The Quotable Manuel Scott Sr.: Words frm a Gospel Genius*. Los Angeles: Manuel Scott Jr Ministries, 2010.

Scott, Manuel L., Sr. *From a Black Brother*. Nashville: Broadman, 1971.

————. *The Gospel for the Ghetto*. Nashville: Broadman, 1973.

Simmons, Martha J., and Frank A. Thomas, eds. *Preaching with Sacred Fire: An Anthology of African American Sermons, 1750 to the Present*. New York: Norton, 2010.

Smith, J. Alfred, Sr. *On the Jericho Road*. Downers Grove: InterVarsity, 2004.

————. *Speak Until Justice Wakes*. Valley Forge, PA: Judson, 2006.

Smith, Robert, Jr. *Doctrine That Dances: Bringing Doctrinal Preaching and Teaching to Life*. Nashville: B & H Academic, 2008.

————. *The Oasis of God: From Mourning to Morning—Biblical Insights from Psalms 42 and 43*. Mountain Home, AR: Border Stone, 2014.

————, ed. *Preparing for Christian Ministry*. Grand Rapids: Baker, 1998.

Smith Jr., Robert, and Timothy George, eds. *A Mighty Long Journey: Reflections on Racial Reconciliation*. Nashville: Broadman, 2000.

Taylor, Gardner C. *How Shall they Preach?* Elgin, IL: Progressive Baptist, 1977.

————. *The Scarlet Thread*. Elgin, IL: Progressive Baptist, 1981.

————. *The Words of Gardner Taylor*. Edited by Edward L. Taylor. 6 vols. Valley Forge: Judson, 2004.

Taylor, Gardner C., and Samuel D. Proctor. *We Have This Ministry*. Valley Forge, PA: Judson, 1996.

Thomas, Frank A. *Introduction to the Practice of African American Preaching*. Nashville: Abingdon, 2016.

————. *They Like to Never Quit Praisin' God: The Role of Celebration in Preaching*. Cleveland: United Church, 1997.

Wade, M. V., Sr., et al. *These Three*. 3 vols. Nashville: R. H. Boyd, 2005.

Willimon, William, and Richard Lischer. *The Concise Encyclopedia of Preaching*. Louisville: Westminster John Knox, 1995.

Bibliography

"The 15 Greatest Black Preachers." *Ebony* 49.1 (Nov 1993) 156–68.

"The 25 Most Influential Preachers of the Past 50 Years." *Christianity Today*, 2006. https://www.christianitytoday.com/anniversary/features/top25preachers.html.

Alcántara, Jared E. *Crossover Preaching: Intercultural-Improvisational Homiletics in Conversation with Gardner C. Taylor.* Downers Grove: IVP Academic, 2015.

———. *Learning from a Legend: What Gardner C. Taylor Can Teach Us about Preaching.* Eugene, OR: Cascade, 2016.

———. "Past Masters: Caesar A.W. Clark—Small Stature, Giant Message." *Preaching* 31.4 (2016) 46–47.

———. "Past Masters: A Poet in the Pulpit: Manuel L. Scott Sr." *Preaching* 30.4 (2015) 54–55.

"America's 15 Greatest Black Preachers." *Ebony* 39.11 (Sept 1984) 29–33.

"Baylor Names the 12 Most Effective Preachers." Baylor University Media Communications, Feb 28, 1996. http://www.baylor.edu/mediacommunications/news.php?action=story&story=1036.

"Baylor University's Truett Seminary Announces 12 Most Effective Preachers in English-Speaking World." Baylor University Media Communications, May 1, 2018. https://www.baylor.edu/mediacommunications/news.php?action=story&story=198528.

Carter, Jerry M. "The Audible Sacrament: The Sacramentality of Gardner C. Taylor's Preaching." PhD Diss., Drew University, 2007.

Cochran, Johnnie L., Jr. *Journey to Justice.* New York: Ballantine, 1996.

Duduit, Michael. "The 25 Most Influential Preaching Books of the Past 25 Years." *Preaching Magazine*, 2010. https://www.preaching.com/articles/the-25-most-influential-preaching-books-of-the-past-25-years/.

Goode, Jo-Carolyn. "Rev. Dr. A. Louis Patterson, Jr. Dies While His Preaching Legacy Lives On." *Houston Style Magazine*, April 24, 2014. http://stylemagazine.com/news/2014/apr/24/rev-dr-louis-patterson-jr-dies-while-his-preaching/.

Hinton, Carla. "Fabric of Faith: OKC Church with Legacy of Civil Rights Is Marking 100 Years." *The Oklahoman*, April 6, 2019. https://oklahoman.com/article/5627809/fabric-of-faithbrokc-church-with-legacy-of-civil-rights-is-marking-100-years.

LaRue, Cleophus J., ed. *Power in the Pulpit: How America's Most Effective Black Preachers Prepare Their Sermons.* Louisville: Westminster John Knox, 2002.

Massey, James Earl. *Aspects of My Pilgrimage*. Anderson, IN: Anderson University Press, 2002.

Mills, Zach. *The Last Blues Preacher: Reverend Clay Evans, Black Lives, and the Faith That Woke the Nation*. Minneapolis: Fortress, 2018.

Phillips, John. *Only One Life: The Biography of Stephen F. Olford*. Neptune, NJ: Loizeaux, 1995.

"Reverend Dr. J. Alfred Smith Sr.: Biography." *The History Makers: The Nation's Largest African American Video Oral History Collection*. https://www.thehistorymakers.org/biography/reverend-dr-j-alfred-smith-sr.

Scott, Manuel L., Jr. *The Quotable Manuel Scott Sr.: Words from a Gospel Genius*. Los Angeles: Manuel Scott Jr Ministries, 2010.

Shellnutt, Kate. "Died: James Earl Massey, the Church of God's 'Prince of Preachers.'" *Christianity Today*, June 26, 2018. https://www.christianitytoday.com/news/2018/june/died-james-earl-massey-preacher-church-of-god.html.

Simmons, Martha J., and Frank A. Thomas, eds. *Preaching with Sacred Fire: An Anthology of African American Sermons, 1750 to the Present*. New York: Norton, 2010.

Taylor, Gardner C. *The Words of Gardner Taylor: Quintessential Classics, 1980–Present*. Vol. 3. Edited by Edward L. Taylor. Valley Forge: Judson, 2004.

Thomas, Gerald Lamont. *African American Preaching: The Contribution of Dr. Gardner C. Taylor*. New York: Peter Lang, 2004.

Willhite, Keith, and Scott M. Gibson, eds. *The Big Idea of Biblical Preaching: Connecting the Bible to People*. Grand Rapids: Baker, 1998.

CPSIA information can be obtained
at www.ICGtesting.com
Printed in the USA
JSHW032045110421
13462JS00004B/4